THE COMPLETE IDIOT'S GUIDE® TO

Beagles

by Kim Campbell Thornton

ALPHA

A member of Penguin Group (USA) Inc.

To Darcy, who taught me all about puppies.

Publisher: *Marie Butler-Knight*
Product Manager: *Phil Kitchel*
Managing Editor: *Jennifer Chisholm*
Acquisitions Editor: *Mike Sanders*
Development Editor: *Nancy D. Lewis*
Production Editor: *Billy Fields*
Copy Editor: *Jeff Rose*
Illustrator: *Chris Eliopoulos*
Cover/Book Designer: *Trina Wurst*
Indexer: *Tonya Heard*
Layout/Proofreading: *Brad Lenser, Vicki Keller*

Contents at a Glance

Contents

Foreword

My very first dog was a Beagle. My older sister and I were six and seven years old when Mom brought home our sweet-faced, silky-eared baby dog. My recollection of Flag, supported by faded home movies, is of a compliant puppy who was cheerfully resigned to being mauled and hauled around by a neighborhood full of young children.

Much has happened in my life since I shared my childhood with Flag. Although I originally aspired to be a veterinarian, I got side-tracked and spent 20 years of my life as an animal protection professional, working at the Marin Humane Society in Novato, California, just north of San Francisco. I left Marin in 1997 to open Peaceable Paws Dog & Puppy Training in Monterey, California, then, three years later, moved the training center to Chattanooga, Tennessee, when my husband was hired as Director of that city's new Animal Services program. During those intervening years I managed to collect, train, and compete with many breeds, from our diminutive Pomeranian to a giant St. Bernard, and including a Bloodhound, Springer Spaniel, Rough Collie, Bull Terrier, Australian Kelpie, Scottish Terrier, and many more.

Now that I'm a professional dog trainer, I'm pleased to see that the Beagle's steady popularity hasn't damaged his easygoing personality. The sturdy little dog has held his spot as fifth most popular breed on the AKC list for at least the last three years, and has long been a family favorite. While I have not had the privilege of having another Beagle in my canine family since Flag, I do see them regularly in my classes, and they are invariably as accommodating as my little dog was so many years ago.

Beagles have long been given short shrift in many canine training and competitive arenas because they—like a number of other breeds—respond somewhat poorly to old-fashioned, force-based training methods. This has unfairly earned them a reputation for being stubborn, defiant, and disobedient. I prefer to think of them in positive terms, as strong-willed, independent, and "otherly motivated." The key to training a Beagle is using something that *does* motivate him, which frequently is food.

Dogs who are bred to work closely with humans, like many of the sporting breeds, will continue to work despite old-fashioned training methods that inflict pain. Many other breeds, Beagles included, are more likely to shut down the more you try to force them. Modern thinking about dog training tells us that it is our job as owners and trainers, and as the supposedly more intelligent species, to figure out how to get our dogs to offer the behaviors we want voluntarily, rather than using brute force to accomplish training goals.

Author Kim Thornton offers up-to-date training advice, advocating gentle methods and frequent use of rewards. This kind of training works well for all types of dogs. The contrast is most vivid, however, with breeds that have traditionally resisted force-based training. With the happy influence of modern, positive training methods, it's no longer a surprise to see Beagles cheerfully and successfully working in training classes, obeying their owners' cues in home and field, or competing in any canine sport. As a positive dog trainer and President of the Association of Pet Dog Trainers (APDT), I am thrilled to read a Beagle breed book that advocates a training philosophy that, like mine and that of APDT, encourages a relationship between dog and owner that is based on mutual trust and respect.

Immerse yourself in this book. Learn about the history of your chosen breed; educate yourself about your dog's health, grooming, and exercise needs; and learn about activities available to you and your canine pal—those specific to Beagles as well as those open to all types of dogs. Be sure to pay special attention to the section on training. Don't let anyone talk you into using forceful tools and techniques with your pal that you know could hurt him or damage his trust in you. Training that opens two-way communication and builds a strong bond between you and your dog will help to ensure that he spends the rest of his life as a well-loved member of your family. Care for him well, train him gently, and he will be your loyal friend, companion and confidante for many years to come.

—Pat Miller

President of the Association of Pet Dog Trainers (APDT)

Introduction

Beagles are classic dogs. Fun-loving, cute, mischievous, always sniffing out good times, they epitomize the dog we all dreamed of when we were growing up.

Not surprisingly, the Beagle has held a spot in the AKC's top 10 breeds for many years. Sometimes it seems as if everyone owns a Beagle or knows someone who has one. The fact is, though, these merry hounds aren't for everyone.

It takes a special person to live successfully with a Beagle. The sweetest Beagle in the world can drive his people to distraction with his propensity for trouble. He wanders, willing to follow his nose to the ends of the earth in search of that intriguing scent. He howls when he's feeling neglected—or just to let you know that he's smelled something interesting. Some people call it singing, but the neighbors usually call it a nuisance. The Beagle has a strong and distinctive personality (read stubborn) that calls for an owner with patience, persistence, and a great sense of humor. This book will help you understand the workings of the Beagle's mind and decide whether this is really the right breed for you.

If your decision is affirmative, I will help you navigate the entertaining but sometimes frustrating path of Beagle ownership. You'll learn about the Beagle's history and why it makes him the dog he is, tips and techniques for housetraining and good canine manners, typical behavior problems and how to cope with them, health issues, and the sports, games, and tricks your Beagle will enjoy.

This book assumes you know nothing about these amusing, smart but stubborn little dogs. If you already have some experience with Beagles, you might want to scan the "In This Chapter" sections at the beginning of each chapter to decide which chapters relate to your individual situation and interests. If you are considering acquiring a Beagle or if you have a new puppy or dog, this book will take you step by step through the fundamentals of raising and training your Beagle pal.

How This Book Is Organized

This book is presented in six sections:

In **Part 1, "Is a Beagle for You?"** you'll learn whether you have what it takes to live life with a Beagle. This section covers the Beagle's development as a breed, the typical Beagle personality, and what the breed should look like.

In **Part 2, "A Beagle in the House,"** you'll discover some of the potential differences between Beagles bred for the field and those destined for the show ring or pet home. The chapters discuss whether to choose a puppy or adult, how to find a breeder, the pros and cons of adopting a needy Beagle, and what to expect when you bring your new friend home.

In **Part 3, "The Civilized Beagle,"** you'll find tips, tricks, and techniques for teaching your Beagle how to live happily in your home. Look for advice on protecting your home and yard from destruction, getting started in training class, housetraining, establishing leadership, dealing with behavior problems, and providing effective rewards and corrections.

In **Part 4, "A Healthy Beagle Is a Happy Beagle,"** is guidance on finding a veterinarian, providing preventive health care, giving medication, coping with emergency injuries, grooming, and nutrition. All are vital to your Beagle's well-being.

In **Part 5, "Fun With Beagles,"** you'll learn about the numerous sports and activities available to dogs, as well as which ones are most likely to appeal to your Beagle. Sports are a great way to keep your Beagle's body healthy and his mind active.

In **Part 6, "Special Needs,"** is information we hope you'll never need to know. These chapters cover hereditary diseases that can affect Beagles, plus tips on living with a Beagle during his golden years. You'll also find advice on deciding when it's time to give your Beagle a peaceful departure to that great rabbit hunt in the sky.

Things to Help You Out Along the Way

Here's a guide to the different sidebars you'll see peppering the pages that follow. These boxes focus your attention on interesting facts, important information, and safety warnings that can help the training and care of your Beagle go more smoothly.

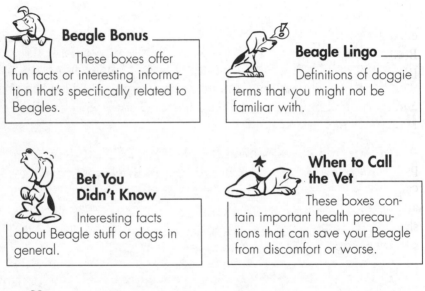

Beagle Bonus
These boxes offer fun facts or interesting information that's specifically related to Beagles.

Beagle Lingo
Definitions of doggie terms that you might not be familiar with.

Bet You Didn't Know
Interesting facts about Beagle stuff or dogs in general.

When to Call the Vet
These boxes contain important health precautions that can save your Beagle from discomfort or worse.

Doggy Do's/Doggy Don'ts
Doggy Do's are special tips for training and caring for your Beagle, as well as shortcuts that can save you time and frustration. Read the Doggy Don'ts boxes to avoid common pitfalls in care and training as well as dangerous or unproductive habits that could affect your dog or your relationship with him.

Acknowledgments

Many people offered encouragement, support, and information during the writing of this book. Their suggestions and advice helped make it the complete guide that it is. I'd like to thank Greg Gustafson, Janiece Harrison, Gary and Lisa Jones, Kristine Kraeuter, Susan McCullough, Carolyn Morgan, Boone Narr, Janet

Nieland, Anne Page, Sherri Regalbuto, Sandy Seward, Donald Skinner, VMD, and Faith A. Uridel for their input, stories, and photos. Thank you all for your myriad contributions.

Special Thanks to the Technical Reviewer

The Complete Idiot's Guide to Beagles was reviewed by experts who double-checked the accuracy of what you'll learn here, to help us ensure that this book gives you everything you need to know about Beagles. Special thanks are extended to Beth Adelman and Deb Eldredge, DVM.

Trademarks

All terms mentioned in this book that are known to be or are suspected of being trademarks or service marks have been appropriately capitalized. Alpha Books and Penguin Group (USA) Inc. cannot attest to the accuracy of this information. Use of a term in this book should not be regarded as affecting the validity of any trademark or service mark.

Part 1

Is a Beagle for You?

Are you considering whether you have what it takes to live life with a Beagle? These little scenthounds are real charmers, that's for sure, but they also come with a few foibles that can make them a bit of a challenge, especially to the novice dog owner.

In this section, you'll learn about the Beagle's development as a breed, the typical Beagle personality, and what the breed should look like. This section also helps you decide between a puppy and an adult Beagle, choose a breeder, and ensure a happy relationship among your children, your new dog, and your other pets.

Chapter 1

How the Beagle Came to Be

In This Chapter

- 🐾 The Beagle's early years
- 🐾 Off to the colonies
- 🐾 Beagles get organized
- 🐾 Differing opinions
- 🐾 The popular Beagle

Ever since dog and human became partners, thousands of years ago, they have worked as a team to hunt for food. Hounds, the quintessential hunters, are perhaps the oldest type of dog known. While Beagles as we see them today have existed for only 150 years or so, we can look back through history and trace their probable beginnings.

Beagle Beginnings

Beagle-type dogs have been around for a very long time in one form or another. As long ago as the fourth century B.C.E., the Greek historian Xenophon, an avid hunter, wrote a treatise on hunting that included mention of small hounds that hunted hare and rabbit. Over the centuries, the hounds spread through Europe and likely made their way to England via Roman traders, and later from France.

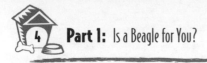
The Home Country: England

Like so many breeds, the modern Beagle developed in England, where love of the hunt was strong and small game was abundant. Small hounds hunted hare and rabbit by scent there as early as the fourteenth century, although they hadn't yet acquired the name Beagle.

Chaucer's Prioress, a literary character created in the fourteenth century, has some "small houndes," but it is not until the fifteenth century that the "small houndes" acquire a proper name. The first known written mention of the Beagle is in a story called "The Squire of Low Degree," an English romance published in 1475 that portrays the medieval delights of feasts, finery, music, and sports, including hunting. The unknown author's lines refer to Beagles in the plural, an early reference no doubt to the breed's pack mentality:

"With theyr Beagles in that place

and seven score raches [harrier-type dogs] at his rechase."

Beagle Bonus

Some people think the Beagle's name comes from the Old French words *bee gueule*, meaning loudmouth, an appropriate nickname for this vocal hound. The phrase *bee gueule* originates from the words *beer*, to gape, and *gueule*, gullet. Other theories suggest that the breed's name came from words that mean "small": the Old English *begel*, French *beigh* or Celtic *beag*.

By the time of Elizabeth I (1533-1603), it was the rare nobleman who didn't keep a pack of hounds, and the Queen herself was an enthusiastic hunter with her own pack of "singing beagles," a reference to the breed's cry when on the scent.

Some Beagles of this time period sported a wire coat, quite different from the smooth-coated dog of today. Others were tiny, small enough to fit in a huntsman's pocket. They were called, natch, pocket Beagles. Paintings from this period depict the pocket Beagles

as being short-legged and pointy-nosed. It was said that 10 or 12 couples of pocket Beagles could be carried in saddlebags.

Following in his cousin Elizabeth's footsteps, King James I of England (1566-1625) also enjoyed hunting hares on horseback and affectionately referred to his wife as his "deare little beagle."

Although they had good noses and plenty of staying power, Beagles lost ground to the speedier, more dashing Foxhounds in the mid-eighteenth century, when sport hunters began to desire a more exciting and fast-paced chase. But that wasn't the end of the Beagles. They remained popular with farmers and lesser landed gentry who couldn't afford to keep packs of the larger Foxhounds.

During this time, the Beagle's looks varied wildly because each pack's master had his own ideas about what he wanted in a Beagle. Type and size often depended on the type of country being hunted. Some, known as Southern Hounds, were cobby with short muzzles and long ears, stout and sure on the trail with deep voices. Their counterparts, North Country Beagles, had sharper muzzles and tight lips and moved swiftly across the field.

Hunting with Beagles increased in popularity in the 1830s, thanks to the influence of Rev. Phillip Honeywood of Essex, England. Honeywood's pack hounds, bred for hunting ability, were the forerunners of today's Beagle.

When dog breeding and showing became popular in the mid-nineteenth century, people formed breed clubs and wrote standards describing the ideal dog for their particular breeds. The Beagle was no exception, and it was recognized in 1873 by Britain's Kennel Club. The rise of dog shows led to the realization that the Beagle's type was in danger of disappearing, so breeders formed The Beagle Club in 1890 and worked to develop a more uniform dog.

Beagles of the American Revolution

Beagles are known to have made their way across the pond with colonists who came to settle the American wilderness. They earned

their keep on farms and were used to hunt in packs, or *braces*, not only to find game but also for sport.

These Beagles for the most part were bandy-legged little critters that were used to hunt just about everything. The early American Beagles were mostly white with few dark markings and often resembled a straight-legged Basset Hound or a Dachshund. Not very attractive in outline, they were nonetheless snappy, tireless hunters, full of vitality, and quick at the turn.

In the mid-nineteenth century, dog showing took hold in America, as it had in England. In the earliest show Beagles were *tall*, often with *pied* or *mottled coloring*. They varied in size from "toy," usually described as 9 inches or under, to 16 inches at the *withers*, or shoulders.

Things took a turn for the better in the 1860s, however. That's when General Richard Rowett of Carlinville, Illinois, and Norman Elmore of Newark, New Jersey, imported some high-class Beagles from British hunting packs. The Rowett line of Beagles became known for their consistent type and outstanding field ability. These hounds imported from the finest hunting packs in England became the foundation of the breed in the United States.

Beagle Lingo

A **brace** is a pair of Beagles. **Pied** or **mottled coloring** looks blotchy or spotted.

The American Kennel Club

The AKC (American Kennel Club) is a registration body, which means that it records birth and title statistics for the breeds it recognizes as being purebred, such as the Beagle. The AKC also sponsors events such as dog shows, obedience trials, and field trials held by its more than 500 member clubs. Be aware that while the AKC only registers purebred dogs of certain breeds, it does not guarantee the quality or health of those dogs. AKC registration papers mean only that a puppy's parents and grandparents were members of his same breed.

The first Beagle registered by the American Kennel Club was Blunder in 1885, only a year after the AKC was formed in 1884.

The National Beagle Club

In 1888, Beagle fanciers formed the National Beagle Club (NBC) with the objective of holding field trials to improve not only field qualities but also type (the characteristics that distinguish a breed). Members held their first field trial in 1890, followed by the first NBC specialty show in 1891.

To help achieve their goal of improving Beagle fieldwork, NBC members searched the country for an ideal location to hold field trials on a regular basis. In the early 1920s, they settled on a 500-acre property in Aldie, Virginia. It's called Institute Farm and is the NBC's present headquarters.

Also in the 1920s, the NBC began having pack trials as well as individual Beagle competitions. The masters of the various packs in the country could go to Institute Farm and compete their packs during the same week that *brace trials* and a *bench show* took place. (To learn more about the different types of field trials and dog shows, including the Triple Challenge mentioned later, be sure to read Chapters 15 and 16!)

Today, the NBC boasts more than 500 regular, supporting, and associate members. The club holds many activities at Institute Farm, including spring and fall *pack trials*, *field trials*, and the annual *Triple Challenge Trial*, open to *conformation* champions, field champions, and members of NBC-recognized hunting packs.

The individual hounds compete in a brace trial, a *three-hour stake*, and *on the bench*. The winner is the dog with the highest combined score. Thanks in part to the Triple Challenge, the Beagle breed has its first dual champion in more than 50 years.

A dual champion is a dog that has earned both conformation and field titles. The first Beagle to earn this title was Dual Ch. Frank Forest (1886-1889), who was a major influence on the breed. The

most recent holder of the coveted title is 13-inch Dual Ch. Pebble Ridge Shadrack (1995–), who broke a more than 50-year dry spell.

> **Beagle Lingo** _____
> A **brace trial** is a competition where two or three Beagles are judged on their accuracy in trailing a rabbit. A **bench show** is one where the dogs are kept on display when they're not in the show ring. **Pack trials** are competition hare hunts involving large packs of 30 or more Beagles; **field trials** are practical demonstrations of a Beagle's ability to hunt rabbits or hares; and the annual **Triple Challenge Trial** is a combination conformation show, field trial, and pack hunt. **Conformation** is the structure of a dog as described by the breed standard. A **three-hour stake** is a time-limited pack hunt; and a dog **on the bench** is one on display at a conformation show.

Breed Split: Different Types for Different Jobs

At the turn of the twentieth century, Beagle looks had become pretty standardized. The people who were importing them from England hunted their Beagles and competed with them in field trials and conformation shows.

Gradually, however, conformation Beaglers became dominant in the breed, and the Beagle again began to vary in type, depending on whether it was a field dog or a show dog. Because many conformation Beaglers had stopped working their dogs in the field, they weren't taking into consideration such elements of the total Beagle as the desire to hunt and a good nose that can tell when a rabbit has turned and then follow that line accurately. (When a rabbit has turned, it has gone in a different direction.)

Besides the differences between field and show dogs, differences developed among the field dogs themselves, depending on whether their quarry, or prey, was rabbit or hare and whether they competed in brace trials or large pack trials. Brace trials favor slow-moving dogs and may last only a few minutes per brace, while large pack trials reward sound dogs with plenty of stamina.

Beagle Bonus _____

In the twentieth century, certain lines of Beagles strongly influenced the breed. The Blue Caps and the Yellow Creeks had the greatest influence until 1950 or so. Then a hound emerged named Willcliff Boogie, who changed the course of brace Beagling in the United States. After he hit the scene, he became so popular that he was bred to extensively. Today, it's almost impossible to find any pedigrees in brace trial Beagles that don't have extensive crosses of Willcliff Boogie.

Up until 10 or 15 years ago, Beagles that competed in brace trials were almost useless for hunting because they didn't have the stamina to hunt all day and go out and do it again the following day.

Then the American Kennel Club approved a new kind of field trial for Beagles: the small pack option. At the same time, the United Beagle Gundog Federation decided to have two components to its field trials: one for field performance and one for conformation. This helped raise awareness among people who competed in Beagle field trials about the importance of having a hound that was not only a good hunter but also well made. The small pack option and large pack on hare trialers all want a Beagle that can last a long time, all day if necessary, and to achieve that goal they need Beagles with better conformation.

Now, after nearly a century of wrangling over what the Beagle should be, the breed is once again on the trail that will take it back to being the beautiful and functional dog that was envisioned by the fanciers who wrote the breed standard back in 1888.

The Twenty First Century Beagle

Beagle people are seeing exciting changes in the breed. The advent of the Triple Challenge Trial has brought together the best and the

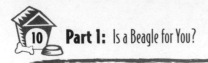

Beagle Bonus

Beagles are popular around the world and can be found not only in Britain and North America, but also in many other countries, including Australia, India, New Zealand, Singapore, the Philippines, and South Africa.

brightest of these merry hounds. Competition is keen in Beagles, and judges see many good ones, both in the field and in the show ring. Breeders are taking into account all the elements that go into a useful hound and are producing a well-rounded dog that can be successful in the home, the show ring, and the field.

What Makes the Beagle So Popular?

Not surprisingly, given his small size and charming personality, the Beagle is a popular companion in many homes. The breed ranks fifth in American Kennel Club registrations, with 50,419 Beagles registered in 2001.

The Beagle is a social extrovert with a warm and cheerful personality. Curious and intelligent, this is a dog with a true zest for life. Being a pack hound, he enjoys the companionship of people as well as other dogs. Although some Beagles can be a bit reserved toward people they don't know, most are people-oriented and bond with all members of the family. Shy and nervous are not words that should be applicable to this breed.

One of the great things about a Beagle is that while he's big in personality, he's small in size. Because Beagles generally weigh less than 30 pounds, they're well suited to living in an apartment or small home. They're equally at home indoors and outdoors, and they make good traveling companions.

While Beagles have a well-deserved reputation for digging, barking, and howling, such misbehavior usually occurs only when they're left alone for long periods. Beagles are pack animals and have a strong need to be part of the family.

While the Beagle is not as energetic as, say, a Jack Russell Terrier, he's exuberant in his youth and demands plenty of activity. Long walks on a leash, a leisurely hike, or a good run in an area away from cars will satisfy his desire for outdoor fun. Many Beagles are enthusiastic retrievers as well, especially if they're encouraged at an early age.

At physical maturity—about 18 months of age—the Beagle can join you in a daily jog. Running him at an earlier age, however, can damage his skeletal development.

Older Beagles tend to become fairly lazy. They're satisfied to lie around on the sofa with you and eat chips while watching television. Don't let them fool you, though. They still need regular exercise to stay trim and healthy.

These merry hounds retain a remarkably puppy-like appearance and attitude throughout their lives. Even after a Beagle's face has grayed with age, he's often mistaken for a youngster. Happily, this is a generally healthy breed that can live well into the teens.

The Nose Knows

Easygoing and affectionate, Beagles are content to be couch potatoes for large parts of the day, but are always up for a long walk or hike, especially if it offers opportunities to sniff new scents.

The most important thing to know about a Beagle is that he is a scenthound. His attention will always be diverted by any odors that waft his way. This is why you most often see a Beagle with his nose to the ground.

The strong desire to follow a scent wherever it may take him means that the Beagle tends to be a wanderer. It takes a clever owner and a well-made fence to keep this breed safe at home. Otherwise, expect them to take off into the wild blue yonder every time they smell something interesting. Beagles have been found miles from home after following a tempting trail.

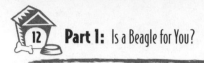

Inside the Beagle Brain

Never underestimate the intelligence of a Beagle. He is an independent thinker and likes to do things his own way. The Beagle is often dismissed as stubborn and untrainable, but he is far from thick-skulled. His problem-solving abilities are legendary, and he is fully capable of learning just about anything when properly motivated.

For most Beagles, motivation comes in the form of food. Their food drive, along with their amazing sense of smell, makes them single-minded in their determination to get what they're after. Beagles are also fond of praise and enjoy pleasing their owners—when it suits them. These two positive reinforcements—food and praise—combined with frequent but short and fun training sessions, can make your Beagle a dream dog to work with in almost any canine sport or activity. You can do anything you want with a Beagle—if you're patient.

The Least You Need to Know

- Beagles were developed in England over many centuries and achieved their modern form in the late nineteenth century.
- The Beagle's name is thought to come from words that describe either its loud voice or its small size.
- Some early Beagles were tiny, small enough to fit in a pocket or on a huntsman's gloved hand.
- Britain's Kennel Club recognized the Beagle as a breed in 1873.
- Beagles can vary in type depending on their purpose, but the ideal Beagle can compete well in the field, look good in the show ring, and hunt all day with his owner.
- The Beagle is a scenthound and is highly motivated by food.

Chapter 2

What Should a Beagle Look Like?

In This Chapter

- 🐾 Why a breed standard is important
- 🐾 Current breed standard
- 🐾 Variations in size
- 🐾 Common faults
- 🐾 Show or pet quality?

The Webster's Ninth New Collegiate Dictionary says the Beagle is a "small, short-legged hound with drooping ears and a smooth coat that has white, black, and tan markings." But there's a lot more to know about how a Beagle is supposed to look and why his looks are important. In this chapter, we'll take a look at the breed standard to see how it might apply to your search for a Beagle.

What Is a Breed Standard?

A breed standard is a picture in words. It describes what the perfect example of each breed should look like. Standards are written by breed experts. They describe perfect type, *gait*, temperament, and other information that describes the ideal member of a particular breed.

Just as there are no perfect people, there are also no perfect dogs, but the standard gives breeders something to aim for. A good breeder's goal is to produce dogs that meet the standard as nearly as possible.

Why does it matter how closely a Beagle matches up to the standard? After all, a good dog is a good dog, no matter how pretty he is, right?

Yes and no. A standard is what keeps a Beagle looking like a Beagle instead of a Harrier or a Foxhound. A standard also spells out the physical and mental qualities that make a dog a good *herder*, *puller*, or in the case of the Beagle, scenthound.

Beagle Lingo

The **gait** is the way a dog moves; for instance, a walk, trot, or jog. A **herder** is a dog that herds livestock, a **puller** is a dog that pulls a sled or wagon, and a scenthound is a dog that hunts prey by scent.

(© *John Kraeuter*)

Breeding to the standard ensures that a Beagle looks like a Beagle, not a Dachshund or Basset Hound.

The standard is important whether you are looking for a Beagle to be a family companion, show dog, or hunter. The Beagle is a versatile dog and ideally should excel at all of these jobs, but each individual dog may have particular flaws in one area or another. By understanding what makes a Beagle a Beagle, you can decide which characteristics are most important to you when choosing your dog.

Field Dog, Show Dog, or Pet?

The Beagle breed has become quite diverse over the years. The factions consist of the following:

- 🏠 Show dogs are bred with the goal of perfect conformation.

- 🏠 Traditional brace dogs are the product of a fad that stresses accuracy of trailing instead of the characteristics necessary for hunting.

- 🏠 Gun dogs are trialed to encourage the characteristics necessary for hunting ability.

- 🏠 Large-pack dogs run on hare (meaning that they hunt the fast-moving hare) and need great stamina.

- 🏠 Pets may come from any of these groups, or they may be bred with little regard for pedigree, with the primary goal being an enjoyable companion.

In the best case scenario, however, there should be no significant difference between field, show, and pet Beagles. The same Beagle, from a reputable breeder with a selective breeding program, can perform all three duties quite nicely. Many people breed for versatility and produce Beagles that not only conform to the breed standard but also retain the hunting abilities for which the breed was developed.

Nonetheless, some traits are useful for success in certain types of competition and are sometimes bred to the exclusion of all else. For example, brace trials reward dogs with a slow and careful working style. Some breeders artificially slow down their Beagles by intentionally breeding for short legs. This type of Beagle, which more closely resembles a Basset Hound, is known as a walkie-talkie. These dogs are a far cry from both the proper gundog Beagle and the show winner.

Likewise, some breeders of show Beagles place more emphasis on correct breed type than on functional aspects of the dogs' conformation. Happily, there are plenty of breeders who strive to produce the complete Beagle, a versatile dog with good health, a pleasant temperament, and sound conformation.

The Big Picture

Whether he's a field dog or a show dog, a Beagle's most important physical characteristic is balance. He should be nicely proportioned, squarely built with a level topline (back), a nice, straight front, and well-angulated hindquarters. When he moves, it looks almost as if he's floating.

The ability to go all day is where field dogs tend to beat out show dogs. A trend toward a back that is too short is part of the problem. When the back is too short, the shoulders are upright and the rear is straighter, affecting the dog's ability to move correctly. Ideally, the Beagle has a good sloping shoulder, a good upper arm, and a driving rear.

Beagle Bonus

It's a common misconception that Beagles were "bred down" from Foxhounds, but this is not the case. In fact, some say just the opposite is true: that Fox-hounds and Harriers were developed by crossing Beagles and other scenthounds.

Problems tend to emerge as the result of fads. Breeders assume that if something is good—a slow pace, for instance—then even slower is better. The next thing you know, you have a bunch of extreme Beagles running around, rather than the balanced dogs the standard calls for.

The Beagle Standard

The standard has not changed over the years, although trends in the breed have come and gone. For instance, people were breeding for a very short back at one point, which often meant a sacrifice of other qualities in terms of movement or shoulder and rear. Such trends come and go in the show ring and in the field.

In general, the Beagle standard is simple and clear. It describes the head, body, shoulders and chest, back, loin, ribs, forelegs, feet, hips, thighs, hind legs, tail, coat, color, and general appearance. Surprisingly, it doesn't discuss gait, or movement, but it describes the parts of the body that create good movement. The standard also covers the two varieties of Beagle, the qualities of a good pack, and recommendations for show livery (the distinctive clothing to be worn in the show ring or field).

General Appearance

This description calls for the Beagle to be a miniature Foxhound, solid and big for his inches, with the wear-and-tear look of a dog that can last in the chase and follow his quarry to the death. If you've ever seen a Beagle intently following a scent, you know just what the standard means.

The well-put-together Beagle has the look of a dog that can go all day in the field and the conformation that allows him to do that: a shoulder that's properly angulated rather than straight; a strong, powerful rear; and a good long ribcage for heart and lungs; and stamina.

Beagle Bonus

Conformation refers to the structure of a dog, the way that he "conforms" to the breed standard.

Height and Weight

Beagles come in 2 sizes: 13-inch and 15-inch. The first variety may not stand more than 13 inches at the withers (shoulders). The

Beagle Bonus

The English standard permits a maximum height of 16 inches. Many fine Beagles that are too tall for the American show ring are happily imported by British breeders.

second variety is for Beagles that are taller than 13 inches but not exceeding 15 inches.

Beagle height at maturity ranges from 10 inches to 16 inches. In the United States, Beagles that stand taller than 15 inches are disqualified from competition in the show ring or in field trials, although they can still compete in obedience and agility trials. In most other countries, 16 inches is accepted as the maximum height.

It's hard to say what size a Beagle pup will grow to be. Thirteen-inch parents can produce pups that grow to 15 inches, and 15-inch parents can produce smaller offspring. Sometimes the same litter can have pups of both sizes. If you want to be sure of the size you're getting, purchase a Beagle that has already reached physical maturity, usually about nine months of age.

(© Kristine Kraeuter)

These two dogs demonstrate the differences in Beagle height. On the left is a dog from the 13-inch category, on the right one from the 15-inch category.

Depending on their height, Beagles weigh anywhere from 15 to 30 pounds. Beagles that stand under 13 inches typically weigh 15 to 20 pounds, while their taller counterparts weigh 20 to 30 pounds.

Head

A pretty Beagle head brings gladness to a breeder's heart. The proper Beagle has a fairly long skull that is slightly domed at the back part of the head. The cranium, the part of the skull that surrounds the brain, is broad and full.

The droopy Beagle ears sit moderately low on the head. They're long. If you pull them forward, they should reach almost to the end of the dog's nose. The forward edge of the ear turns slightly in toward the cheek, and the ear is rounded at the tip. It should not stand up at all.

Gentle, melting eyes are large and set wide apart. Brown or hazel in color, they display the soft, pleading expression for which this breed is famous.

The Beagle's *muzzle* should be moderately long, straight, and square. The *stop* is moderately defined. The nostrils are large and open (the better to scent with, my dear). The jaw is level, meaning that the incisors (front teeth) of the upper and lower jaws meet exactly edge to edge. Avoid choosing a dog with a noticeable overbite or underbite.

When all these parts come together properly, the result is a soft, pretty face.

Beagle Lingo

The **muzzle** is made up of the nasal bones, nostrils, and jaws. The **stop** is the indentation between the eyes where the nasal bones and cranium meet.

Neck and Throat

The Beagle's medium-length neck rises free and light from the shoulders. The neck shouldn't be wrinkled, although a slight wrinkle below the angle of the jaw is allowable.

Shoulders and Chest

Sloping shoulders are clean and muscular without looking too heavy or muscled. In other words, the proper Beagle has a nice build without the pumped look of a body builder. Think Tom Cruise, not Arnold Schwarzenegger. The standard says the shoulders should convey the idea of freedom of action with activity and strength.

The chest is deep and broad, without interfering with the free play of the shoulders.

Beagle Lingo
The **back** is also known as the top-line. The top-line stretches from just behind the shoulders to the root of the tail.

Back, Loin, and Ribs

The Beagle's *back* is short, muscular, and strong. The loin—the area about the hips—is broad and slightly arched, and the ribs are well sprung. This means that they curve enough to provide plenty of room for the lungs to work, an important consideration for a dog that's expected to hunt all day.

Forelegs and Feet

Because this is a breed that should be able to go all day in the field, a Beagle's feet and legs are especially important. The Beagle's front legs are straight, with plenty of bone in proportion to the size of the dog. The pasterns, the area between the wrist and toes, are short and straight. Feet are close, round, and hard with full, hard pads to protect the feet from wear, not to mention hazards such as brambles.

Hips, Thighs, and Hind Legs

Strong, well-muscled hips and thighs power the Beagle as he chases his quarry. Strong stifles, or knees, aren't too long, and firm hocks (the bones that form the dog's heel) are symmetrical and moderately bent.

Movement

The Beagle standard doesn't discuss how the Beagle should move, but the foregoing attributes all contribute to good movement. If a Beagle has a good rear and a good front, he'll have good movement.

A Beagle should move freely, covering ground effortlessly. He has good drive and reach with no wasted movement to the side such as weaving in and out. Many descriptions of hunting in old English books refer to hounds galloping, and that's what they do if they're running for an extended period of time. Being able to move effortlessly means they don't have to expend excess energy.

Tail

The Beagle's slightly curved tail is set moderately high and carried up, although it shouldn't come forward over the back. It's called a brush tail, meaning it's bushy or heavy with hair.

Bent or crooked tails are fairly common in Beagles. Don't let a breeder persuade you that this type of tail will correct itself in time. A bent tail doesn't affect a Beagle's "pet"-ability, but it would be a serious flaw in a show dog.

The Beagle's tail is referred to as a flag. Packs are to work with flags up, obeying all commands cheerfully.

Coat

This is a double-coated breed. A medium-length, close, hard coat covers the Beagle's body, protecting the dog from brush and inclement weather. Beneath the top coat is a finer undercoat.

What Color Can My Beagle Be?

When we think of a Beagle, we usually picture the classic tricolor dog of black, brown, and white. The standard simply says a Beagle may be any true hound color. This leaves a lot of room for variation

Bet You Didn't Know Beagles shed. They shed a lot. Be prepared to brush your dog regularly to keep the hair under control.

and dissension. For example, the British standard permits "any recognized hound color except liver" (for the U.S. folks, liver is the color brown).

So what exactly is a hound color? According to the AKC and the NBC, hound colors include all shades and combinations of white or cream, black, tan/lemon/red, brown/liver, blue/gray, and the colors of the hare or badger. Keeping in mind the adage that no good hound can be a bad color, let's take a look at some of the colorations seen in Beagles.

The Classic Model

The tricolor Beagle has a black saddle overlaying a brown body and head with white on the feet, face, neck, and tail tip. This placement of white is called an Irish spotting pattern. The saddle is just what it sounds like: a black marking over the back, like a saddle in the horse.

When white is the predominant color, the pattern is called an open, or broken, tricolor. The term open refers to the white on the back, which breaks up the color. In such a case, the dog is described as white, tan, and black. Neither pattern is preferred over the other; it's all a matter of personal taste.

Two-Tone

The second most commonly seen color combination is the red and white bicolor. These dogs may be described as lemon and white or tan and white, depending on the depth of their coat color. Beagles can also be a predominantly solid black and tan.

Tricolor Varieties

Sometimes the black on a tricolor is replaced by a faded, or dilute, color such as blue, chocolate or liver, or lilac. Blue dogs may have light eyes that appear almost yellow, or slate-blue noses rather than black. Sometimes a blue dog is so dark that the only clue to its true color is the blue nose. Others develop a dark nose that makes them indistinguishable from a normal tricolor. Then there are shaded blue tricolors, which exhibit much lighter tan areas than their dark blue counterparts.

A liver or chocolate tricolor is described as a dog whose black has diluted to dark brown, including on the nose. As with blue dogs, Beagles with chocolate coats sometimes darken as they mature.

The lilac tricolor has not only the liver or chocolate factor but also a blue dilute factor. Combined, they give a bluish cast to the blanket, which is the color of the coat on the back and upper part of the sides.

Beagle Bonus

Often there's a white tip on the Beagle's tail, which is desirable because it makes it easy to spot the dog in the field. Not to mention it just plain looks cute. The British standard calls for the tip of the tail—they call it the stern—to be white, but the American standard does not specify such a requirement.

Pied Pipers

The term pied refers to comparatively large patches of two or more colors and is sometimes called particolor or piebald. Pied Beagles come in three shades: hare pied (darkest), badger pied (medium), and lemon pied (lightest). The predominant color on these dogs is more of a pale cream than a clear white. The patches of color usually appear on the dog's sides or across the back. Breeders sometimes disagree over whether a dog is a true pied or simply a shaded or faded tricolor.

A badger-pied Beagle has an almost-white base coat. Pigmented areas are a mixture of black, silver, and fawn hairs all together, resembling the coat of a badger. Thus the name. The colors fade into each other and into the white, marking the main difference between a faded tricolor and a true pied.

The hare-pied Beagle has a similar pattern, but with more tan hairs and fewer black hairs. Again, the color blends in with the creamy base coat.

Lemon-pied Beagles mingle cream or lemon hairs with the off-white base coat. Sometimes the colors can be so dilute as to give the appearance of a pure white dog.

Ticked Off

A ticked coat is one with small, isolated areas of black hairs on a white ground. Ticking is seen more often in Beagles bred for field work. In the show ring, excessive ticking would likely be considered a fault.

Mottled Crew

A mottled hound has a pattern of dark roundish blotches superimposed on a lighter background. A mottled coat can be identified when a puppy is as young as four or five days by looking at its feet. A tricolor puppy has soles that are pigmented in patches, while the pads of a mottled puppy start out mulberry and then turn black. There are no patches of pink on a mottled pup.

Markings

The markings on a Beagle pup can change as he matures. Small white markings may fade around the edges, and faint areas of white sometimes fade completely. Tan areas can deepen, and sometimes black markings will turn to tan. Like the Cheshire Cat in Alice in Wonderland, a mask of black around a puppy's eyes may gradually vanish until only a spot between the eyes and ears remains by the time the dog is grown.

The Great Debate: Show Quality vs. Pet Quality

We all want the best when we make a purchase. Especially when that purchase is going to become a beloved member of the family. It's better, then, to demand a show-quality Beagle, right?

Well, not necessarily. Although the term "pet quality" may sound derogatory to your anxious ears, it simply means that certain of the dog's characteristics are not good enough for him to succeed against the tough competition in the breed ring or the field.

The qualities that can lead to a Beagle being placed in the pet category may include such cosmetic flaws as light eyes, short ears, or a long muzzle. While these faults aren't acceptable in the show ring, they don't detract at all from the dog's ability to be a great companion. And you're still getting a dog, ideally, from parents that have been tested for hereditary diseases before being bred and from a breeder who will stand with you for the life of the dog.

Less Than Perfect

A number of faults can cost a Beagle points in the show ring, although they may not affect his ability to hunt or to be a great pet. Some are cosmetic faults, while others are actual physical flaws. For instance, being too tall—measuring more than 15 inches—can actually disqualify a Beagle from the ring, rather than merely costing him points. What you plan to do with your Beagle will determine whether these flaws are important to you.

Standard Defects

The Beagle standard lists the following faults:

- 🐾 A very flat skull, narrow across the top
- 🐾 An excessively domed head

🏠 Eyes that are small, sharp, or terrier like

🏠 Prominent protruding eyes

🏠 Roman nose (one with a high bridge that forms a kind of hump or curve from the forehead to the tip of the nose)

🏠 Ears that are short, set high on the skull, or that have a tendency to rise above the point of origin

🏠 A thick, short, cloddy neck

🏠 Too much loose skin under the throat (throatiness)

🏠 Straight, upright shoulders

🏠 A disproportionately wide chest

🏠 A chest with lack of depth

🏠 A long, swayed, or roached back (a roached back is curved or humped looking)

🏠 A flat, narrow loin

🏠 Flat ribs (these don't curve out enough to give the dog's heart and lungs enough room to work)

🏠 Elbows that turn out from the body

🏠 Knees knuckled over forward or bent backward

🏠 Crooked forelegs

🏠 Long, open, or spreading feet

🏠 Hocks that turn in, with the rear feet toeing out (cow-hocked)

🏠 Straight hocks

🏠 Lack of muscle and propelling power

🏠 A long tail or one with a teapot curve (where the tail is carried in an arch up and over the back)

🏠 A rat tail (one that has a hairless tip)

🏠 A short, thin, or soft coat

Whew! That's a long list, but it's unlikely that any one Beagle will have all of these faults. If you're planning to show your Beagle, you will of course want to take such things into consideration, but a Beagle that's going to be a family friend is no less loving and fun for having a rat tail, a roman nose, or short ears. Minor faults such as these won't affect his health or life span, and that's the most important thing.

Bet You Didn't Know

Ask the breeder to go over the standard with you so you understand the fine points that make the difference between a Beagle that has show potential and one that doesn't. Avoid breeders who claim all their puppies are show quality. A dog goes through many changes as it matures, and one that had promise as a puppy may not always turn out exactly as expected.

Temperament Faults

In general, the Beagle is a happy-go-lucky soul. He may have behaviors that become problematic, such as howling or digging or running away, but these things don't detract from his overall nice disposition.

Occasionally, however, a Beagle comes along who has a less than stellar temperament. He may be shy, either because he wasn't socialized properly as a pup or because his parents and their parents before them were shy. It's often tempting to feel sorry for a shy animal, but this is not an appropriate trait for this breed. It's best to look for a more outgoing pup who will enjoy interacting with people.

The opposite of shyness, which is aggression, should be just as uncommon in the Beagle. While these pack hounds may defend their territory by barking, they should never be aggressive toward people or other dogs or family pets. (Squirrels, on the other hand, are fair game.)

**Bet You
Didn't Know**

Spoiled Beagles can become snappy and irritable. They need good leadership and training to retain their merry temperament.

If a Beagle does become aggressive, it's likely to be food-related. Beagles do love their meals and some may growl or bite if they perceive that their food supply is being threatened. A trainer or behaviorist can help solve this problem before it gets out of control.

Aggression can also occur during adolescence, when the Beagle is trying to establish his place in the family and with other dogs. He may become aggressive toward other males. Neutering can reduce this tendency, as well the desire to urine-mark territory or seek out females in heat.

Aggression is different from challenging authority. The independent and pack-oriented Beagle is keenly aware of his family's social hierarchy. He will certainly try to run the household if you let him, but this is simply the normal canine attempt at dominance. Establish that you're in charge by setting firm, consistent rules and teaching appropriate manners. It's only when you fail to do so that behavior problems are likely to begin.

The Least You Need to Know

🐾 The breed standard explains what a Beagle should look like.

🐾 Beagles come in two sizes: 13-inch and 15-inch.

🐾 A Beagle may be any hound color.

🐾 A pet-quality Beagle has flaws that make him unsuited to the show ring or to the field, but don't affect his ability to be a great companion.

🐾 Beagles should never be shy or aggressive.

Chapter

Beagle Mania

In This Chapter

- A nose for news
- Vocal yokel
- Mmmm ... food
- Blah, blah, blah, Baxter, blah, blah
- Problem Beagles

If you're thinking about getting a Beagle companion, there are a few things you need to know about what he's like to live with. That nose, for instance. And why he likes to howl. And his strong desire to eat anything that even slightly resembles food. You get the picture.

Beagle Personality Quirks

Pretty much everything a Beagle does relates back to his nose. That powerful scenting organ is what causes him to wander away from home and eat everything in sight in the hope that it might be food. It's what makes the breed prized by termite inspectors and government agencies, both of which use the Beagle to sniff out termites and contraband.

Beagles are also known for their voices. Some liken Beagle vocalizations to music, while others simply call it noisy howling. The Beagle's "Aaaroooooh" can make you laugh or growl, depending on what time of day or night he lets loose with it.

The Beagle's foibles are an integral part of his merry nature. Living happily with a Beagle requires understanding and embracing all the facets that make him the bright, inquisitive dog he is. Take a few minutes here to learn more about the inner scenthound.

Follow That Scent!

His sense of smell may well be a dog's most valuable asset. The canine nose is amazingly well designed for sniffing or smelling. A dog's nasal passages are built to receive and trap odors, and an estimated 220 million scent receptors (cells that specialize in identifying odors) help dogs define the world around them. Beagles have especially good scenting ability in part because of their large, open nostrils.

Bet You Didn't Know

Dogs sometimes cannot recognize people or other dogs they know until they get close enough to identify them by scent.

Beagle Bonus

Dogs don't become accustomed to scents and lose them after a few minutes, the way humans do, but they can block out scents other than the one they're searching for.

A dog's nasal cavity is lined with turbinates, bony plates containing specialized cells that send sensory information about odors to the olfactory nerve. This nerve runs directly to the brain, which then processes the scent information and stores it, in much the same way as a computer stores files. With training, dogs can learn to recognize and indicate many different odors.

Scenthounds such as Beagles are particularly well suited to using their sense of smell. Their noses have large, open nostrils to pull in smells. As the Beagle's nose sniffs along the ground, his long ears fall forward, sweeping the scent up toward the nose. A Beagle's nose is so finely tuned that he can detect and identify even faint or diluted odors that are beyond the measuring capacity of high-tech equipment.

The Beagle Brigade

Because of their scenting ability, small size, and friendliness toward people, Beagles became the dog of choice when the USDA's Animal and Plant Health Inspection Service (APHIS) established a detector dog program at Los Angeles International Airport in 1984. The program was so successful that APHIS now has a national training center in Orlando, Florida. There, members of the Beagle Brigade learn their trade.

If you've done much flying at all, chances are you've seen these green-coated Beagles sniffing luggage at airports, in search of forbidden plants, fruits, and other food products that might carry pests or disease. The Beagle's love of food makes him a natural at this job. He's happy to work for treats, and he remains calm at busy baggage claim areas.

The leashed dogs sniff the baggage of passengers entering the United States. If they smell prohibited items, they sit to alert their human partners, who then inspect the bags, confiscate contraband, and reward the dog with a treat.

Dogs that work for the Beagle Brigade are donated by their owners or adopted from animal shelters. Because these dogs work so closely with the public, trainers evaluate them to make sure they aren't shy or aggressive. Each dog is paired with a handler who's responsible for training and care.

Beagle Bonus

APHIS has provided expertise and training to agriculture officials in other countries who want to start their own detector dog programs. Canada, Australia, New Zealand, Guatemala, Mexico, and South Korea have all sought the assistance of USDA's Beagle Brigade and APHIS officials.

Training takes 8 to 12 weeks. Scents the dogs learn to identify include citrus fruit, mango, beef, and pork. Only positive training techniques are used since Beagles don't respond well to force or harsh handling. They're rewarded for making correct decisions and ignored or gently redirected for making incorrect decisions. By the end of their first year on the job, the Beagles have a success rate of 80 percent, which rises to about 90 percent after 2 years' experience.

Bet You Didn't Know _____

Scent forms when the bacteria that inhabits skin cells release volatile substances. As a person or animal moves, scent floats off the body. When a rabbit's paws touch the ground, or its body brushes against greenery, or it sheds flakes of skin and hair, it leaves a trail for a Beagle to follow. Scent stays near the ground when conditions are damp or cool and rises into the air when the weather is warm or hot.

A typical day for a member of the Beagle Brigade might involve sniffing baggage, taking part in a demonstration at a school, or visiting the veterinarian for routine health care. Each work hour includes 20 minutes of rest time. A Beagle Brigade dog works for about six years. When he retires, he's adopted by his trainer or placed in a home where he'll be a pet. Dogs that wash out from training class are also placed in pet homes.

The Termitinator

Beagles are also capable of sniffing out the location of termite nests. Termite-detection dogs have been used in the industry for about 15 years. Beagles tend to be the favored breed for this job not only for their keen sense of smell but also because they're able to reach tight spaces that people can't get to.

Bet You Didn't Know _____

In comparison to dogs, people have a relatively low level of scenting ability. Humans have only about five million scent receptors. These cells are concentrated in a small area at the back of the nose. People have only about 1 square inch of olfactory membrane, while dogs may have an olfactory membrane of up to 22 square inches.

Training and certification for this job takes 8 to 10 months, and dogs can be recertified every 90 days to ensure that their skills remain up to snuff. The dogs sniff out live termites and above-ground nests. When they make a find, they're rewarded with food.

Howl-o-rama

Beagles have a reputation for being noisy, but it's not always deserved. Like most dogs, they bark when strangers arrive, at squirrels in the backyard, or at unusual events—say, a moving van next door. They're likely to howl along with sirens, and because of their hunting heritage, they often bark when they happen upon an interesting scent. Of course, they tongue on the trail, to let the hunter know where they are and that they're in pursuit of quarry.

Nuisance barkers they're not, though, unless they're left alone for long periods every day. Beagles get bored, and when they're bored, they bark or howl to entertain themselves or to express their displeasure at being by themselves.

To prevent nuisance barking, give your Beagle plenty of daily attention and exercise. Make sure he has interesting toys to keep him occupied while you're gone. And teach him to bark or howl on command, as well as to stop barking on command. You, your neighbors, and your dog will all be happier. It's also a good idea to keep your Beagle indoors when you're not home, so he isn't distracted by outdoor scents, sounds, and passers-by.

Is It Food?

When in doubt, the Beagle will always attempt to eat something, just in case it might taste good. Most of the funny stories about Beagles involve the strange things they eat.

Beagles have been known to eat a sack of potatoes stored in a cabinet, socks, and shelled pecans. They'll attempt to eat anything left within their reach. One Beagle in Tennessee stole a head of lettuce off the kitchen counter and then pretended it was something he had really wanted.

When to Call the Vet

Beagles can suffer from pancreatitis if they pig out on rich table scraps or fatty foods found in the garbage. This condition is an inflammation of the pancreas and can be serious if left untreated. If your Beagle suddenly begins vomiting and appears to have abdominal pain—indicated by a tucked-up belly or a hunched position as if he's saying his prayers—call the veterinarian. Acute pancreatitis requires hospitalization. A milder version of this condition is called garbage can enteritis and is commonly seen in Beagles.

Less pleasantly, Beagles are also known to eat poop, a habit formally known as coprophagy. Beagle owners learn quickly to keep the poop scooped in the yard and to keep the cat's litter box off limits.

Because Beagles are so motivated by food, it's next to impossible to teach them to leave it alone. Instead put food away that you don't want your dog to have or chances are he'll find a way to get to it.

Having a cocktail party? Don't plan on serving hors d'oeuvres on your coffee table unless your Beagle is confined to quarters. Keep dining room chairs pushed in when there's food on the table, and don't leave food too close to the edge of the kitchen counter.

(© *Janiece Harrison*)

No matter how much you try to teach them not to, Beagles will take any opportunity to snatch food. Keep it out of reach.

Selective Hearing

Like all hounds, Beagles tend to go their own way. They're independent thinkers (read stubborn), and they'll expect a good reason from you before they'll consider doing things your way. Easily bored or distracted, the Beagle is quite capable of suddenly developing a form of deafness known to parents as selective hearing.

You can call and call and call, but if they're doing something they enjoy, such as following a trail or eating a meal, you're unlikely to get much of a response. Far from stupid, the Beagle pays attention only when paying attention seems worthwhile. Training is no fun anymore? The Beagle simply wanders off to better things, like rolling in something stinky. The only thing that might regain his attention is the sound of a box of treats being shaken.

Bet You Didn't Know

If the sensory membranes that line the inside of a dog's nose could be removed and stretched flat, their total surface area would be greater than the total surface area of the dog's body.

The secret to understanding a Beagle is the knowledge that his only interests are scents and food. Those interests are the key to successfully molding a Beagle into the warm, outgoing, trustworthy companion he's meant to be, without stifling the intelligence and independence that make him a scent-hound.

Problem-Solving Ability

While selective hearing can certainly be a problem in this breed, when a Beagle wants something, not much is going to stop him from getting it. Canine intelligence has been defined as a dog's ability to meet and adapt to novel situations quickly and effectively. Based on this description, the Beagle is a brainiac.

In canine intelligence tests that involved problem-solving situations, short- and intermediate-term visual memory, and the ability to discern where sounds were coming from, Beagles were among the highest scoring dogs. The tester commented that of all the dogs tested, hounds were the most methodical and analytical when faced with a problem-solving task. They also had good concentration and visual memory.

The Least You Need to Know

- 🏠 The secret to understanding a Beagle is the knowledge that his only interests are scents and food.

- 🏠 Almost everything a Beagle does is linked to his scenting ability.

- 🏠 Beagles are likely to become nuisance barkers if they're left alone every day for long periods.

- 🏠 Beagles will eat anything, so keep all food items—or anything that even looks edible—out of reach.

- 🏠 Beagles are good problem-solvers, quick to work out solutions to obstacles that are preventing them from getting what they want—usually food.

Part 2

A Beagle in the House

Now that you've definitely decided on a Beagle, you have a few other decisions to make and some research to do. Like what you want in a puppy, where to get him, what you need to know to make the right choice, and what kind of environment you need to provide for him.

In this section, you'll learn how to evaluate a breeder, select a puppy, choose a dog from a shelter or breed rescue group, and introduce your pup to his new home and family members—two-legged and four-legged. This is an important part to read if you're still not entirely sure that a Beagle is the right breed for you. Remember, Beagles are a lot of fun, but they're not always the easiest breed to live with.

Chapter

Decisions, Decisions

In This Chapter

- 🏠 Do you really want a Beagle?
- 🏠 Deciding between a puppy and an adult
- 🏠 Choosing the right Beagle for your needs
- 🏠 One Beagle or two?

Now that you know a little something about the Beagle, be honest with yourself. Is this really the right dog for you? The best owner for a Beagle is a person who has plenty of time to spend with a curious hound who loves to follow his nose wherever it may take him.

Club Beagle or Escape from Alcatraz?

This is not a breed that can be trusted off-leash—ever. You'll need a secure yard to keep him safely at home. This means a tall, sturdy fence with a properly latching gate and no areas he can dig under or jump over.

Besides a good fence, the ideal Beagle yard has a nice grassy area for running and rolling around, a supply of fun toys rotated on a

regular basis, and fresh water and food. In case of inclement weather, there's an insulated doghouse to provide shelter from wind, rain, or snow. A shady spot is nice for days when the mercury climbs high.

Puppies are adorable, but they have lots of energy and need constant attention unless they're safely confined.

However nice his yard is, the Beagle is not a dog that will enjoy being tied outside for long hours. If he is left alone frequently, he will express his displeasure vocally. Not to mention loudly. And often. This pack hound wants to be with his people, and that means in the house. To help make him a good housedog, the Beagle needs firm, consistent training to learn the manners you require.

The Urban Beagle

Does a Beagle require a home with a yard? Not necessarily. Beagles are the ideal size for apartment living and can live quite happily in the city. Just think of all those fascinating smells that will attract

them. As long as they get a couple of daily walks, city Beagles have just as much fun as country Beagles.

You can make apartment dwelling or city life fun for your Beagle with daily outings to a park where he can sniff, chase squirrels, and meet other dogs and people. Other ways to give a city Beagle the sensory satisfaction and socialization he needs include car rides to a drive-through bank teller or fast food spot (no, you don't need to buy him his own burger, but a couple of fries wouldn't come amiss), a meal at an outdoor cafe, or a walk to the dry cleaners or video store. A well-behaved dog is welcome at most such places.

Beagle Pros and Cons

Beagles are stubborn, and their intelligence can make them a challenge for the new dog owner. Unless they're motivated, it's their way or no way. Besides being firm and consistent, you must be kind to win a Beagle over to your way of doing things.

On the plus side, the Beagle is a lovable critter and good buddy who's always ready for a walk, a car ride, or a rabbit hunt. His small size makes him a good travel companion. Beagles are smart and can learn all kinds of things when they're motivated.

The short Beagle coat is easy to groom and has no odor (unless the dog has been rolling in smelly dead things so he can enjoy their scent). A Beagle's coat does shed, though, so be prepared for hair on furniture and clothes.

Beagles are good playmates for children old enough to interact with them, but their care and training requires supervision by an adult.

Doggy Do's/ Doggy Don'ts

Never rely on children's promises to care for and play with a dog. If you get a family dog, it must be because you would enjoy having a dog and are willing to be responsible for its care.

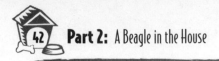

Before you decide to get a Beagle, ask yourself the following questions:

- Are my home and yard set up to contain a questing Beagle? If not, can they be modified to meet a Beagle's needs?

- Do I have the time to give a Beagle the training he needs to become a full-fledged member of the family?

- Am I willing to continue this training throughout my dog's life?

- Are family members home often enough that my Beagle won't become lonely and bored, or are we too busy with work and school to give him the time he needs for play, exercise, and training?

- Do we have the discipline to keep food and other potentially edible items out of reach?

- Do we have time for a dog at all, let alone a Beagle?

Don't run out and get a Beagle until you've asked yourself these questions and answered them with a resounding "Yes!" Despite his good nature and charming demeanor, the Beagle is a demanding dog who's been known to drive his owners to the brink of madness. He doesn't mean to; he just gets distracted by his nose, and the next thing he knows, he's in trouble again.

Beagle Bonus

Patience and a strong sense of humor are pluses when it comes to living with a Beagle. If you can laugh at his antics, even if they've made you a little mad, you're well on your way to being an understanding owner.

If you have any doubts about whether the Beagle is right for you, wait to get one. Try to meet a few on a recurring basis or, better yet, borrow one from a friend. Too many Beagles end up in shelters because people purchased them on impulse without knowing the breed's quirks.

The Versatile Beagle

The great thing about a Beagle is the variety of activities for which he's suited. The same Beagle can be a fine hunter, a winning show dog, a heartwarming therapy animal, and a loving companion to his family. He's limited only by the amount of time and effort you put into training him.

It's important to know, however, that different types of Beagles can have different characteristics. While some Beagles are well rounded, some come from strictly *field lines*, meaning they and their ancestors have been bred only to hunt rabbits, and others from strictly *show lines*, meaning they might not ever have seen a rabbit, but they're very familiar with the show ring. Which you choose can determine what kind of Beagle experience you have. Know what you want to do with your Beagle before making a decision on which one to buy.

That Dog Won't Hunt

If your Beagle will be a pet or show dog, it's probably a good idea to avoid buying a puppy from field lines. Field dogs tend to be more active and vocal than dogs bred for the show ring. Their desire to hunt is strong, and they can be more difficult to train and to contain. They may also have a greater tendency toward shyness. These characteristics don't apply to every field Beagle pup, of course, but you should be aware of the possibility.

Remember that the typical Beagle isn't shy. Shyness can result from heredity or lack of attention from the breeder.

Doggy Do's/ Doggy Don'ts

Don't buy from any breeder who isn't willing to let you to come out and see her Beagles in person or who makes excuses for not letting you see the mother, such as "She doesn't like strangers much."

Before buying any puppy, you should always meet the parents, or at least the mother. She can pass on shy or other undesirable behavior to pups, especially if they stay with her eight weeks or longer. While it's usually best for pups to stay with their mother and littermates for 8 to 10 weeks, some breeders have found that a pup from a shy mother is best taken to his new home at about 7 weeks of age. At that age, he's less likely to have picked up his mother's shy behavior. Given plenty of interaction with a variety of people and other dogs, he'll be more likely to develop into a friendly, outgoing dog.

Family Friend

What if you want "just a pet"? There's nothing wrong with that. A Beagle can be the best friend your family ever had. That doesn't mean you shouldn't get your money's worth, though. You want a healthy dog that looks like a Beagle, not a Dachshund or Basset. And you want a Beagle that has the breed's characteristic friendly nature, not a shy guy that's fearful of his own shadow.

Your best bet for finding a Beagle with all these qualities is a reputable breeder. This is someone who breeds only the nicest dogs with the fewest faults. A good breeder has the mother tested for parasites and brucellosis, a sexually transmitted disease, before breeding her.

If a problem such as *hip dysplasia* or eye disease occurs in a breeder's lines, she has hips and eyes checked before breeding her dogs so they don't pass on serious health conditions. She requires that

Beagle Lingo

Hip dysplasia occurs when the head of the leg bone doesn't fit properly into the hip socket.

A **stud dog** is a male dog used for breeding.

Beagle Bonus

While line breeding and inbreeding can intensify desirable traits, they can also increase the incidence of hereditary faults such as bent tails or bad bites.

the *stud dog* she uses has the same good health, nice temperament, and excellent conformation. A good breeder will always be there to help you with your Beagle if you have questions or problems.

Visit the breeder and meet her dogs. The adults should have outgoing personalities, and their pups should follow in their pawprints. A clean, well-kept living area is a must. Look at the dogs' paws to make sure they aren't caked with feces or dirt.

Choose a color or markings that you like. Since this won't be a show dog, appearance isn't as important, but you should still like the way the dog looks.

Personality is most important. You want a dog that everyone in the family will enjoy. If you have kids, they'll like an active Beagle that has fun chasing a ball and isn't afraid to roughhouse. If you and your spouse are an older couple with no children, look for a more laidback pup. They're out there. Some Beagles are hams and may tickle your funnybone. It never hurts to have a dog that can make you laugh.

Most people are best off choosing a puppy whose personality is somewhere in the middle of the pack: not too aggressive and not too hangdog. Nonetheless, this is one area of choosing a dog where it's good to go with your gut instinct.

Whatever your plans for your Beagle—show dog, hunting dog, or pet—look at the overall picture he presents. He should have a nice, shiny coat. A dog with a dull coat is likely to have intestinal parasites or some kind of nutritional deficiency. Bright, shiny eyes are another good sign. Avoid pups with dull or goopy eyes. They may have an infection. Remember, you're paying a lot of money for this animal, and you deserve to get a high-quality pet, show, or hunting puppy in exchange.

Youth or Wisdom?

Is it better to get a Beagle as a puppy or an adult? There are advantages and disadvantages to each option. The best choice for you depends on your lifestyle.

Puppy Pleasures

Puppies are cute, and they're awfully hard to resist. The main advantage of getting a puppy—besides the cuteness factor—is that you have control over how he grows up. You can make sure his training starts early, that he meets lots of different people and goes to lots of different places, and that he becomes accustomed to a variety of sounds, sights, and situations. All of these are crucial to raising a well-adjusted Beagle who loves other people and dogs, enjoys being handled, and is willing to have food and toys taken away if necessary.

(© Janet Nieland)

Before you start looking for a Beagle, decide whether you want a puppy or adult. Each has advantages and disadvantages.

Puppy Pains

On the other hand, puppies are a lot of work. They take as much effort as a toddler, if not more so. At least toddlers wear diapers and aren't usually known for nibbling on drywall.

Puppies need regular feedings, lots of potty trips (as often as every hour or two in some cases), and training, training, training. Puppies have a seemingly never-ending supply of energy, and

sometimes they don't calm down until they're 18 to 24 months old. Puppies can be loud and destructive. And puppies must fully mature physically before they can start going jogging with you or competing in *agility*, a fun sport that involves completing an obstacle course in a given amount of time. To learn more about agility and other dog sports, see Chapter 16.

Adding a puppy to the mix can heavily increase your workload if you already have young children. Are you really ready to have another toddler in your home? It's fun to have a dog, but don't make it harder than you have to. That's not to say that you can't acquire a puppy if you have children. Simply be fully aware of what you're getting into.

Nonetheless, if you're willing and able to take on the extra work of having a puppy, it can be an experience you'll enjoy and remember with pleasure for the rest of your life.

Adult Advantages

What about an older Beagle? Does a preowned model have any advantages over a puppy? Quite a few, as a matter of fact.

With an older Beagle, what you see is what you get. There's no wondering whether he'll turn out to be 13 inches or 15 inches, 15 pounds or 30 pounds. As little as five pounds can mean the difference between a Beagle that's allowed in an apartment complex and one that's banned.

An older Beagle may already be experienced with household routine. He can stay home without the supervision that a puppy requires. Since few people have the luxury of staying home with a new dog for a week or two to help him adjust, an older dog that already has some experience with home life can be a good choice. Such a dog may already be housetrained or even have some obedience training. Older dogs are also less active and may well be content to snooze on the sofa while you're at work.

You may think that a puppy will be a better choice for a household with kids, but often just the opposite is true. Older dogs may have prior experience with kids. They're calm enough that the noise and sudden moves of a child don't faze them.

Adult Dog Difficulties

Often, adult Beagles are placed in a shelter or rescue organization because they have behavior problems such as barking or chewing. While this type of behavior is a drawback, it's important to remember that it's normal for dogs to bark or dig or chew. These behaviors can be managed with supervision, companionship, and training. In many cases, the dog is simply bored. If he goes to a home where his mind and body are kept busy with constructive activities, his behavior problems are likely to disappear.

The other drawback of adopting an adult Beagle is simply missing the fun of puppyhood. Balance that with the notion that you're giving a Beagle a second chance, though, and I think you'll see that you come out ahead.

A Compromise

What if a puppy sounds like too much work but you're worried that an older dog will be set in his ways? Look for an older puppy, one that's six or seven months old instead of eight weeks old. A puppy this age is still cute and rowdy and rambunctious, but he's young enough to adapt quickly to a new home, and his attention span is greater than that of a younger pup.

Many breeders keep pups to "run on," waiting to see whether they blossom into show dogs. Not all do, and they're often available for sale to a good pet home.

Double the Fun

What's more fun than one Beagle? Two Beagles, of course! While a *brace* of Beagles may sound like a lot of work, it can actually work in your favor, especially if you're not home during the day. Two dogs have each other to play with and are less likely to become bored and destructive. (Then again, two can do twice as much damage as one, and if you get them at the same time they may bond with each other rather than with family members.)

Beagle Lingo
A **brace** is pair of Beagles. Some dog shows have brace competitions in which the dogs are shown to-gether. Ideally, their color and markings are as similar as possible. It's a real crowd-pleaser when they wag their tails in unison.

Unless your Beagle has another dog as a companion, he'll probably sleep most of the day—when he's not barking at squirrels, other dogs, the mailman, every car that passes by—you get the picture. When you come home from work, he'll be ready to play, just when you're ready to drop. A doggie pal can help him work off a little of that energy.

Because Beagles are such highly pack-oriented dogs, they tend to be very social with other dogs, especially other Beagles. Most Beagles seem to thrive on the companionship of another dog. Two or more will entertain each other and are more inclined to exercise by running and playing together. That helps keep them in better physical condition, an important consideration for a breed that can be prone to obesity.

Beagles with buddies are also less likely to develop separation anxiety. Even if their human "pack" isn't at home, they still have each other.

The main drawback to multiple Beagles is economic. You'll have greater expenses for food, equipment, toys, and veterinary bills. There's also the strength factor: Are you capable of hanging on to two or more Beagles tugging on their leashes?

If you decide to get two Beagles, remember that you'll have to train each of them as individuals and provide each with one-on-one playtime. Seasoned Beagle owners advise against getting two puppies at the same time. Puppies need lots of individual attention to develop a loving and lasting bond with you as well as to learn

household rules. For instance, housetraining two puppies at the same time is a real chore and often extends the time it takes to have a reliably trained dog.

It can be easier to acquire and train one Beagle and see him through adolescence, an often difficult time. Then add a second Beagle to the household.

Remember that Beagles are highly intelligent with excellent problem-solving abilities. Owning more than one means you not only have to be smarter than one Beagle, you have to worry about outthinking two of them. They're fully capable of joining forces and working against you.

If you decide to go for two Beagle pups, most experts recommend getting one of each sex. No, not so they can make puppies together. It's just that a male and female are more likely to get along better than two males or two females.

The Least You Need to Know

- Beagles need secure yards to keep them contained, though as long as they get daily exercise, they can live happily in the city or country.

- Beagles are smart and require lots of motivation in the form of positive reinforcement such as treats or praise.

- Both puppies and older dogs have advantages and disadvantages. Decide which is best for your situation based on your lifestyle. An older Beagle is often a better choice for a family with young children.

- Beagles from field lines can be more active and noisy than Beagles from show lines.

- Beagles should not be shy. Avoid choosing a puppy or older dog that doesn't warm up to people after a few minutes.

- Put some time into your search for a Beagle, and buy from a breeder who is concerned about health and temperament.

The Search

In This Chapter

- Where to look for your Beagle
- Questions and answers
- Beagle price
- Choosing the right puppy

When you're ready to go hunting for a Beagle pup, you may be overwhelmed by the choices you have. Beagles come in lots of different colors and personalities. While each puppy is cute, cute, cute, all are unique individuals.

To help make your selection easier, it's a good idea to write down exactly what you're looking for in a Beagle. Sit down with the whole family and talk about everyone's expectations. Do you want a boy or a girl? What color? Size? Laidback or wild and crazy? What are your plans for the dog? Will you show or hunt him or is his primary purpose to be that of a family companion? By writing down exactly what you want and sticking to your list, you're less likely to be swayed by the first adorable face you see.

Finding Your Beagle

There's no shortage of Beagles. The small hounds are available from a variety of sources. Beagles can be found through breeders, breed rescue groups, animal shelters, and pet stores. Each has advantages and disadvantages.

A Tale of Two Breeders

Like Beagles, breeders come in a couple of varieties. Hobby breeders are experts in the breed. They've developed a breeding program that lays out exactly what kind of Beagle they want to produce. They show their dogs to see how they stack up against other members of the breed. They study *pedigrees* carefully to choose the best bloodlines to achieve their breeding goals. The Beagles in their breeding program are healthy with correct conformation and good temperament. Any Beagles that develop hereditary health problems such as hip dysplasia or epilepsy are removed from the breeding program and neutered. You're most likely to find a hobby breeder at a dog show or through a recommendation from a satisfied Beagle owner.

Backyard breeders have a pet Beagle and think it would be fun to have puppies or a good way to recoup the cost of purchasing their dog. They find a neighbor or friend who has a Beagle of the opposite sex and mate the two dogs. They're usually not aware of hereditary health concerns, so they don't have the dogs vet-checked before breeding them. When the puppies are born, they discover that they're a lot of work. They let new owners take pups before they're really ready to leave their mom and littermates. Backyard breeders usually advertise their pups in the newspaper.

Beagle Lingo

A **pedigree** is a dog's family tree. It shows three, four, or sometimes five generations of his ancestry. For a breeder, a pedigree lays out a dog's heritage and genetic qualities. When you read a pedigree, the male relatives are on the top side, females on the bottom.

By far, your best option of the two is the hobby breeder. A puppy from a backyard breeder may cost less, but you really get your money's worth when you buy from a hobby breeder.

Why Do Breeders Charge So Much?

You are paying for the generations of quality champions in your pup's heritage, the time the breeder spends *whelping* and caring for the litter, the high-quality food the pups eat, and the costs of deworming and vaccinating the litter.

Other expenses involved in producing a high-quality litter include the stud fee or the costs of maintaining a home-based stud dog, the shipping of the bitch to the stud, her care during pregnancy, and the pre-breeding health checks. What you get in return is a beautiful Beagle that looks and acts the way a Beagle should.

There's a more intangible benefit of buying from a hobby breeder. A caring breeder wants only the best homes for her pups, and she can help you decide if a Beagle is really right for your lifestyle. An honest breeder will discourage a purchase if she's concerned that you might not enjoy life with a scenthound. If you are right for Beagle life, she can help you choose the puppy that will best fit your lifestyle and desires for a dog.

Beagle Lingo

A newborn puppy is called a **whelp**. When the mother gives birth, she's said to be whelping a litter.

Breeder Pros and Cons

The advantages of buying from a reputable breeder are the quality of the dog you'll get and the—ideally—lifelong relationship you'll build with her as a partner in your Beagle-owning adventure.

The disadvantage is that the process takes time. You have to seek out a good breeder, and she may have a waiting list for her puppies. Remember that patience is a virtue. Your Beagle will be with you for 10 years or more, so you want to be sure you get the right one.

Adopting a Beagle

Because Beagles are so popular, it's inevitable that some of them end up in the wrong homes or become homeless through no fault of their own. They may have owners that die or must enter a nursing home, families that move and can't or won't take them along, or people who give them up because they weren't trained properly and have become noisy or destructive. Some are found as strays or in animal shelters. Others come from loving families who must give up their dogs for reasons beyond their control. That's where breed rescue groups and animal shelters come into the picture.

Breed Rescue Groups

A breed rescue group is just what it sounds like: an organization that takes in and places members of a particular breed. There are many Beagle rescue organizations, with at least one in almost every state or region. Some large states, such as Texas, have several Beagle rescue groups.

Most Beagles helped by rescue groups are adults. It's rare that these organizations have puppies available. Sometimes the dogs have health problems that must be dealt with.

Beagle Bonus

When choosing a Beagle from a rescue group or animal shelter, pick one that makes eye contact with you, that seems to be glad to be in your company, and that responds when you speak to or move toward him. A dog that shows no interest in you, even after several minutes, is going to be tougher to win over than one who immediately seeks your affection.

(© *Janet Nieland*)

Many nice Beagles are available from rescue groups. Usually they are adult dogs; it's
rare to find a puppy through a rescue organization.

When a Beagle comes into a rescue group, his temperament and
health are evaluated if he doesn't come from a known background.
He receives a veterinary exam and vaccinations, if needed. Usually
he's placed in a foster home until a permanent adoptive home is
found. The foster owner studies the dog to see what kind of home
and family will best suit him.

Rescue groups conduct the same thorough questioning a breeder
might. They want to make sure the Beagle goes to a family that will
love him and understand his needs. Before a rescue Beagle goes to a
new home, he or she is neutered or spayed. Breed rescue is not a
place where you'll find a dog you can show or breed, but lots of loving pets are available. Many rescue Beagles become successful competitors in obedience, agility, and tracking.

Animal Shelters

There's no one-size-fits-all description of animal shelters. Some are
rundown and make little or no effort to screen or appropriately

place dogs. Progressive shelters with healthy budgets may offer animal placement services, community education, vaccination clinics, and other animal protection efforts.

You may think of the animal shelter as a place to get a mixed breed, but plenty of purebred dogs, including Beagles, can be found at shelters, too. Look for a Beagle at an animal shelter (or rescue group) if you prefer the idea of giving a home to a dog that really needs one.

If your local shelter doesn't have any Beagles, ask if it keeps a list of people who are interested in specific breeds. Local shelters often are willing to give you a call if a litter of puppies comes in or an adult dog is given up.

Beagles on the Net

Another way to adopt a Beagle is to take to the Internet. Many breed rescue groups have websites (see Appendix B), or you can turn to an organization called Petfinders, which plays matchmaker for people and dogs nationwide.

Rescue groups and shelter employees post descriptions and sometimes photos of dogs that need homes on Petfinder's website: www.petfinders.com. Potential adopters can search by breed, size, area, and other parameters.

Beagle Bonus

It can be impossible to predict the size a puppy will grow to be, even if both parents are small. Birth weight can be a good indicator of adult size, as can size at eight weeks, but these indicators aren't totally reliable. If you want a small Beagle, get one that's at least nine months old so you can be reasonably sure he has stopped growing.

If you find a dog that meets your needs, you can contact the rescue group or shelter directly. You may be required to go through the shelter's screening process before being permitted to adopt the dog.

Once you're approved, you can make arrangements to pick up the dog or have him shipped to you.

Breed Rescue and Shelter Pros and Cons

These groups are good sources for older Beagles. They screen homes carefully, so you're likely to get a Beagle that suits your lifestyle. Often these dogs are already housetrained or have some obedience training. The price is right. Breed rescue groups require an adoption fee to help cover their costs, which can range from $100 to $200, but that's usually far less than the cost of a puppy and includes vaccinations and neutering. That's a pretty good deal!

On the flip side, you miss out on the fun of having a puppy. You also may not have as much choice in color or markings. And instant gratification isn't possible. The screening process helps ensure that you don't just walk in and pick out a dog that's not right for your lifestyle.

Pet Stores

Why not just go to the pet store? They almost always have Beagles.

The advantage of a pet store is certainly its convenience, but it's next to impossible to determine the quality of the dogs found there. At a pet store, you'll pay the same price—or more—as you would from a breeder, but you won't get a puppy of the same quality. That's because reputable breeders don't sell to pet stores. They want to meet puppy buyers themselves to ensure that the fruits of their hard work go to great homes.

Pet store puppies usually come from commercial breeders who churn out large numbers of puppies without regard for health or quality. Puppies acquired from pet stores are often difficult to housetrain because they've spent all of their young lives soiling the cages they live in. Teaching them not to eliminate in their new den—your home—is a long and sometimes unsuccessful process.

Beagle Bonus
Small Beagles tend to be more active than larger ones, although there can be exceptions.

If you're going to pay several hundred dollars for a dog, you should be able to talk to the breeder, check out the environment the puppy comes from, meet one or both parents, and see the health certifications. That's just not possible with a pet-store purchase. Make the effort to find a good breeder instead, or give a rescue Beagle a home.

Cost

Don't let price be the only deciding factor when you're choosing a puppy. Certainly it's important to consider your budget, but the cheapest puppy is not always the best buy. Consider the dog's temperament and markings, too, as well as the breeder's personality and location. A nearby breeder with whom you have a good rapport can be a valuable asset, especially if you need help with training or a good place to board your dog.

The cost of a Beagle varies, depending on where you buy him and the gender and quality of the puppy. Beagles are most numerous in the South, Midwest, and East Coast, so they tend to cost less in those areas, with prices ranging from $300 to $500. West Coast Beagles are a little more expensive, usually going for $600 to $800. Females generally cost more than males.

Finding a Breeder

Start your search with the National Beagle Club. The NBC can refer you to Beagle clubs in your area. Most clubs have a contact person who makes referrals to breeders. The NBC has a website with lots of good information, or you can write to the club directly. The NBC's website and snail mail address are listed in Appendix B.

Go to dog shows. You can talk to several breeders all in the same day and get a good look at their dogs. When you approach a breeder at a show, ask first if she has time to talk. If she's trying to set up her equipment or getting ready to go in the ring, she will probably suggest that you come back at a different time. After you talk to breeders, get their business cards so you can contact them later to talk puppies.

Ask your veterinarian for a referral. He may have clients who breed Beagles and can be a good source of information about their dogs' health and whether they have puppies available.

If you have friends or neighbors with a nice Beagle, ask if they're still in touch with the breeder and whether they'd buy from her again. Referrals like this are a great way to meet a reputable breeder.

Top 10 Signs of a Good Breeder

The following is a list of signs of a good breeder:

1. She belongs to the NBC as well as a local all-breed or Beagle club.

2. She shows her dogs. Bonus points if she competes with her dogs in field trials, obedience, or some other dog sport.

3. She wants to know why you're interested in a Beagle.

4. She asks what kind of home you'll provide for one of her pups.

5. She explains the hereditary problems that can affect the breed and what steps she takes to avoid them.

6. She offers a written guarantee of puppy health.

7. She doesn't twist your arm to get you to take a certain puppy, or any puppy.

8. She doesn't say nasty things about other breeders or their dogs, and she can provide references not only from satisfied puppy buyers but also from other breeders.

9. She asks you to keep in touch and offers to help if you have any problems.

10. She requires that the dog be returned to her if there's ever any reason you can't keep it.

Buying From a Breeder

Once you've found the perfect breeder, you and she will want to get to know each other. Expect the breeder to grill you about why you want a Beagle, what you expect from a dog, and what kind of home you'll offer. She's not being rude or intrusive; she's just making sure that you know what you're getting into and that you'll provide a good home for one of her special puppies.

In fact, you might want to take a second look at a breeder who doesn't ask you any questions. She may not have the puppy's or your best interests at heart.

More Questions

In turn, you should thoroughly interview the breeder. Ask if she belongs to the parent club or a local dog club. How long has she been breeding and showing Beagles? Why does she like the breed? What's the downside of owning a Beagle? What's the goal of her breeding program? What steps does she take to ensure healthy and temperamentally sound puppies? Does she put working titles on her dogs? (Field or obedience titles aren't a must, but they're a nice plus. See Chapters 15 and 16 to learn more about the titles Beagles can earn in dog sports.)

A reputable breeder will answer your questions honestly and forthrightly. Be wary of someone who's offended by your questioning or who brushes aside your questions as being unimportant.

Meet the Parents

Most breeders have the *dam* on the premises, and you should be able to meet her. If the *sire* is local, try to meet him too. Often, however, bitches are shipped to sires in other parts of the country or are impregnated through artificial insemination.

It's okay if you can't meet the sire. The dam is the one who spends all the time with the puppies, so she has a much greater influence on their development. To paraphrase the old adage, like mother, like puppy. A happy, well-adjusted mother is likely to produce nice puppies, while a shy or aggressive mother is likely to produce shy or aggressive puppies.

Beagle Lingo

The terms **sire** and **dam** refer to a puppy's parents. The sire is the father and the dam is the mother.

(© Kristine Kraeuter)

A new mother will be protective of her puppies, but avoid pups whose mother seems overly shy or overly aggressive.

Remember that you're new to this dog's house, so give her time to get to know you. She may be a little protective of her pups until she's had a chance to become accustomed to your presence. Be concerned if she remains fearful of you or seems unusually hostile. It's probably a good idea to pass on pups from that dam.

(© Kristine Kraeuter)

By seeing a puppy's parents, you can form an opinion as to how the pup will look and act when he's grown. Here, father and son are pictured.

Health Issues

Beagles are generally healthy. That's one of the reasons they've been great pets for so many people. That said, they can be affected by certain hereditary conditions. These include cherry eye, epilepsy, and chondrodysplasia (dwarfism), a type of skeletal *dysplasia*. These health issues are explained in greater detail in Chapter 18.

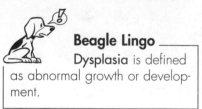

Beagle Lingo
Dysplasia is defined as abnormal growth or development.

Cherry eye, although unattractive, is easily repaired with surgery. Epilepsy often doesn't show up until later in life, so it can be passed on unknowingly until the sire or dam is diagnosed with it. If that happens, the reputable breeder removes that particular dog from her breeding program and notifies others who might be using dogs from that line.

Dwarfism is defined as a disorder that causes a dog to be markedly smaller than the size established for a given breed. Dwarfs are usually the smallest puppies in the litter, less vigorous, and tend to be slow to nurse.

Beagles with dwarfism may or may not have physical deformities. Potential defects include crooked front legs, a hunched back, cow-hocks, bad bites or other dental problems, and short toes. They may also have light bones, high ear sets, and toyish heads, all of which are faults according to the breed standard. These dogs often have itchy skin. As if to make up for their physical problems, dwarf Beagles are usually very smart and loving.

Dwarf Beagles or even just very small Beagles are sometimes referred to as pocket Beagles. Less reputable breeders or pet stores may try to pass them off as being "rare" or "special," even charging extra for them. Don't fall for it. Extremely small dogs of any breed are more likely to have health problems than their larger brethren of proper size. Avoid heartache and veterinary bills by selecting a normal-size Beagle.

Another form of skeletal dysplasia that can affect this breed is called Chinese Beagle syndrome. Chinese Beagles usually have short outer toes and slanted eyes, hence the name. Other than these differences, they have normal bone and joint development and can be expected to have a normal life span, barring other *congenital, hereditary,* or *genetic conditions.*

> **Beagle Lingo**
> A **congenital** condition is one that exists from birth. A **genetic** or **hereditary** condition is transmittable from parent to offspring and may or may not be present at birth.

Love at First Sight

Now comes the fun part: looking at the puppies. You run a real risk here of falling in love with the first furry face you see. It's tempting to take home a pup from the first litter you visit, but try to keep a hold on your emotions. Evaluate several litters if possible, and keep looking at your list to make sure you finally go home with exactly what you want.

Look and Learn

When you meet the litter, stand back and just watch the puppies play with each other. Who's on top? Who's the laggard? How do they play with their toys? Which ones come marching right up to you, and which ones run away? Are they more interested in you or in each other? Does a particular pup immediately attract your attention?

The typical puppy should be trusting and curious, willing and even eager to approach people. Gentle or slightly reserved puppies may stand back and watch for a couple of minutes before they make a move toward you. Shy puppies run away and hide. Make note of all these things before you begin to handle the pups individually.

Handling 101

Pick up the puppy that appeals to you and walk with him away from the other pups. Note his reaction. Does he relax and let you stroke him, or is he struggling to get back to his littermates?

Offer him a toy and see if he wants to play with it or otherwise interact with you. Is he hesitant or feisty? Ask yourself how this puppy matches up to the requirements on your list.

Temperament Assessment

Continue interacting with the puppy to see how he responds to you. Does he roll over for a tummy rub? A pup who does this willingly is sure of himself and comfortable with people. It's a great sign that he'll be amenable to training.

A pup who fights you tooth and nail if you try to give him a tummy rub is going to be more of a challenge. That's not necessarily a bad thing, but a potentially stubborn nature is something you should be aware of before you take him home. Be prepared to take a firmer hand with him than you might with his more compliant brother. (And don't let the easygoing guy trick you into letting him do whatever he wants because he's so sweet and cute.)

Beagle Bonus _____

Very small Beagles that stand only 9 or 10 inches high are some-times called pocket Beagles. Pocket Beagles are not a special breed or variety of Beagle and are not recognized by a registry such as AKC or UKC. Beagles this small are often that way be-cause their legs are shortened from poor breeding or dwarfism.

As you handle the pups, keep in mind what it is you want from a dog. If you're a couch potato, you want the puppy that's more laid-back, likes people, and gets along well with the other pups. For an active child's playmate or a dog that will be competing in canine sports, consider the more rambunctious pup.

Ask the breeder for her advice. She has been watching the litter for weeks and can give you lots of good information about each puppy's personality. Tell her what you're looking for in a Beagle and she can put you on the right scent. Sometimes the breeder may choose the pup for you since she knows their personalities best.

Aim for the Center

Usually the best choice is going to be a nice, middle-of-the-road puppy. He's not too wild, not too mild.

If you choose a puppy that's more extreme—he's very active or very assertive or very reserved—accept that you're not going to be able to change him. What you see is what you get. Don't assume that he'll "grow out of it." He might, but you can't count on that. If you do, you're sure to be disappointed.

Be aware that very shy puppies can become fear biters if they're not handled correctly. Very outgoing or assertive puppies might be just fine for an older child, but they can be frightening to a toddler.

**Doggy Do's/
Doggy Don'ts**
Make sure everyone in the family likes the puppy that's chosen. This is a big decision, and you should all be pleased with it. After all, this dog is going to be with you for 10 years or more.

Puppies jump up—that's a fact of life—and they can knock down a small child without meaning any harm.

Remember, trying to change a scenthound is a thankless task. Resistance is futile. Instead pick a pup that suits your personality and lifestyle.

Boy or Girl?

When it comes to Beagles, there's not much difference between the sexes. They're all equally nose-oriented. Beagles typically don't have any strong gender-related differences as some breeds do. Males and females can be equally bossy and dominant or, conversely, equally sweet and obedient. In this breed, temperament is more an individual trait than something that's gender-related.

There are, of course, physical differences to consider. Males are more likely to urine-mark their territory—your home and the things in it—unless they're neutered at adolescence. They have no qualms about licking their genitals in public or humping inanimate objects or even people. Males are more likely to challenge your authority during adolescence.

Females, unless they're spayed, go through regular heat cycles. During this time, they must be kept closely confined to prevent males from miles around getting to them.

When Can We Take Him Home?

In most cases, the best age for a Beagle pup to go to his new home is eight weeks (two months). By this time, he's fully weaned, he's learned all he can from his mother and littermates and the breeder, and he's ready to sniff out new adventures. His mind is open to new experiences, and he'll learn rapidly.

No Gift Puppies, Please

The idea of presenting a child (or even an adult) with the gift of a puppy on Christmas morning or for a birthday is irresistible. It is, however, a bad idea. Holidays and birthdays by definition are stressful times. They usually involve lots of screaming kids, wrapping paper, food, and other elements that can stress or cause harm to a puppy. When the puppy starts piddling on the carpet or destroys another gift because no one was watching him, it just adds to the uproar.

Rather than giving the actual puppy as a gift, present a gift certificate entitling the bearer to a puppy that will be picked up at a later date. Or give the recipient a box containing a collar, leash, and book on the breed (like this one!) with a card or note stating that a puppy will follow.

If the puppy is a surprise for an adult, this method gives the person an opportunity to say that maybe now isn't the best time for her to have a dog and prevents a return trip to the breeder to take the unwanted puppy back.

Beagle Bonus

Be wary of breeders who try to get you to take puppies before they're eight weeks old. The only time this can be a benefit is if the mother is very shy. Then it can be a good idea to get the puppy away from her influence a week early.

Paper Chase

When you pick up your puppy, expect the breeder to provide you with a copy of his pedigree, his vaccination and deworming records, and the paperwork you'll need to fill out if you want to register him. You don't have to register your puppy—there is a fee—but it's a must if you plan to show him or compete with him in AKC dog sports such as obedience or agility.

> **Beagle Lingo**
>
> **Limited registration** means that the dog is listed as a purebred Beagle, but his offspring cannot be registered. Some breeders give limited registration to pet-quality puppies to ensure that buyers don't breed dogs that are less than the best. Limited registration can be changed to **full registration** at the breeder's discretion. Limited registration doesn't mean there's anything wrong with your puppy, simply that he's not suitable for breeding purposes. Beagles with limited registration can still compete in dog sports such as obedience, agility, and tracking.

Many breeders require you to sign a sales contract. This usually spells out the price of the dog and any conditions of sale. Such conditions might include agreeing to show the dog or to spay or neuter the dog. The contract may specify that the puppy is being given only *limited registration* until or unless he develops into a show-quality dog worthy of being bred, in which case the breeder can amend his papers to give him full registration.

The registration application you will receive is called a blue slip. The breeder will fill out the sections calling for the puppy's breed, date of birth, sire and dam, breeder's name and address, and the litter registration number. All you have to do is complete the remaining information, sign the form, and send it in with the required fee. When the form is received by the American Kennel Club, your puppy will be registered and ownership is transferred from the breeder to you. If your Beagle's papers are important to you—for your own satisfaction or because you plan to breed or show him—don't leave the breeder's premises without the necessary paperwork. Promises that "the papers will be along later" are all too often broken and it's not the kind of dispute the AKC can resolve.

Health Hints

Find out from the breeder when the puppy's next set of vaccinations is due. She should also let you know what she's been feeding and how often your puppy is used to eating.

Try to keep him on the same food and the same schedule so he doesn't get an upset tummy. If you plan to feed a different food, you can gradually wean him onto it over a 10-day period. The breeder will probably send you home with a supply of the food she's been using. Be sure to find out where you can get more of it if it's a brand you like.

Take the puppy to your veterinarian for a complete exam within 48 hours of getting him. You want to make sure he's healthy before you all become too attached to give him up.

Return Policy

If all goes well, you won't even think of returning your new puppy, but sometimes things go wrong. You realize how much work a dog is, your kids get bored with the puppy after three days, or you find that he has a health problem that you don't want to deal with.

Most reputable breeders will ask that you return the puppy to them in any of the above instances—or any other situation where you can't keep the dog. Some even include that provision in their sales contract. Usually if a dog is returned within the first week or two of purchase, the full price is refunded.

This is a good sign. When a breeder is willing to take a dog back, no matter what the reason, you know it's because she's concerned for the dog's welfare and isn't just out to make a quick buck on Beagles.

The Least You Need to Know

- 🏠 Before you begin to look for a Beagle, write down what you want in a dog. Then choose the puppy or dog that most closely meets the list you made.

- 🏠 A breed rescue group or animal shelter can be a great place to get an older Beagle.

🏠 If you plan to get a puppy, the most important step is finding a reputable breeder. Visit several litters before making your decision.

🏠 Ask lots of questions, and don't be offended if the breeder questions you.

🏠 Walk away from breeders who aren't interested in finding out about you or who try to push a puppy on you.

🏠 Ask the breeder for advice on which puppy is best for you and your family.

Chapter **6**

Home Sweet Home

In This Chapter

- 🏠 Beagle buying guide
- 🏠 The big day
- 🏠 A kid's best friend
- 🏠 Meet the other pets

You've finally found the perfect Beagle, and you're ready to bring him home. Well, almost. You still need to load up on a few supplies, especially if you're a first-time dog owner.

What You'll Need

Beagle necessities include a sturdy collar and leash, an identification tag, a kennel or crate, food (number one on your dog's list) and dishes, a brush, and toys. You can find all of these items at your local pet supply store. Before you go shopping, ask the breeder if there are any particular brands or styles of equipment that she recommends. She may be able to save you a few dollars by suggesting items that are particularly long-lasting or well-suited to a Beagle.

(© Kristine Kraeuter)

Go shopping before you bring your new Beagle home. He'll need food and water dishes, a collar and leash, toys, a carrier, and more. The breeder can advise you on appropriate sizes to purchase.

Collar and Leash

A flat or rolled buckle collar made of leather or nylon is usually a good choice. Leather is durable and has a classic look. It smells good, though, so your puppy might try to chew on it. Nylon is also durable and comes in lots of colors and patterns. Choose it if you want a more stylish look.

Some nylon collars are adjustable and grow along with your puppy. The 10-inch to 16-inch size is a good fit for the typical Beagle throughout his lifetime. A collar should fit snugly without being too tight. Make sure you can get two fingers between the collar and the dog's neck. Check the collar's fit on a regular basis as the puppy grows. You don't want it to get too tight. On the other hand, you don't want your Beagle to be able to back out of the collar and escape, a typical puppy trick.

Doggy Do's/Doggy Don'ts _____
Never use a chain or nylon choke collar as your dog's every-day collar. This type of collar is strictly for training sessions or the show ring. It can strangle a dog if he gets it caught on something. Many trainers are moving away from the negative reinforcement of a choke collar, so don't buy one unless it's called for in your dog's obedience class. A 16-inch fine chain fits most adult Beagles.

Matching leashes are usually available for leather and nylon collars. A young puppy does well with a slip lead, one that has a noose at the end that slips over the dog's head. A slip lead tightens up as the dog pulls and prevents a frightened pup from backing out of his collar and escaping. Purchase a snap lead—one that snaps onto a ring on the collar—for an older puppy or adult dog.

For best control of your Beagle, choose a leash that's four to six feet in length. Any longer and he'll always be getting tangled up in it. If you plan to do tracking with your Beagle, you'll eventually need a 30-foot tracking lead.

If you want to give your dog some freedom to roam while still keeping him under control, consider getting an extendible leash. Just be sure your thumb is fast on the brake. This type of leash doesn't offer a high level of control, and you'll need to be good at reeling your dog in quickly if need be.

Identification

A tag is the classic method of identifying a dog. Have it engraved with your name, home and work phone numbers, and maybe your veterinarian's phone number. That's all a finder needs to return your dog safely if he gets lost. Brass ID tags are durable and attractive, or you can purchase a colorful plastic tag. Your dog should also have a license tag issued by your city, county, or state.

Doggy Do's/ Doggy Don'ts

Look for a tag that attaches directly to the collar and lies flat rather than one that hangs from an S hook. Anything that dangles could get snagged on something and cause your dog to choke.

Beagle Bonus

Whether your Beagle is microchipped or tattooed, you'll receive a tag to put on his collar indicating where a finder should call to report that he's been found. This is especially handy for microchipped dogs, since there's no outward sign that they're chipped.

More high-tech identification is available, too. No, you can't put LoJack on your dog yet, but a microchip is the next best thing. It's implanted by a veterinarian between your dog's shoulder blades and takes about as much time to do as a vaccination. Once the chip is in place, it can be scanned and your contact information or your veterinarian's contact information will come up on a reader. Many animal shelters and veterinary clinics have scanners now to help identify and return lost dogs. It's a good idea to register your dog's microchip number with a national registry (see Appendix B) so you can be located and your Beagle returned to you. If you move, be sure to provide the registry with your new address and phone number.

A tattoo is a permanent, visible form of identification. It can't fall off or be removed the way a tag can, and it can be seen, unlike a microchip. If you choose to tattoo your Beagle, be sure you register the tattoo with a national organization so that you can be contacted in case your dog is found. A tattoo isn't of much value if the person who finds the dog doesn't have any way of reaching you.

Kennel

A kennel, or crate, may well be the single most important piece of equipment you buy. It serves as your dog's bed. It's a safe, comfy place for him to be when you can't be there to supervise. And it's a housetraining tool, the best one you can have. In future chapters, you'll learn what size and type of crate your Beagle will need (Chapter 10), as well as ways to use it for housetraining and puppy-proofing (Chapters 7 and 10).

Food

Ask the breeder what the puppy has been eating so you can have some on hand when you bring your puppy home. She'll probably send you home with a small bag to get you started. Dogs have sensitive digestive systems, so if you plan to switch your new dog to a different food, do it over a 10-day period. See Chapter 14 for advice on choosing a diet as well as other nutritional tips.

Food and Water Dishes

Dog dishes can be made of stainless steel, ceramic, or plastic. Some dogs are allergic to plastic and develop skin discolorations from it, so stainless steel or ceramic items are probably your best choices.

Stainless steel is indestructible, but it's lightweight and easily shoved around. A bouncy Beagle puppy can make a mess with metal dishes unless you get the kind that sit in a stand. The 1-quart size works nicely for Beagles.

Ceramic dishes are heavier, but they can break if dropped. On the plus side, they come in lots of different colors and patterns, so you can choose them to match your decor. Both ceramic and stainless steel dishes are easily cleaned.

If possible, buy dishes that are about 5 inches in diameter. They're wide enough that your Beagle can stick his nose inside them but not so wide that his ears will drag through the food or water.

Beagle Bonus

Because they're lightweight and inexpensive, stainless steel dishes are nice to have if you plan on traveling with your Beagle.

Toys

Beagles are fond of most types of toys, from balls to stuffed animals. They enjoy chewing, especially during puppyhood when chewing helps to exercise and develop their jaws.

Safe chew items include Nylabone, Gumabone, and Nylafloss products. Because of the appetizing odor, special Beagle favorites are smoked cow or lamb's ears and cow hooves. Heavy knotted or pressed rawhide chews will also keep your hound entertained for hours. These products should be given only when you're there to supervise, however. Dogs, especially Beagles, will try to swallow large pieces and could choke on them or develop an intestinal blockage.

Grooming Tools

Happily, your Beagle doesn't require nearly as much grooming equipment as a Poodle or Afghan Hound. All he needs is …

- Hound glove or curry brush. These have rubber nubs that pick up and remove loose hair. It fits over your hand or sometimes right in the palm of your hand. Use the hound glove daily to distribute skin oils, remove loose hair, and help keep down shedding.

- Nail clippers. Trim your Beagle's toenails every one or two weeks, depending on how quickly they grow. If you can hear his nails clicking on the floor, they're too long. Choose guillotine-style clippers with a sharp blade. To use this type of clipper, put the tip of the dog's nail inside the metal loop. When you squeeze the handles, a sharp stainless steel blade slides out to trim the nail. These clippers are nice because it's easy to see just how much nail you're clipping. If the clipper blades get rusted or dull, you can buy replacements at a pet supply store.

- Styptic powder. Use this to control any bleeding in case you accidentally trim a toenail too short and cut the quick.

Tearless puppy shampoo. This will keep from irritating their eyes.

 Dog toothbrush and dog toothpaste. Do not use human toothpaste; it can make them very sick.

Refer to Chapter 13 for more helpful hints and advice on grooming your Beagle.

Cleanup in Room Two

No matter how careful you are puppy accidents are inevitable. Don't be without a bottle of enzymatic stain and odor remover. You'll be amazed at its ability to leave your carpet looking and smelling like new. See Chapter 8 for more tips on cleaning up after pup.

Puppy's First Day

Now you're finally ready to bring your new puppy or adult Beagle home. He's at least eight weeks old, and you have all the items you need to care for him in style.

When you pick your new friend up, make sure you leave with all the paperwork you need. Many breeders provide a care package with food and written tips on taking care of your dog. Put your dog's new collar and tags on him before you leave the breeder's home.

It's a good idea to have the puppy ride in the crate on the way home. The kids will probably want to hold him in their laps, but remember that puppies are squirmy. You don't want an escapee jumping around in the car while you're trying to drive. And if the puppy gets excited and has an accident, it will

Doggy Do's/ Doggy Don'ts

Stress to your kids the importance of always making sure doors and gates are closed and latched. Your Beagle will take any opportunity to escape and go exploring.

be contained in the crate, which is much easier to clean up than car upholstery or clothing.

At Home

Put the puppy's leash on before you get out of the car. Lift him out and let him sniff around the yard for a few minutes to take stock of his new territory. If he potties, praise him.

Then take him into the house, still on the leash. Training begins now. Don't give your puppy free run of the house until he's reliably housetrained, which is likely to be a matter of months rather than days.

Place the crate in the family room or kitchen, wherever everyone spends the most time. He'll enjoy being in the midst of family goings-on. Let the kids play with him for a few minutes and then put him in his kennel for a nap. It's been a big day!

**Doggy Do's/
Doggy Don'ts**

Don't let your kids tease or talk to the dog while he's in his kennel. That's his special place where he can enjoy some Beagle R&R.

Take your puppy out every couple of hours to go potty. An older dog doesn't need to go out that often, but for the first week or two it's a good idea to take him out fairly often just to make sure he doesn't have any excuse for eliminating in the house. Gradually extend the amount of time between potty breaks until you're sure your older dog knows the drill.

Bedtime

Your puppy is used to sleeping in a big, warm pile with his mother and brothers and sisters. This is his first night away from them, and he'll probably be lonely and frightened.

Sleeping in your bedroom will help make his transition easier. Put his crate at your bedside so he'll be comforted by your scent. By having the crate in your room, you'll know when he awakens. Carry him outside as soon as you hear him stir so he can do his business.

The Child-Beagle Relationship

In the right situation, kids and Beagles are ideal playmates. They both are filled with curiosity and boundless energy. A Beagle will play ball for as long as a child will throw it. He's great for going on rambles through the neighborhood. His love of attention—and food—makes him good at learning tricks. Sturdy and built for action, he enjoys roughhousing as much as the next dog, but he can also be gentle with youngsters. Because he's small and unthreatening, he can be a good choice for kids who might be fearful of a bigger dog.

A Beagle, or any dog for that matter, is best suited to families with no children under the age of six. That's the age of reason, the point at which children understand that the dog is a living being that can be hurt, not just a mobile stuffed toy. That's not to say that a Beagle won't do well in homes with younger children; simply that it takes more effort on your part to make sure he's not harmed by ear-pulling and tail-tugging. Take an honest look at your child's maturity level and your ability to provide supervision before adding a dog to the family.

Children six years and older can take on simple dog-care tasks such as giving the dog food and water, but they shouldn't be held solely responsible for any aspect of the dog's care. Kids are forgetful and self-centered, and even teenagers need reminding to brush the dog's teeth or give him fresh water. If a dog joins your family,

Beagle Bonus

Remember that Beagles take their food very seriously. Teach your child not to reach into the dog's bowl or tease the dog while he's eating. At the same time, teach your Beagle to allow people to add food to his dish or to take his dish away without fuss.

he's your responsibility, no matter how much the kids may promise that they'll take good care of him.

Beagles and Younger Children

If you want a Beagle but have children younger than six years, consider getting a kid-savvy older dog. A well-socialized Beagle that's past the wild puppy stage can be a good introduction to dogs for a young child. He's more tolerant of heavy petting and less likely to knock a toddler on her rear by jumping up on her. A puppy, on the other hand, may treat a young child like a littermate and play too rough.

In any case, never leave a dog and young child without supervision. No matter how nice the dog, he's not a furry babysitter. Many dogs have a reputation for being as patient as saints, but saintly patience is not something that you can expect or demand from any dog, especially if he's being poked and prodded. Teach your child how to pat the dog softly, and keep an eye on things to make sure they don't get out of hand.

Making Introductions

When you bring your new Beagle home, remind the kids that he's in a new place and will need their help to feel comfortable. No squealing or screaming, please! Let them show him around the fenced yard and introduce him to some of his toys.

Show younger children how to pet the puppy nicely. Keep reminding them not only to stroke softly but also to speak softly. Dogs have very sensitive ears.

After 20 or 30 minutes of play, it's probably a good time to let the pup have a nap. Gently put him in his crate and let your child give him a treat before you close the door.

Home Rules

Many young children think it's their job to yell at or hit the puppy if he has an accident in the house. Never allow this. The puppy is a baby, and he will make mistakes. You, as the adult, can shout "No!" or "Aaaaght!" if you catch him in the act, but teach your children that it's never okay to hit the dog.

Another good rule to establish is that the children can only hold the dog when they're sitting on the ground. No picking puppy up and hauling him around like a rag doll. It's not comfortable for the dog, and he runs the risk of being injured if a child accidentally drops him.

Teach your children as well to keep their hands away from the puppy's mouth. Puppy teeth are sharp, and pups haven't learned yet not to bite or how to moderate the force of a bite. If they get excited, they may clamp down on whatever's in the way, without meaning any harm.

Beagle Bonus

Be sure your children and the dog know your expectations for good behavior. Just as if the dog were a sibling or playmate, establish the rule that no one is to bite or hit the other.

A New Baby in the Home

Beagles adapt quickly to new situations and new people, so the advent of a baby is not something to fear. Be matter of fact and let your Beagle sniff the new arrival so he can add the baby's scent to his repertoire of family odors.

Avoid the temptation to swoop the baby out of the dog's reach every time he tries to sniff her. That just adds to his curiosity. Instead give him a chance to satisfy that curiosity and he'll quickly come to accept the baby as a new member of the family.

Beagle Bonus

If you can, bring home a blanket from the hospital that the baby has been wrapped in. This will give your Beagle an opportunity to smell the baby in advance.

For an even more positive association, include your Beagle in your outings with the baby. Take him along on his leash while you're pushing the stroller around the block or to the park. That way, all three of you get some fresh air, and your Beagle gets a walk in the bargain.

Animal Pals

Before marriage, couples often undergo counseling to ensure that their personalities and lifestyles will be compatible and help them deal effectively with conflicts. Bringing a new pet into a household entails many of the same concerns, albeit on a different level. While you can't exactly sit down with all your animals to talk out their potential problems, you can take steps to keep tensions to a minimum and develop cordial relationships.

This is especially important when introducing your Beagle into a home where you already have small animals such as mice, rats, hamsters, guinea pigs, ferrets, or rabbits. Although these animals are very different in size and nature, they can live together successfully with the right beginning. Some even become the best of friends.

Proper Introductions

This is not the time to just throw everyone together and hope for the best. That sometimes works at cocktail parties, but animals tend to prefer more ritual and structure in their lives.

Take it slow, and take each animal's personality into account. The introduction technique you use depends on which animals are involved.

Other Dogs

If you already have another dog or dogs, arrange to introduce your new Beagle to them on neutral territory. This can be at a park near your home or at a neighbor or friend's house. Ideally, it will be within walking distance of your home.

Doggy Do's/Doggy Don'ts _____

If you already have an adult dog or cat, they're more likely to welcome a puppy than an animal of their own age. If your current dog or cat is very old, however, a puppy may be too rambunctious, and you'll want to supervise their interactions until the pup learns to slow down around them. Always make sure your older pet has a quiet place where he can go to get away from the puppy.

With each dog on his leash, let everyone start sniffing. This is the canine equivalent of shaking hands and exchanging business cards. Keep leashes loose. Tension on the lead makes the dogs think something's wrong, so they're more likely to posture and behave aggressively. A loose lead indicates that everything's cool.

When everyone has met and seems to be getting along, walk everyone home so your Beagle can get to know the home territory and your other dogs can slowly come to the realization that the new guy is here to stay.

Feline Friend or Foe?

Have your Beagle on-leash when you introduce him to the cat. A rambunctious puppy may try to lunge at a cat—especially if he's never encountered one before—and might receive a painful swat on the nose in return. Say "No" or "Aaagh" and restrain the puppy with the leash if he tries to play too roughly with the cat. Reward him with praise and a treat if he ignores the cat or tries to sniff her gently.

Another option for introducing cat and Beagle is to have one or the other in a crate the first time they meet. That way they can see and smell each other before any physical get-together takes place. A good time for a cage-free meeting is when both animals are relaxed, even a little tired.

If your cat stands her ground and lets the Beagle know who's in charge, they'll likely get along well. A cat that runs, however, may stimulate the Beagle's prey drive, and their interactions will need close supervision until the dog learns that the cat is off limits.

Play Dates

While Beagles get along with most dogs, they especially enjoy the company of other Beagles. Get to know some other Beagle owners and schedule regular play dates at a nearby park, preferably one where your dogs can safely run off-leash.

Your veterinarian may be able to put you together with other Beagle owners, or you may make new friends through puppy kindergarten class or a Beagle mailing list. You'll soon find yourself looking forward to the get-togethers as much as your dog.

Living on BQT (Beagle Quality Time)

It's impossible to spend time around a Beagle without being amused and impressed by the breed's brains and ability to entertain. To enjoy your Beagle to the fullest, you need to spend time with him so you can learn to recognize the quirks that make him a special individual. By knowing what makes him unique, you'll be better able to understand why he does certain things and how best to motivate him to be the best Beagle he can be.

It takes a real commitment of time to ensure that a Beagle becomes a true member of the family rather than a noise-making lawn ornament. It doesn't require a lot of effort, though. Plan to devote 15 to 30 minutes once or twice a day solely to your Beagle. This time can be used for play, training, a walk, or just hanging out together.

This one-on-one time is a great way to make sure your Beagle is getting enough activity to keep him from becoming bored and destructive. Contrary to our imaginings, most dogs sleep during the day. They're not much more motivated to exercise on their own than we are. By scheduling a regular playtime, you ensure that your dog has something to look forward to.

Don't forget that quality time doesn't always require loads of activity on your part. Walking together to the mailbox, snuggling on the sofa while you watch TV, and sleeping in the same room are all great ways to bond with your Beagle.

If all of this sounds like too much work, think twice about getting a Beagle, or consider getting an older dog who's past the energetic and demanding puppy stage. You'll be happier if you're honest about the time commitment you're willing to make.

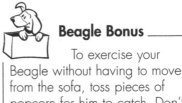

Beagle Bonus

To exercise your Beagle without having to move from the sofa, toss pieces of popcorn for him to catch. Don't do this too often, or he'll quickly grow fat!

The Least You Need to Know

- 🏠 Buy all the supplies you need before you bring your new dog home.

- 🏠 Don't give your new dog free run of the house until you're sure he's reliably housetrained.

- 🏠 Sleeping in your bedroom will help your dog bond with you.

- 🏠 Supervise all child-dog interactions to make sure no one gets hurt.

- 🏠 Introduce other pets gradually and supervise all pet interactions until you're sure everyone gets along.

- 🏠 Spending quality time with your Beagle is the best way to understand him.

Part 3

The Civilized Beagle

Hounds by nature are stubborn, independent thinkers. They are just as smart as other dogs, but not always as easily trainable. They like to know why you want them to do certain things, and if they're not impressed by your rationale, they may choose to ignore you or do things their own way.

In this section, you'll learn about Beagle-proofing your home and yard, the art of housetraining, the value of manners training, effective rewards and corrections, and establishing leadership. It also covers behavior problems you might encounter, such as barking, digging, and chewing, and how to deal with them.

Chapter 7

The Danger Zone

In This Chapter

- 🏠 A Beagle-proof house and yard
- 🏠 Unsafe plants
- 🏠 Good fences make good beagles
- 🏠 In-home confinement options

The first step in living successfully with a Beagle is to make sure your house is safe from him and that he's safe from your house. Just like toddlers, Beagles will explore any area they can get to and put anything into their mouths that will fit. (And if it doesn't fit, they'll chew it down to size.) Read on to learn how to protect your home and yard from a curious Beagle, as well as how to protect your Beagle from his own curious nature.

Beagle-Proof Your Home

No, not burglarproof, Beagle-proof. These dogs may have sweet faces, but the amount of damage they can do in just a short amount of time boggles the mind.

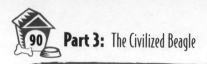

One minute they're innocently playing with a toy, the next thing you know, they've nibbled away a large portion of drywall. Puppies have been known to eat hardwood floors, gnaw furniture to flinders, strew garbage throughout the house, chew the tops off child-safe pill bottles, mummify themselves in toilet paper, decorate eyeglasses with toothmarks, and eat dish towels, socks, and rocks.

Beagle Bonus

The curiosity and destructiveness of puppies, especially Beagle puppies, can confound even the most experienced or careful dog owner and is usually beyond the belief of new puppy owners, who tend to assume that such stories are the exception rather than the rule.

Puppies can and will chew, eat, or otherwise destroy anything interesting that's within their reach. And there isn't much that's *not* of interest to a scenthound puppy.

In-Home Security Evaluation

Before you bring your Beagle pup home, take a walk through the entire house. Do you have special items that are fragile or irreplaceable because of sentimental value? Put them away. Puppy-proofing an area means having out of reach any and all items of great value and household items that you want kept intact, such as shoes, home accessories, books, or magazines.

Do the same thing with items that pose a safety risk, such as electric cords. Unplug what you can, bundle cords and put them out of sight if possible, and try to keep them from dangling invitingly.

What else might your puppy get into? Think medicine bottles, cleaning supplies, dental floss, yarn, sewing gear, rodent poison, toilet bowl cleaners, diaper pails, trash containers, cat litter boxes, dirty laundry, cigarettes, candy, coins, and toys, especially those with dangly parts. Put such items up high or behind closed doors.

Sometimes it's necessary to temporarily rearrange your home to keep a puppy out of trouble. This could involve putting something in

front of an outlet with a plugged-in cord, moving furniture to minimize risks, or raising such items as lamps or trash containers off the
ground.

> **When to Call the Vet** _____
>
> Any time you discover that your Beagle has eaten something
> harmful, such as chocolate, medication, or cigarettes, call
> your veterinarian or take your dog to the clinic. Try to estimate
> how much the dog might have ingested, and be sure to bring
> the packaging or container with the label information.

Multilevel homes with railings and open stairways make for
additional concerns. You may need to use baby gates or other barri-
cades to keep your pup safe.

An open door is an invitation to any self-respecting Beagle.
Screen doors can help prevent your Beagle from making a run for
freedom. Just make sure he doesn't figure out how to unlatch them.
Beagles can also easily rip through screen doors. One Beagle owner
I know has had to replace his screen door several times, at consider-
able expense. Consider using a baby gate to keep your dog away
from screen doors.

When you think you've puppy-proofed your home, get down on
your hands and knees to check it out from a puppy's-eye view. Anything below 18 inches is fair game to a puppy. Protect chair legs by
wrapping them in aluminum foil—yucky to chew on—or coating
them with a foul-tasting substance.

Living Room, Den, Home Office, and Bedroom

Think twice about storing dangerous or desirable items underneath
things. Your puppy will crawl under the sofa, bed, or workbench.
Keep closet doors closed, and make sure they latch securely so they
can't be pushed open. Remind your kids to keep toys and clothes off
the floor.

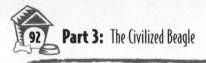

Beagle Bonus

Look for cable ties at electronics stores. They're simple to use, and they can only be removed with scissors. Don't use the simple coated wire ties that come with garbage bags. Those are too easy for a Beagle to chew off.

Use tough plastic cable ties to wrap up cords for clock radios, computers, phones, stereos, and televisions so they're not accessible. If you can't keep cords out of the way, coat them with a nasty-tasting substance. Bitter Apple, Bitter Grape, and Tabasco sauce are all good for this purpose. Whatever you choose, reapply it regularly, and understand that it's going to make a mess.

Kitchen and Bathrooms

Put child locks on bathroom and kitchen cabinets. Keep that toilet lid down. All pups are born with toilet water sonar. A curious puppy could fall in the toilet and drown before being found. Put trash out of reach.

Dangling dishtowels are favorite puppy toys. They're not so much fun if they get eaten, though. Intestinal obstructions can require surgery to repair and may even cause a dog's death if not caught in time.

Garage

Install high shelves or locked cabinets for antifreeze, weed killers, pesticides, herbicides, paint, turpentine, dried-up paint rollers, and anything else that might conceivably cause your puppy harm. When in doubt, get it out.

Automatic garage doors are potentially dangerous, too. Pets have been known to get caught beneath them. Make sure your Beagle is under control or not in the garage when you open or close the door.

If the garage houses the cat's litter box, consider getting a covered box or placing the box in a spot that's accessible to kitty but not to puppy. You don't want your Beagle to develop the nasty habit of snacking out of it. One couple solved this problem by cutting a small hole in the bottom of a baby gate. Their cats could slide through, but the puppy didn't fit.

Beagle Bonus

All antifreeze is hazardous to pets, even brands that are labeled animal-safe. They're just less toxic than other types. If you suspect that your Beagle has ingested antifreeze, get him to the vet pronto!

The Great Outdoors

Check your yard for safety as well before you bring your Beagle pup home. What looks secure to you may be a minefield for him. Make sure the yard is completely safe for your puppy before letting him loose in it.

Walk around the fenceline. Are there areas that need to be repaired? Holes that a puppy could wiggle through or under? Does the gate latch properly? Could your puppy jump onto a doghouse, playhouse, or garbage can and use it as a launching pad to go over the fence?

Fence Facts

Speaking of fences, is yours really capable of containing a Beagle? These dogs are escape artists and must be confined to a safe, secure area when outdoors to prevent them from wandering off. So many Beagles die of HBC—vetspeak for "hit by car"—that breeders often won't sell to people without a fenced yard.

Four feet is the minimum height your fence should be, and 5 or 6 feet is probably a better choice. If the ground is soft and diggable at the base of the fence, you may need to reinforce the area with buried rocks or a concrete base to keep the little Houdini from digging out.

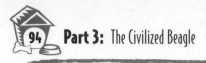

Choose a chainlink or solid wood fence if possible. Concrete or stucco walls are good, too, as long as they're the right height. Small picket fences are pretty but easier to escape through unless you plant shrubs or thorny roses to serve as a barrier.

What about electronic fences that are buried underground? Those are unlikely to contain a Beagle who's hot on the trail. A momentary shock isn't going to stop him from going after that intriguing scent. And this type of fence doesn't keep other intruders—animal or human—out.

Don't ignore bodies of water such as swimming pools, hot tubs, or fish ponds. Pups aren't born knowing how to swim. Don't assume that if they fall in, they'll be able to get out on their own. Supervise Beagles when they're around water or fence off pools and spas, just as you would with a child, and show your Beagle how to swim to the steps and climb out. Practice this frequently until you're sure your Beagle knows how to swim.

Bet You Didn't Know

The dog paddle is a simple form of swimming in which the arms paddle in the water and the legs maintain a kicking motion.

Plant Safety

Make a list of the plants you have and ask a veterinarian if they're safe. Or check your list against those included in the bible of dog health care, the *Dog Owner's Home Veterinary Handbook, 3rd Edition* (Carlson and Giffin, New York: Howell Book House, 2000).

Check your houseplants, too. Even if they're not poisonous, put them out of reach. Puppies love chewing on leaves and digging in dirt.

Just as you need to keep your Beagle safe from your plants, you need to protect your plants from your Beagle. Many dogs are connoisseurs of fresh fruits and vegetables, such as tomatoes and avocadoes, and they enjoy digging up bulbs, which are usually toxic.

To protect a garden, surround it with chicken wire or some other type of fencing. Home-maven and dog-owner Martha Stewart recommends using bamboo criss-cross edging to keep dogs out of gardens. If fencing or edging isn't feasible, consider buying or building a dog run. Your pup will have a safe place to play outdoors, and the rest of your yard will be protected from digging paws or nibbling teeth.

When to Call the Vet

Signs of poisoning may include vomiting, staggering, drooling, convulsions, and collapse. Take your dog to the vet immediately if he displays any of these signs.

Toxic Plants

A number of plants can cause skin reactions, irritation, respiratory problems, gastrointestinal upset, or even death if eaten. Avoid the following plants in your home and yard, or keep them well out of reach.

- Amaryllis
- Asparagus fern
- Azalea
- Boston ivy
- Caladium
- Calla lily
- Chinaberry
- Chrysanthemum
- Daffodil/Buttercup
- Dieffenbachia (dumbcane)
- Elephant's ear
- English holly
- Jasmine
- Jerusalem cherry
- Lupine
- Monkeypod
- Mother-in-law plant
- Nightshade
- Philodendron
- Pothos
- Privet
- Tomato vine
- Tuberous begonia
- Wisteria
- Yew trees

A thoroughly puppy-proofed home and yard isn't much fun for a Beagle, so make sure you have a variety of dog-safe items for him to play with. Plenty of toys, exercise, and playtime are essential to keeping your dog out of trouble.

> **Beagle Bonus**
>
> How long does Beagle-proofing take, anyway? When can your household go back to normal? That depends on the dog. Some dogs look for trouble all their lives and can never be left unsupervised or unconfined. Others prove themselves trustworthy by six months of age. Expect your Beagle's puppyhood to last until he's at least two years old.

What's the most important thing to know? Never underestimate the creative energy of a puppy. He will crawl into, under, and over impossible places to do mischief. With proper supervision and prevention, however, you can ensure that he grows into a happy, healthy adult dog.

Sanity Savers

The best way to avoid problems is, well, to prevent them. Keep your puppy at your side instead of giving him the run of the house. Tether him with a leash so that you're always aware of what he's doing.

It's impossible to constantly give a puppy the level of supervision he needs. When you need a break, don't just give up and let him play by himself. Instead confine him safely to an area where he can't do any harm.

> **Beagle Bonus**
>
> Remember that dogs are perfectly capable of thinking out and executing a plan to achieve a goal. Beagles may be stubborn when it comes to training, but they're plenty smart when it comes to getting what they want.

The Safe Room

This can be a place such as the bathroom, kitchen, or laundry room, all areas that usually have easy-clean tile or linoleum floors. Or use dog crates, baby gates, puppy playpens, or a dog run to create a safe haven that allows you and your Beagle to relax. A dog door can give your Beagle the option of going out whenever he needs to instead of relying on you to open the door for him.

Confine your mischievous Beagle to an x-pen (pictured here), crate, or safe room when you can't directly supervise him.

Dog Crates

The right crate is the canine version of a comfy recliner. It's the place he can go to relax and feel secure. When he's in his crate, he can't get into trouble, so you can't get mad at him.

The ideal setup is to have a crate in every room where you spend time with the dog. That means one in the bedroom, one in the living room, and maybe one in the home office or den. That can get expensive, of course, and one crate is plenty if you aren't at the

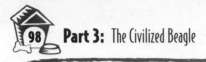
same income level as Bill Gates. Beagle-size crates are easily portable from room to room.

Plastic airline crates are lightweight and easily cleaned. Coated wire crates with removable bottom trays are fine for female Beagles, but males are likely to lift their legs and shoot a stream of urine through the wires.

A good size for at-home use is 32 inches long by 22 inches high by 23 inches wide. This is a medium-size crate from most manufacturers. For car travel, look for something slightly smaller: a crate 27 inches long by 20 inches high by 19 inches wide will hold your Beagle comfortably and fit conveniently into the back seat of the average car.

Baby Gates

Look for this type of barrier at pet or baby supply stores. Be sure the gate you choose has safety features that will prevent your pup from getting his head stuck in the bars. It should be high enough that he can't jump over it, although a determined dog can find ways.

One dog, safely stashed behind a 3-foot baby gate in the guest bathroom, escaped in five minutes. Her owner put her back in the room. She was out in less than five minutes. The owner put her back in the room a third time and then stood where the dog couldn't see her. The escape artist jumped from the floor to the toilet, the toilet to the vanity, then walked across the vanity and jumped over the gate.

If you choose to use a baby gate instead of a crate, be aware that some dogs are more inventive than others. The kitchen may seem like a safe place for them until you come home to find out that they've jumped from a chair to the table to the counter, knocked a package of scone mix to the ground, and then returned to the floor to destroy the box and eat the contents. Remember, too, that an uncrated dog may still nibble on cabinets or drywall. Keep a can of spackling handy for repairs.

Beagle Bonus

To test your Beagle's maturity, start slowly. Leave him alone for 10 or 15 minutes and see how he does. If he behaves, gradually extend the amount of time he's on his own to an hour or two. You'll find out quickly whether he's dependable or still needs the restraint of a crate or other safe area.

Playpens for Pups

If you like the confinement that a crate gives but you want your Beagle to have a larger play area, consider getting what's known as an x-pen, short for exercise pen. An x-pen is an uncovered octagonal wire enclosure that can be set up in the home or yard. It's a good place to keep a dog if you're busy in the same room and want him to be able to play without getting into trouble. Think of it as the canine version of a baby's playpen.

X-pens range in size from 24 inches high by 24 inches wide to 48 inches high by 24 inches wide. They're lightweight and easy to move around. An x-pen can be folded up and packed in the car for a trip, and you can add or remove panels to change its size. The cost of an x-pen can range from $75 to $135.

Make the x-pen a comfy place to be by lining the area it surrounds with a towel or blanket (or newspapers if your pup isn't potty-trained yet). Provide a couple of favorite toys and fresh drinking water.

Dog Runs

A dog run in the yard provides your Beagle with a covered or uncovered play area or safe haven if you're not home. A dog run is a good idea if you don't have a fenced yard but need to confine your Beagle outdoors sometimes. It's also a way to give the dog part of the yard as his very own, while protecting the rest of it from being dug up. Dog runs are usually made of chainlink and can have grass, pea gravel, or concrete flooring.

Dog runs vary in size. A 6- × 8-foot run set on concrete is a fine size for a Beagle. Provide an insulated doghouse for shelter. Be aware that Beagles confined to dog runs can get bored, which leads to barking and howling. If this becomes a problem, try crating your Beagle indoors. If you do this, however, limit the time he spends in his crate to no more than four hours without a break.

Dog Doors

Letting a Beagle in and out of the house can be a never-ending chore. If you want to give him the option of going out on his own, consider installing a dog door. Besides giving your Beagle access to the great outdoors to play or do his business, a pet door prevents him from scratching doors and marring the paint.

The original concept—a pet-size, pet-level portal to allow a dog to make his own way from house to yard—has expanded to include pet doors that fit into screens, sliding glass doors or windows, or that operate electronically, ensuring that only a particular animal can enter and exit through it. You may be able to set up a dog door that leads directly into your dog's run.

(© Janet Nieland)

These Beagles have access to the outdoors via a dog door but are prevented from roaming the rest of the house while their people are gone.

Pet doors are installed by cutting a hole in an existing door or wall, or by inserting a same-size panel into a screen or patio door. Flaps provide weather resistance, preventing drafts and precipitation from entering the house. A medium-size dog door with a frame size of about 13 inches by 17.25 inches should be the right size for a Beagle.

The Least You Need to Know

- Puppy-proofing prevents injuries to your puppy and to your possessions. Put out of reach anything you don't want your Beagle pup to have.

- Your Beagle is as curious as a toddler. If you wouldn't let a baby have something, keep it away from your dog as well.

- Many common plants are toxic to dogs. Check your home and yard for poisonous plants and remove them or put them out of reach.

- A securely fenced yard is a must for keeping your Beagle at home. Check your yard for gates that don't latch and weak areas of the fence where a dog could dig under or push through. Repair them before letting your Beagle loose in the yard.

- Good ways to confine your dog when you can't watch him are crates, x-pens, baby gates, and dog runs.

- Holidays require extra vigilance to keep your Beagle out of harm's way.

Chapter **8**

Housetraining 101

In This Chapter

- 🏠 The whys and wherefores of potty training
- 🏠 A pup-proof confinement area
- 🏠 The great crate
- 🏠 Potty trips galore
- 🏠 The difference between boys and girls

Beagles have a reputation for being difficult to housetrain. Experienced Beagle people say this bad rap is undeserved though. A Beagle can be housetrained, as long as you're patient and consistent. That's the most difficult aspect of housetraining for people though. Remember that toddlers can also take weeks or months to potty train, so be as patient with your pup as you would with a child.

To succeed in housetraining, you'll need three more things: good timing, the right equipment (a crate and a leash), and an understanding of dog physiology—the way his body works. By following a schedule based on puppy potty needs, using appropriate confinement to prevent accidents, and giving praise for successful potty outings, you'll soon have a Beagle that understands and displays good house manners.

Begin at the Beginning

Start housetraining the minute you bring your Beagle pup home. Before you take him indoors, walk him around so he has an opportunity to go potty. When he performs, name the action and tell him what a good dog he is. "Gooood go potty!"

Before you bring your puppy home, decide on a room where he can stay when you can't be there to supervise. This is his safe room and can also be his bedroom if you choose not to have him sleep in your room.

The best choice is usually a kitchen, bathroom, or laundry room—any small area with a tile or linoleum floor for easy cleanup. If the room is large and you want to limit where he goes, use a puppy playpen (see Chapter 7 for more details). Keep a supply of newspapers or housetraining pads in this room; you'll need them to line the floor.

The Crate Is Your Friend

A dog kennel, or crate, serves a number of purposes. It keeps your Beagle safe when he's riding in the car, it keeps him out of trouble when you can't watch him, and it's a place for him to sleep at night. By far, though, the crate's most valuable role is as a housetraining tool.

Beagle Bonus

Choose a crate that's just large enough for your puppy to stand up, lie down, and turn around. Anything bigger will give him room to eliminate in one corner and sleep in the other.

Before you think to yourself that it's mean to keep your puppy in a crate, stop a minute and review the facts. To a dog, a crate is a nice, cozy spot for a nap, not a jail. He doesn't understand the concept of freedom versus confinement. All he knows is that when he goes in the crate he gets a treat and it's time for a break from play.

As a species, dogs are accustomed to making a den for them-selves. In the wild, it might be a cave or a hole in the ground. In your home, it's the crate. Once your Beagle pup recognizes the crate as his den, he won't want to soil it because that's his sleeping place. It's deeply ingrained in dogs not to mess up the den. So your Beagle is ready-made to accept the idea that the crate is his den and that he needs to avoid soiling it. The scheduled trips outside will reinforce the idea that the entire house is his den and that the outdoors is his potty area.

When's He Gotta Go?

It's easy to predict when your puppy will need to go out. When he wakes up in the morning or after a nap, his first act will be to step away from his sleeping area and squat. He'll need to go again a few minutes after eating or drinking. The excitement of play can also prompt a puppy to potty. Sometimes he'll just stop in the middle of a game and squat.

The Schedule

Make it a habit to take your puppy out first thing in the morning so he gets the idea that outside is the place to go. Carry him if you have to, so he doesn't have a chance to stop and pee before you get to the door.

Any time he goes outside, take him out on-leash. If you don't go out with him, you won't be able to praise him when he goes, and that's a must in the potty-training process. Yes, it's a hassle, but it's the quickest route to success. Before you get your pup out of his crate, place your filled coffee cup by the

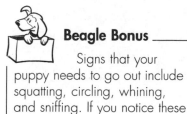

Beagle Bonus

Signs that your puppy needs to go out include squatting, circling, whining, and sniffing. If you notice these behaviors, scoop him up and take him outside fast!

door so you can grab it on the way out. It'll help wake you up while he's sniffing around for the perfect spot.

After he eliminates (and you praise him), let him play for a few minutes. Then take him inside for breakfast. After he eats, it's back outdoors again. When he goes, praise him and then take him inside. It's time for him to go back in his crate while you get ready for work or get the kids off to school.

Mealtimes and Housetraining

Part of setting up a housetraining schedule includes feeding your puppy on a regular schedule. If you leave food out all the time, you won't know when he's likely to need to go out. Set down food at given times during the day and don't leave any out for him to nibble on.

Outside Again!?

It can be a shock to discover just how frequently a puppy needs to go out. Even at four months of age, it's not unusual for a puppy to need to go out every couple of hours.

Don't get mad about this. It's not something he can help. Puppies aren't physically capable of "holding it" until they're at least six months old. They just don't have the muscle control. Be patient.

Obviously, unless you work at home, you're not going to be able to take your Beagle out every couple of hours during the day. If you can take a week off from work when you first get him, that's a smart step in getting him used to the idea of going outside when nature calls. If that's not possible, though, consider some other options.

🐾 Ask a neighbor to come over and take him out two or three times during the day.

🐾 Confine the puppy to a kitchen, bathroom, or laundry room with linoleum or tile floors. If he has an accident, it will be easy to clean up.

🏠 Get a doggie door so he has access to the yard from his "safe" room. (He's not old enough to have the run of the house.)

🏠 Hire a petsitter to come in and take him out and play with him.

🏠 Arrange to come home during your lunch break.

Using the Crate

Your Beagle's crate is his safe haven. Take steps to make sure being in the crate is a pleasant experience for him. Place the crate in an area where he can watch the family activities. You don't want to move him off to a room where he won't feel a part of what's going on.

Every time you put him in the crate, say "Crate!" in a happy tone of voice and give him a small treat, such as a bite-size dog biscuit. He'll learn very quickly that the command "Crate!" comes with a nice, tasty reward. Amaze your friends by showing off how quickly he runs to his bed when you say the magic word. Don't forget to reward him with that treat!

Put the dog in his crate any time you can't watch him. Don't leave him there for more than two to four hours at a time. Remember, he's not old enough to control his bladder or sphincter for much longer than that. You don't want him to get used to the idea of having accidents in his crate, because that will make the crate much less effective as a housetraining tool.

Beagle Bonus

Housetraining pads are impregnated with a scent that attracts dogs to urinate or defecate on them. They're more expensive than newspapers, but they can be an effective way to teach your pup to go in a particular spot in the room instead of just any old place. With their water-resistant backing, puppy pads are easier to clean up than papers.

When you leave for work, place the crate in the puppy's safe room with the door open. He should be able to go in and out as he pleases. If you're going to be gone all day, lay down papers or housetraining pads for him to use. Place them away from the crate.

Accidents Happen

Despite all your precautions, your puppy is bound to have a few accidents in the house. Review the circumstances and see where you can do better. Did you wait a little too long after his meal to take him out? Did you let him roam around on his own while you were distracted? Get back on schedule and keep him on a leash at your side or make better use of the crate.

Remember that the more accidents your puppy has in the house, the longer it will take to fully housetrain him. Any time he gets the opportunity to go in the house, it's going to reinforce the idea that the house is an acceptable place to eliminate. You want him to think that outdoors is the only place to do his business.

Should you punish your puppy if he has an accident? Keep in mind that he's only doing what comes naturally. You wouldn't spank a baby for soiling his diapers. You also don't want your pup to get the idea that the act of eliminating makes you mad. That will only encourage him to sneak around and potty in out-of-the-way places. Some dogs become so nervous that they won't pee or poop in front of their owners at all—not even outdoors! That's a bad habit for a dog to learn, so hold your temper.

When to Call the Vet

Pay attention to your puppy's output. If you see blood in his urine or stool, take him to the veterinarian.

If you see that your pup is about to go in the house or you catch him in the act, make a disapproving sound—"Aaaaght!"—yell "Outside!" and hustle him outdoors. But forget that whole idea of rubbing his nose in the mess or swatting him with a newspaper. Those techniques—which are more properly described as common housetraining mistakes—are from the dark ages of dog training. Throw them in the garbage along with your Beagle's poop.

Advanced Training

As you get to know your Beagle's habits, you'll start to see the sometimes subtle signs that he needs to go out. Some Beagles are forthright and go stand at the door. Others may just look at you a certain way.

Bet You Didn't Know _____

Lots of dogs at least make the attempt to go outside. Often, when accidents are discovered, they're located in front of the door, sometimes as close to the edge of the door as the dog can get. This is a positive sign. It means that your dog knows he's supposed to go outside; he just didn't have the opportunity.

To increase the chances that your dog will alert you to his needs, hang a bell on the doorknob and ring it before you open the door to take him out. Some dogs catch on quickly to this trick and learn to ring the bell themselves when they need to go out. It's worth a try!

Spot the Patterns, Not the Carpet

As you learned earlier, Beagles—and dogs in general—are programmed to go potty at certain times. You can count on them needing to go when they wake up in the morning or after a nap, after every meal, and after or during playtime.

By observing your Beagle's habits, you can recognize the behavior patterns that will allow you to take him out almost before he knows he has to go. These include whining, sniffing, circling, squatting, or even a particular facial expression. Each dog is an individual, so get to know your own dog's signs.

It might help to keep a chart with notes on such things as the time of elimination, how many minutes it takes for him to eliminate after each meal, and what body language indicates a need to go. This may sound a bit anal, so to speak, but it can really help you get a handle on your Beagle's routine.

Make sure everyone in the family understands and responds to the dog's routine. Waiting "just until the commercial comes on" often means waiting too late. Remember, the more accidents your pup has in the house, the longer it's going to take to housetrain him.

Boys Vs. Girls

Male Beagles are often more difficult to housetrain than females. Males have a natural instinct to mark their territory—warning off potential adversaries and attracting potential mates—by lifting their leg. Chronic leg-lifters will baptize anything at leg height, from furniture to bedding to plants.

An intact male can be almost impossible to housetrain effectively. Neutering at six to nine months of age can help solve this problem. See Chapter 12 for further discussion on the benefits of neutering.

Housetraining the Adult Beagle

You can use the same techniques to housetrain an older Beagle as you would a puppy. The only difference, of course, is that the mature Beagle doesn't need to go out as often. Do put him on a schedule, including regular mealtimes instead of free-feeding, so that you can better gauge when he needs to go out. Once he learns the boundaries—that indoors is his den and outdoors is the potty area—he should be good to go.

Housetraining the Pet-Store Puppy

Puppies that come from pet stores often have spent their entire lives in a little wire cage. They eat in that cage, and they pee and poop in that cage. Puppies that have learned that it's normal to eliminate in a cage can be difficult if not impossible to housetrain. Sometimes they even "hold it" until they're placed back in the crate. For all they know, that's the way things are done. If you're faced with this problem, try the following technique.

When you're at home, keep the puppy on a leash by your side. All the time. Take him out even more often than you might otherwise. Praise him wildly when he goes outside. He needs to learn that outside is the place to go.

Doggy Do's/Doggy Don'ts _____

Don't assume that your puppy is fully housetrained until he has shown himself to be reliable for several months. Setbacks can occur occasionally until he's as much as one year old (or older if his training hasn't been consistent). Be patient and calm, and review what might have gone wrong.

If he still messes in his crate at night, try to forestall the problem. If you took him out at 9:30 P.M., take him out again at 10 P.M. Stay outside for as long as it takes him to perform. If he doesn't do anything, take him inside, on-leash, and watch or crate him to make sure he doesn't do anything in the house. Take him out again in a half hour.

Your goal is to learn his schedule as well as to teach him what you want. Because you can't speak Dog, he has to guess what you're asking him to do. Be patient and give him time to learn.

Clean It Up

In the event of an accident, clean up the mess quickly and thoroughly. A dog, especially a scenthound such as the Beagle, is wired to return to the same elimination spot over and over. Unless you do a good job of getting rid of the smell, you could have problems.

Keep a good enzymatic cleanser on hand. These products "eat up" the bacteria that produce the odor that attracts your Beagle. In a pinch, vinegar and water works too. Avoid ammonia-based cleansers. Canine urine contains ammonia, so the scent of such a cleanser will simply draw your dog back to the spot of the crime.

Doggy Do's/ Doggy Don'ts

Remember to praise your dog every time he goes where he's supposed to. Use a happy, excited tone of voice. "Gooood potty!" Beagles thrive on positive reinforcement.

Clean up after your dog outdoors, too. It's just good dog-owner etiquette to pick up your dog's poop so others don't run the risk of stepping in it. Purchase a poop scoop at the pet supply store or use a plastic sandwich bag or grocery bag. Simply place the bag over your hand, pick up the poop, then turn the bag inside out. Toss it in the nearest trash receptacle.

To clean up urine on carpet, use a towel to soak up as much of the liquid as possible. Then saturate the area with the cleanser. Use it in the immediate vicinity of the wet spot, too, to make sure you don't miss anything. Blot again.

For solid loads, use a towel or plastic bag to pick up as much of the mess as possible and flush it down the toilet. Apply the cleanser to the area and use a clean towel to blot up the rest of the stain.

In both cases, finish by placing a dry towel on the area and stacking books or some other heavy object on top of the towel to help draw out the remaining moisture.

Practice Makes Perfect

The real secret to housetraining success is consistency. Often people give up far too soon, simply deciding that their dog is untrainable. You need to set a schedule, use a crate, take him out early and often, and praise, praise, praise.

Remember that your Beagle isn't deliberately having accidents in the house. If he has more than a few, you aren't watching him carefully enough or giving him enough opportunities to go outside. He would much rather hear you praise him than yell at him, so don't sabotage his efforts.

Housetraining takes time. If the amount of time you have to spend with your Beagle and teach him is limited by work or school, you need to understand that the learning curve will be greater. Even under the best circumstances, it can take six to nine months for your Beagle to be reliable in the house.

Remember when you're about to get mad over an accident, stop and review the situation. What could you have done differently to ensure success instead of failure? Be patient, back up to a point in housetraining where your Beagle was being successful—say, going out every four hours instead of every six hours—and try again. Your positive attitude will help you get through this often trying time and reach your goal of a well-mannered Beagle.

Doggy Do's/ Doggy Don'ts
Don't crate your puppy for more than four hours at a time. That's about the limit for a puppy to hold his urine, as well as the limit for a social animal like a Beagle to go without human attention.

The Least You Need to Know

- A crate is your secret weapon in the housetraining wars, and a consistent schedule is a must for successful housetraining.

- A puppy isn't physiologically capable of "holding it" until he's four to six months old.

- A dog door gives your Beagle access to the outdoors when you can't be there to let him out.

- Use an enzymatic cleanser rather than an ammonia-based one to clean up accidents.

- Praise your dog every time he potties where you want him to. Punishment is counterproductive. Never hit your dog or rub his nose in his urine or feces.

- The signals that indicate your puppy needs to go out include whining, circling, sniffing, squatting, or a particular facial expression.

Chapter **9**

School Time, Rule Time

In This Chapter

- 🏠 When should training begin?
- 🏠 The benefits of puppy kindergarten and obedience class
- 🏠 What every dog should know
- 🏠 Setting goals and staying focused
- 🏠 Choosing a trainer

Any family pet needs rules to live by. This is especially true of Beagles, who will gladly make up their own rules if given half a chance. Besides housetraining, your dog needs to learn certain behaviors and commands that will make him more pleasant to live with. The best place for him to learn is in a puppy kindergarten class, followed by a more formal obedience class.

Never assume that your Beagle is too young to learn. When you bring him home at eight or nine weeks of age, he is in prime learning time. His brain is like a sponge, soaking up and storing every new experience. Turn this learning ability to your advantage by teaching him tricks and commands at home and signing him up for puppy kindergarten class.

What Is Puppy Kindergarten?

This beginner class teaches basic manners and provides socialization. It's usually offered for puppies three months of age and up. Some classes start pups at 10 weeks of age, which is fine, but most trainers and veterinarians prefer that puppies be fully vaccinated before being exposed to other dogs. If you have an opportunity to start a class when your Beagle is 10 weeks old, ask your veterinarian what she thinks.

A puppy kindergarten class is a great place for dogs and people to socialize. You may even make new Beagle friends there. Under the guidance of a trainer, you and your dog can learn the basics while having fun. This early introduction to a class setting also benefits Beagles that will be going on to formal obedience training or the conformation ring.

Class Benefits

Why a class when there are dozens of dog-training books on the market? While you can certainly teach your Beagle at home, attending puppy kindergarten and obedience class offers the opportunity to learn in a structured setting and socialize with other dogs and people. It also teaches your Beagle to work despite the distractions of other dogs and people.

The real point of a training class is for the trainer to teach the owner—you—how to train a dog. In a class, you and your Beagle will learn to work together as a team. By the time you're through, you will have taught your Beagle how to sit, stay, come when called, lie down, and walk nicely on a leash. With practice and positive reinforcements such as praise and treats, he'll learn faster than you could have imagined.

Doggy Do's/ Doggy Don'ts

Even before he's old enough to go to class, you can teach your puppy simple commands such as sit. Young puppies learn rapidly, and early training will help you establish good Beagle habits.

Remember that training class isn't just for puppies. Adult dogs can benefit too, especially if they've been a little spoiled. Taking your Beagle to training class every year or two is a good way to reinforce the things he's learned, as well as to teach him new things.

An obedience-trained dog is nice to live with, but training brings other benefits as well. A trained dog is capable of going to public places without embarrassing you, riding in the car without causing an accident, traveling with you, and becoming a therapy dog, bringing smiles and companionship to people in nursing homes and hospitals.

Setting Goals

Part of teamwork involves setting goals. In an obedience class, you can talk to the trainer about what you want your Beagle to learn. She can guide you through the steps you and your dog need to take to achieve those goals. You'll also have the support of the group. It can be helpful to see how other people and dogs achieve their goals. You might be able to try some of their techniques if you're having trouble with your dog.

Staying Focused

A class setting provides the structure and incentive you need to continue training. Knowing that you have to go every week helps motivate you to practice at home, especially if the trainer assigns homework and expects to see you demonstrate the results. And if you're like most of us, once you've paid for something, you're going to use it.

Emotional Support

A class is a great place to ask questions and get help with problems. The trainer and other class members can help you work through any frustrations you're having with your Beagle. It often helps just to know that other people are going through the same thing. A book is

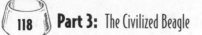

not going to have any new answers for you, no matter how many times you look in it, but a trainer can draw on her vast experience with many dogs to offer different suggestions for coping with your Beagle's behavior bombshells.

Socialization

Public poise is a result of being accustomed to meeting new people and dogs and going lots of places. Puppy kindergarten is where your Beagle's social life begins. It can mean the difference between a dog that enjoys new people and experiences and one that is fearful of anything unusual.

Doggy Do's/Doggy Don'ts

Besides the weekly class meetings, take your Beagle on other outings. Outdoor shopping malls and sidewalk cafes are good places for pups to interact with people and have new experiences. Ask your trainer if there are any places she recommends. Outdoor youth sports events such as baseball games are great places to expose your dog to children. Just make sure your adorable pup isn't mobbed by kids wanting to pet and hold him.

Charting Progress

Most classes include a brief lecture each week on puppy development and physical and mental abilities at that stage. In a class, the learning pace proceeds at your puppy's developmental rate. The trainer can tell you if what you're expecting is too advanced for your puppy's age.

What Your Beagle Should Learn

The basic commands every Beagle should know are "Sit," "Down," "Come," and "Stay." Walking nicely on a leash is a requirement as well. These are all behaviors your Beagle can learn in a kindergarten class. The more advanced obedience class teaches higher levels of these skills, such as long sits and downs, and can be the introduction to obedience competition. It also reinforces what was learned in puppy kindergarten, which is crucial as your Beagle enters adolescence and begins to challenge your authority.

With practice and persistence, Beagles are perfectly capable of displaying appropriate manners for any occasion. They can understand the difference between training walks, where they have to heel, and walks where they are allowed to sniff to their hearts' content. They can differentiate between young children, with whom they must be gentle, and older children, with whom it's okay to roughhouse. When you take them places, they know how to handle themselves in public.

Choosing a Trainer

There are several routes to finding a trainer. If she's local, your Beagle's breeder may train dogs or know someone who does. You can ask a friend, neighbor, or co-worker for recommendations. You can look in the Yellow Pages under Dog Training. Or you can ask your veterinarian for a referral. He or she may even have a staff member who offers training. Sometimes animal shelters offer training classes, and you need not have adopted your dog from them to sign up.

If these routes fail, contact the American Kennel Club (see Appendix B) to see if there is a dog club in your area. Many dog clubs offer training classes themselves or can recommend a trainer.

Whatever the source of the referral, sniff out the trainer's bona fides (bona fidos?) for yourself. Be sure the trainer uses positive training methods and has experience

Doggy Do's/ Doggy Don'ts
Remember that Beagles are individuals. Some learn quickly and love to work, while others seem incapable of picking up and remembering the simplest command. Tailor your training style to your dog.

with Beagles or hounds in general. No matter how good, a trainer who is used to working with easily trained Golden Retrievers or Border Collies may find her first experience with Beagles a challenge. Some trainers view Beagles as untrainable and unreasonably stubborn. If this is the trainer's attitude, you may want to look elsewhere or ask her to keep an open mind.

Be Positive

We all learn more quickly and eagerly in an accepting environment, and dogs are no different. Positive reinforcement works well with any aspect of training, primarily because it's stress-free. The attention a Beagle receives when he performs correctly encourages him to repeat the behavior for which he was rewarded or received attention.

While most trainers now accept that positive reinforcement techniques work, some old-school trainers believe that their use—especially when food is involved—doesn't result in precise, reliable dogs. Trainers who have tried both methods, though, usually find that they get more out of the dog and that the dog retains more of what he's taught when positive training methods are used. Training sessions can last longer, too. One of the advantages of having a Beagle is that you've chosen a breed that will happily work for food or treats.

Before signing up for a class, go to a session and evaluate the trainer's methods. If you see a lot of jerking and frequently hear harsh tones, look elsewhere. You're better off training the dog yourself than exposing your Beagle to such a negative experience.

Practice at Home

Once you've signed up for a class, don't think that's all you need to do. Like any educational pursuit, dog training requires homework. Luckily, your Beagle pup's attention span is short, so a few daily practice sessions of only five or ten minutes are perfectly okay. Keep practice time fun and avoid repetition. Remember, Beagles get bored fast. Most important, encourage your puppy to watch you and pay attention to you. That's how all training begins.

The basic commands you and your Beagle will learn are "Sit," "Down," "Stay," "Come," and "Heel." I've thrown in "Leave It" too, because it's an important one for this breed. Let's take a look at the best ways to teach these behaviors.

Sitting Pretty

What's so great about "Sit"? "Sit" is the default behavior your puppy learns instead of jumping up on people or rushing out an open door. It's handy for him to know when you're having a long conversation with someone and don't want to be interrupted by your dog.

"Sit" is not only a useful command, it's also pretty easy to teach. The simplest method is to hold a treat above your puppy's head and say "Sit!" As his head moves up to look at the treat, his body will naturally move into a sitting position. Voilà! He sits, you give him the treat and say "Good sit!" After a few repetitions of this, he'll get the hang of it and start associating the word "sit" with the action of sitting. As he gets good at it, you can give treats only for exceptional performance, such as a nice, straight sit or a very fast sit.

Another way to teach "Sit" is to place the dog at your left side, leash on. Hold the leash tautly so your puppy is encouraged to look up at you. Say "Sit!" and gently push down on the pup's rear to encourage him to move into position. When he does, praise him or give him a treat. Continue as described previously.

Doggy Do's/ Doggy Don'ts
Make sure your puppy is paying attention when you give a command. You can't work effectively with him if he's not focused on you. Say his name and wait until he looks at you before you give a command.

Down Dog

Teaching "Down" has the same benefits as teaching the "Sit" command. Another good reason to know it is for quieting a dog that's barking. For whatever reason, dogs that are lying down don't bark.

"Down" can be a little more difficult to teach than "Sit" because it's a more submissive position, so many dogs don't like to do it. Here are some tips to help smooth your Beagle's downward path.

Lying down is a natural position for dogs, so start by rewarding your Beagle any time you see him in the down position (the Sphynx look, on his stomach with paws in front and back legs stretched out). When you see your dog assume the position, say "Good down!" and give him a treat. After you've done this repeatedly, he'll associate the word "Down" with the act of lying down. Next, when you see him start to move into position, say "Down!" When he completes the act, click and treat. Eventually you'll be able to give the command and have him respond.

You can also teach "Down" by luring the dog into position with a treat. Hold the treat in front of his nose and then drop your hand down and forward. The dog should automatically move into position. If he doesn't, you can give him a hint by gently pushing down on his back as you pull the treat forward.

If you have a slippery linoleum, tile, or wood floor, use it when you're teaching the "Down" command. Tell your Beagle to "Sit," then take the treat in front of his nose and bring it down and forward. He'll slide right into a down.

Stay Right There!

"Stay" has the same benefits as "Sit" and "Down," plus one more: The Beagle who learns it no longer rushes out open doors. Because they're so curious and eager to explore, Beagles are notorious for running through open doors. This is a command your dog needs to perform when you are opening the door for delivery people or getting out of the car and don't want him to move yet.

Doggy Do's/Doggy Don'ts _____
When your Beagle gets good at performing these commands, add some distractions to test his resolve. Jump up and down, wave your arms, sing, anything that might cause him to break his sit, stay, or down. If he moves out of position, put him back in place and start over. He needs to learn that there's no reason to break his command except for your release word "Okay!"

To teach "Stay," place your dog in a sit or down. Hold your hand palm facing the front of his face and say "Stay!" Slowly back a few steps away from him. If he gets up to follow you, say "Aaaght!" and start over. At first, your Beagle may only hold a stay for a few seconds. That's okay. Start by expecting a stay of only 5 or 10 seconds. You'll probably be able to tell when he's about to break his stay. Quickly, before that happens, say "Good stay!" and reward him. Gradually extend the length of time before you release him as well as the distance you go.

A release word is a signal to your dog that he can relax. Just as an army sergeant tells his troops "at ease," you need to let your dog know when it's okay to stop sitting or staying or whatever else you've told him to do. Choose a simple word. Many people use "okay," although some trainers prefer to use a less common word since you might accidentally say "okay" without meaning to release your dog.

Come When Called

This is the most important command your Beagle will ever learn. Responding instantly to it can save his life if he's ever running toward danger.

To teach "Come," you'll need a box of treats and a long lead. A clothesline will work well. Walk away from him, keeping the lead loose. Rattle the box of treats and say "Baxter, Come!" He'll probably come running at the sound of the box rattling. When he does,

Beagle Bonus

Another easy to way to teach your dog "Come" is to whistle a particular tune every time you set down his food dish. Like Pavlov's dogs, your Beagle will soon come running every time he hears that special whistle.

shower him with praise and give him a treat. "Gooood come, Baxter!" If he's reluctant to come because he's following an intriguing scent, use the long line to encourage him your way. Again, praise and reward him when he gets there. Gradually increase the distance you go before you call him to you.

Work on "Come" all the time until you are sure your Beagle will come without fail. Practice this command throughout your dog's life and make it well worth his while to heed your call. On the other hand, don't ever call him to you when you're going to do something he doesn't like, such as trim his nails. And never call your dog to you and then yell at him for something he did wrong. That's the surest way to teach your Beagle not to come.

Walk Nice

Before you try to walk your puppy on-leash, let him get used to his new "tail." Attach the leash and let him run around with it dragging behind him. When he's worn himself out, pick up the leash and walk outside for some practice sessions. Note: Never leave your Beagle unsupervised with the leash still attached. It could get caught on something and injure him.

Hold the leash in your left hand with your puppy at your left side. Have a treat or favorite toy in your right hand to hold his attention. Walk forward, encouraging your puppy to come using a happy tone of voice.

Don't drag him if he seems reluctant. Keep the leash slack and encourage him with the treat or toy. Reward him after a few steps. As he grows used to the leash, increase the amount of time between rewards.

If your Beagle pulls on the leash, don't jerk the leash or yell "No!" Simply stop walking. When he reaches the end of his tether and looks back at you, wait a few more seconds before moving forward again. If he pulls again, stop again. Teach him that neither of you will be moving forward until he walks politely at your side.

Doggy Do's/ Doggy Don'ts

Encourage your puppy to look up at you frequently when you're walking together. This ensures that he'll be aware when you're about to make a turn or might be planning to stop.

Once your puppy gets the hang of walking on a leash, assign a name to the command. You can use the formal "Heel," which you'll want to do if you plan to participate in obedience trials, or a phrase such as "Walk nice!" Don't forget to praise him as you walk.

Next, practice "Sit" when stopped. After you've walked a few feet, stop and tell your puppy "Sit!" He should sit at your side until you move forward again, commanding "Heel!" Some puppies do this automatically, while others need a little work. Practice this at curbs or intersections so that your Beagle learns not to run out into the street before you check for traffic.

Use a release word such as "Okay!" when you're willing for him to forge ahead on an extendible leash or sniff around on his own.

Leave It!

Because Beagles are led around by their noses, it's a good idea to teach them not to approach certain items. The "Leave It" command comes in handy when a Beagle sniffs out garbage on the ground or some other substance that he shouldn't get into.

To teach "Leave It," place something enticing, such as a dish of dried liver bits, on the floor. With the dog on lead and a liver treat in the right hand, walk by the dish. The dog will show interest, but say nothing and keep walking. At some point, the dog will look away

Doggy Do's/ Doggy Don'ts

Avoid giving your puppy attention for bad behavior. Even if it's negative attention, such as yelling at him, he learns that he can get a response from you. Instead reward him every time you see him doing something you like.

from the liver, although not necessarily at you. When that moment occurs, say, "Yes," and give the dog the treat in your hand.

Repeat this scenario only a couple of times during each training session—remember the Beagle's limited attention span. It shouldn't take long before your dog walks by the dish and looks at you instead of at the liver. This is the time to link the command to the action. As you walk by the dish, say, "Leave It." When the dog looks away from the dish, click or say, "Yes," and give the treat. Once the dog understands "Leave It" in this context, you can start using it with other distractions that might come along.

Training Tips

You can take certain steps to ensure that each training session is both fun and effective. The following hints will help you and your Beagle achieve training success.

Be Prepared

Gather everything you need before you start a training session. Leash and treats should be at hand so you don't have to interrupt your work. Seeing you get ready will also cue your Beagle that it's time to train.

Train Before Meals

Because Beagles are so food-oriented, they'll do anything for a treat. They'll be even more eager to perform if they're hungry. Plan to have a training session before each meal so that your Beagle is more focused on his rewards. Besides, aren't you a little sleepy and sluggish after a big meal? Your dog is too. Train when he's at his most alert.

Vary Your Rewards

To keep your Beagle working his hardest, he should never know what to expect. When you first start training, reward him every time he performs correctly. As he gets better, reward only his better performances: his straightest sits, his fastest downs.

Remember, too, that while treats are highly effective, they shouldn't be the only thing your Beagle responds to. Throw in praise and a play session with a favorite toy to keep things interesting.

Short and Sweet

To engage a Beagle's attention, incorporate plenty of variations in exercises practiced and reinforcements used, and avoid endlessly repeating an exercise. If your Beagle has performed correctly, move on to something else.

Beagle Bonus _____

The rewards that make a dog's efforts worthwhile range from tone of voice to tug-of-war games to well-timed treats. Words themselves are not especially meaningful to dogs, but a high-pitched tone of excitement or a soothing monotone can get results, no matter what you're actually saying. The promise of a ball to be thrown or the offer of a treat can lure a dog, prodding him to try things he might not have the gumption to do on his own.

A training session can be as brief as 30 seconds or as long as 10 minutes. Besides being tailored to a Beagle's attention span, short sessions make it easier to fit in several each day, whenever you have time. End a session when the dog has performed a task correctly, so that he leaves with thoughts of praise and treats dancing in his head.

Keep It Simple

Ideally use only one word when you give a command: "Sit," "Down," "Stay," "Come," "Off," "Over." You get the picture. Your Beagle can learn a lot of different words; just make sure they're very specific. Use a distinct tone of voice when you give a command so your dog learns to distinguish between normal conversation and your training voice.

Accentuate the Positive

Training sessions should be fun for your Beagle. If they aren't, you'll lose his attention because he'll look for something better to do.

Doggy Do's/Doggy Don'ts _____

Take note of what motivates your dog. If you see that he responds well to gestures or to a particular toy or tone of voice or type of treat, write it down. Make note of his negative responses as well, such as shying away from gestures or turning up his nose at dry cat food (a particular favorite of many dogs).

Take every opportunity to reward your dog for doing something right. If he doesn't respond to a command, guide him into place and then reward him. If you get frustrated, switch to a command that he does well. Always end a session on a high note.

Patience Pays

Remember that Beagles are individuals. Some learn quickly and love to work, while others seem incapable of picking up and remembering the simplest command. Tailor your techniques to your dog, and allow time for learning to take place. Sometimes you just have to wait for things to sink into your Beagle's brain.

Besides being creative in finding rewards, you must also be creative in solving problems. While it's easy to yell at a dog for doing something wrong, it's not so easy to find a positive way to motivate him or to prevent failure. One of the tenets of positive reinforcement is that a dog is never allowed to fail. If the dog has a difficult time learning a command, you need to be willing to help him work through it.

If positive reinforcement seems like a lot of work, well, it is. The rewards, however, are proportionately greater.

Higher Education

Sometimes toys, treats, and praise just aren't enough to motivate your Beagle. That's when it's time to bring out the big guns. The following techniques will help get your Beagle's attention when he's bored or not paying attention. They may help jump-start his interest in the training process.

Truth or Consequences

Show your Beagle just how costly his misbehavior can be. This works especially well if you're training two or more Beagles at once. Put the dogs in a "Down-Stay" or "Sit-Stay." If one gets up, immediately release the other one and make a big production of giving him a treat. This can make a major impression on the dog who broke the command.

If your dog isn't interested in working, you can cut the training session short without making it seem as if you're giving in to the dog. Take your attention away from him by calmly putting him in his crate. If you have a second dog, work with that dog instead. The "punishment" for the first dog is loss of the opportunity to earn a treat or praise.

Doggy Do's/ Doggy Don'ts

Keep training fun and interesting. Be excited when it's time for training, and your Beagle will think of it as a game rather than as work.

Ignoring Is Bliss

Walk away from behaviors you don't like. If your Beagle is jumping, mouthing, or not paying attention, just turn your back on him and leave. Refuse to give him attention or a treat until he behaves correctly. This is a form of negative reinforcement that's easy to do and harmless to the dog. Remember, when a dog is stressed because of physical or verbal correction, he can't readily take in what you're trying to teach.

The "N" Word

The good thing about the word "No" is that it's short and easy to yell. The bad thing is that your dog soon learns to ignore it if he hears it too often. This is especially true if you yell "No!" at him several times in succession.

To use "No!" effectively, limit it to a diversionary tactic. Say "No!" if you see him start to do something forbidden or if his attention starts to wander during training. If he turns his attention back to you, give a command, such as "Sit!" and reward him when he complies.

Avoid using "No!" in combination with your dog's name. You don't want your dog to associate his name with being yelled at. And try not to give your dog a name that rhymes with "No" such as Joe, Mo, or Beau. If you do, avoid using "No" at all; instead substitute "Aaaght" or some other unpleasant sound.

Other Diversionary Tactics

If you want to redirect your puppy's attention without yelling at him, try using a shake can. What's a shake can? It's a noisemaker that's easy to make at home. Rinse out an empty soda can, put a few pennies inside—you knew they'd come in handy someday, didn't you?—and tape over the top. When you see your puppy chewing on your best shoes or an electrical cord, toss the can in his direction (don't hit him with it!). Don't say anything when you toss the can and if possible don't let your Beagle see you throwing it. He should think that the correction just came out of nowhere.

> **Beagle Bonus**
>
> Trying to figure out what reward will work with a particular dog is one of the challenges of training. It often requires creativity and the constant reminder that each dog is an individual.

The noise will distract him. Once his attention has been drawn away from the forbidden item, offer him an acceptable chew toy and praise him for using it.

A squirt bottle works in much the same way. Use it, say, if you see your puppy about to squat in the house. The stream of water will break his concentration. Then rush him outside and praise him for pottying there.

Why Training Is Important

A dog that's not trained has an unhappy future. He ends up howling his head off in the backyard because he's not allowed in the house. Eventually his owners get tired of him and drop him off at the shelter. There, his outlook is bleak unless he's lucky enough to receive some training that will give him a chance at a second home.

Beagles need to love the person they're working with and know that the person loves them back. Then they'll do just about anything for them.

The Least You Need to Know

🏠 Beagles are fully capable of learning, and learning quickly, as long as they have the right motivation. Keep practice sessions short and always end on a high note.

🏠 Use positive reinforcement techniques to teach your Beagle right from wrong.

🏠 Beagles are capable of learning from an early age, so take steps to teach them the right things instead of letting them pick up bad habits.

🏠 Puppy kindergarten is a great place for your Beagle to learn the basics, as well as to socialize with other dogs and people. Or try to find a trainer who has experience working with Beagles.

🏠 The most useful and important commands for your Beagle to know are "Sit," "Down," "Stay," "Come," "Heel," and "Leave It."

🏠 Catch your dog doing something right and praise him for it rather than catching him doing something wrong and yelling at him for it. Instead of always yelling "No!" at your dog, use diversionary tactics to get his attention.

Chapter 10

Who's in Charge Here?

In This Chapter

- 🏠 The chain of command
- 🏠 Establishing leadership
- 🏠 Effective rewards and corrections
- 🏠 Dealing with dominance
- 🏠 Using the crate

Training a Beagle is not for the faint of heart or ego. This is a willful dog who likes to think for himself. He's fully capable of "forgetting" the rules or working around them. If you're going to stay ahead of him, you need to establish yourself early and often as the leader of the pack.

This doesn't mean, however, that you should use harsh tones and physical force. Both are tactics that will make any right-thinking Beagle dig in his paws and refuse to listen. Firmness and patience, rewards for good behavior, and mild negative reinforcements will get your point across faster and more effectively than the long-discredited swat with a newspaper. A mild verbal reprimand—"Aaaght!"—or withdrawal of food rewards are techniques that are likely to get your Beagle's attention.

Your Beagle is smart, there's no doubt about that. You've got to be even smarter to train him successfully. That means not losing your temper, not checking into the local insane asylum, and not failing to set boundaries.

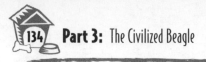

Beagles Need Boundaries

From the very first day you bring your Beagle home, you need to set limits for him. Without your guidance, he'll wreak havoc in the household, chewing your favorite loafers, raiding the dinner table, and howling 'til the cows come home. By setting boundaries, you can help him understand his place in the family pack. Lacking them, he'll test and push and guess, causing all sorts of trouble in the process.

Remember that hounds are masters at diversion and negotiation. Decide in advance what the rules are going to be and stick to them.

Will you allow your Beagle on the sofa? On the bed? Only on certain pieces of furniture? What about jumping up on people? You might not want him to do it, but other people will encourage it. Will you be firm about enforcing the rules or give up after the twenty-fifth person says "Oh, I don't mind. It's cute." One rule you'll definitely want to enforce on your family is "no feeding him from the table." Given half a chance, your Beagle will become a table-beggar faster than you can say "Jackrabbit."

Begin training as soon as you bring your Beagle puppy home. Puppyhood is prime learning time, and if you don't teach your Beagle early on how you want him to behave, he will quickly pick up bad habits instead. The same is true for an adult dog.

Leader of the Pack

Beagles are natural pack dogs. They recognize and accept a chain of command, and they're not hung up on advancement or ambition. They're willing to abide by the rules, as long as they're set by a strong and obvious leader. Providing a structured family life with the adults at the top, the kids next, followed by the dogs—in whatever order they determine for themselves—is the best way to help your puppy find his place and become a happy member of the team.

If you are consistent from the beginning in what you expect, your Beagle will come to recognize you as top dog. It's easy to let

puppies get away with things
when they're young, thinking that
they'll eventually grow out of the
behavior. Not gonna happen. The
longer and more often a puppy is
allowed to get away with things,
the more difficult it will be to train
him.

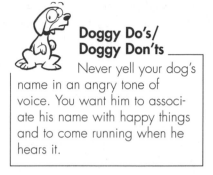

**Doggy Do's/
Doggy Don'ts**
Never yell your dog's
name in an angry tone of
voice. You want him to associate his name with happy things
and to come running when he
hears it.

Beagle owners must walk a fine
line between setting boundaries
and totally dominating their dogs. There's no reason your dog
should ever fear you. If he shies away from you, you're being too
harsh. Lighten up! You live with a Beagle.

While it's important to lay down the law, it can be difficult to
enforce it when a cute puppy is grinning at you, tongue lolling out
the side of his mouth. Be firm but not harsh—and try not to laugh
when you correct him. A low-toned verbal correction is more effective than a loud, harsh "No!" or "Stop that!" which are more likely
to frighten the puppy than keep him on the straight and narrow.

Speaking of straight and narrow, that's a path the Beagle will
rarely take. He can always find a new way to do something, just to
mix things up a bit and keep them interesting. Simply point him
back in the right direction—metaphorically speaking—without losing your temper. Remember that faint heart ne'er won fair Beagle.

Catch Him in the Act

The act of doing good, that is.
When you see good behavior,
reward it, even if it's not something you asked the dog to do.
Such actions could include sitting,
lying down, chewing on a toy, or
ignoring the cat.

Beagle Bonus
Early training and
plenty of attention and playtime
are the best ways to ensure a
well-behaved Beagle. Long
walks or runs will help work off
excess energy.

Keep a running list of good behaviors you want the dog to learn and track his progress. Every day, note the dog's achievements, and reward yourself and your dog for improvements.

Effective Rewards

Beagles have strong drives and desires that you can use to achieve your training goals. Any form of positive reinforcement works well with Beagles, but because they are scent-oriented, they are highly motivated by food.

The offer of a treat as a reward for a particular behavior is irresistible to almost any self-respecting Beagle. Strong-smelling items such as cheese, hotdogs, freeze-dried liver, or dried beef heart will be warmly welcomed and instantly snarfed by your Beagle. (Be sure you clean out your pockets before doing laundry and don't leave clothes with food in the pockets where your Beagle can reach them or you will be sewing up many holes.)

Although treats are a great incentive when training is just beginning, it's important to use them prudently. Remember that your Beagle is smart and conniving. Unless you dole out treats on a random basis, your dog will quickly learn to refuse commands until you hand over a reward.

Circumvent this highway robbery by frequently changing your pattern of offering rewards so that he never knows when a treat might be coming.

Nonfood Rewards

A reward doesn't always have to be food-related (although the Beagle will never turn down a treat of any kind). Beagles crave praise and attention as well. When your Beagle does something right, hug him, pet him, really love him up. Your little love hound will wiggle with delight because he's pleased you.

Play and activity are other great ways to reward good behavior. Take a "dog's choice" walk and let him sniff wherever he wants or

play a favorite game. If he has a preferred toy, don't leave it out all the time. Produce it only on special occasions so it doesn't lose its value as a reward.

Bored Now

Beagles also respond well to clicker training. The chirp of a clicker gives a dog immediate feedback: "Yes, that was right!" Follow the click with food or praise and you'll soon have a Beagle that "asks" for training sessions by handing you the clicker.

Clicker training results in rapid learning not only because it's fun and easy for dogs and people, but also because the instant approval it signals is reinforced by the payoff of a treat or praise. It's an exciting change of pace for the easily bored Beagle. See Appendix B for more information on learning about clicker training.

Crime and Punishment, Dog Style

If you see your Beagle developing problem behaviors, always offer a positive alternative. For instance, teach him to sit to greet you instead of jumping up. When he's chewing on a shoe, don't scold him. Instead quietly take it away and replace it with a chew toy. Then praise him for chewing on the toy.

Doggy Do's/Doggy Don'ts

Give your Beagle a timeout when he gets overexcited or destructive. In a calm manner, pick him up and put him in his crate. Don't tell him that he's been bad, don't say anything, just put him up. You can let him out after he has calmed down. Be sure you don't let him out when he's whining or scratching at the door, or he'll learn that making noise gets him released.

Even though it's tempting to yell at or swat your Beagle when he does something you don't like, remember that negative reinforcement can backfire when used with sensitive or stubborn dogs. When your Beagle makes a mistake, the best response is to ignore the error

and gently refocus him on the task at hand. Any number of things could have caused the mistake, from inexperience to eagerness to confusion. If you punish him, you may actually stifle his ability to blossom into the well-trained dog he has the potential to be. You have to expect mistakes.

When necessary, correct any display of defiance or aggression. Remember, however, that correction and punishment are two different things. When you make a correction, you show the dog what action is right. When you punish him, you merely inflict a penalty without any opportunity for rehab. The best corrections reinforce your position as leader.

A dominant Beagle, for instance, might require a series of steps that clarify to him his place in the pack. One such step is to require him to perform an obedience command for each handful of food, establishing your position as provider and controller of meals. Another is to forbid furniture privileges. This teaches him that he's not on an equal level with human pack members.

When your Beagle does something you don't like, avoid yelling at him or hitting him. Instead turn the tables on him. Call him to you and praise him for coming. Then require him to perform a command such as sit or down. Repeat your praise when he complies. Again, this establishes you as the leader because you are calling the shots. It also gives you an opportunity to praise the dog for doing something right.

Bet You Didn't Know

The dictionary defines the word "dogged" as "marked by stubborn determination; obstinate." And would you believe there's a picture of a Beagle next to the definition? Well, not really, but you get the idea.

Confusion and fear are often the reasons behind aggression in dogs. Hiding inside many dominant or aggressive Beagles is a nice dog that just doesn't know how to show it. By setting boundaries and establishing rules, you give him a solid framework in which to live.

Beagles and kids can be great friends.

A rare sight: a Beagle pup at rest.

15" Beagle Ch. Nieland's Lucky Break winning Best of Variety at the Westminster Kennel Club.

Maddie is a top flyball competitor.

Trim your Beagle's nails weekly or as needed.

Begging is one trick Beagles know by instinct.

Growing puppies need to eat about twice as much volume of food per pound of body weight as adult Beagles.

A Beagle's nose is always working.

Beagles can live to a ripe old age. Here are a father and son, with dad celebrating his seventeenth birthday.

Many Beagles enjoy playing in and near water.

Living with a Beagle is fun but requires a good sense of humor and lots of patience.

Father and son pose for the camera. Try to meet one or both of your puppy's parents before buying.

*Beagle puppies
Sportsman and
Olive explore the
Halloween
decorations.*

Give your Beagle a variety of toys so he won't get bored.

This advice is appropriate for a puppy that is just beginning to show signs of aggression. Persistent aggressive behavior such as biting or growling, especially in an adult dog, must be dealt with by a professional behaviorist or trainer who's experienced in dealing with aggression. Or seek out the services of a veterinarian who is trained in behavior (not all are).

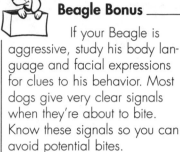

Beagle Bonus

If your Beagle is aggressive, study his body language and facial expressions for clues to his behavior. Most dogs give very clear signals when they're about to bite. Know these signals so you can avoid potential bites.

Using the Crate

Besides its uses as a bed and a housetraining tool, a crate is a good spot for your Beagle to be when he's on sensory overload. If he's barking wildly or is overexcited for some reason and can't seem to calm down, give him a break in the crate. In his hideaway, he can get a grip and return to normal.

It's very likely that your Beagle will protest his confinement by whining, howling, or scratching at the door. Ignore him. Close the door to the room he's in if you have to. Eventually he'll settle down. When he does, give him another 15 minutes or so to relax and then let him out.

By giving your Beagle this chance to calm down, he learns to temper his excitement over new people and experiences. This is an important part of his journey to adulthood.

The crate should be a pleasant place for your Beagle. Line it with a soft towel or blanket, and be sure it's equipped with fresh water and a sturdy chew toy such as a Kong,

Beagle Bonus

Love and respect are crucial. Your Beagle needs to know that you're on his side, not an adversary. Spend time just hanging out with him, playing together with a favorite toy. You may find that he becomes more pliable and less bullheaded.

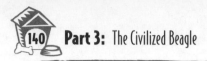

a pyramid-shaped hard rubber toy that's a favorite of many dogs. The Kong has a hole in the bottom that can be stuffed with goodies such as peanut butter and tiny dog biscuits. Your Beagle will spend hours trying to get out every last yummy bit.

Vocal Values

With their excellent hearing, dogs are highly sensitive to vocal tones. They often respond better to the higher pitched voices of women than to the deeper tones of men.

Sounds can also be used to get your Beagle's attention and create interest in what you're trying to teach him. One trainer couldn't get any reaction out of a particular Beagle until she started making a high-pitched squirrelly noise. That was all it took. Play around with different noises until you find one your dog responds to.

If your Beagle isn't responding well to your commands, make an effort to change your tone of voice. Try a higher pitch if you're male. You may be surprised to see that your dog offers less resistance to doing what you ask. Save deep, gruff tones for serious verbal corrections.

Consistency Is Key

The best way to get what you want out of your Beagle is to be consistent in your expectations. For starters, this means using the same commands all the time. People often alternate between "Down" and "Off" to mean the same thing—"Stop jumping on me"—but these should be two separate commands. "Off" is for "stop jumping on me" or "get off the furniture" while "Down" means "assume the down position on the ground." Be precise in what you're asking of your dog.

Consistency also means expecting to be obeyed the first time, every time. Many people repeat a command rapidly in an ever-escalating tone of voice: "Sit. Siiit. Sit! Sit!!" Your Beagle simply learns that he doesn't actually have to sit until the fourth or fifth time you yell the command at him. He learns that "Sit" doesn't always mean "Sit"—or at least not right away. He begins to test you, to see if he really has to respond every time. If you teach him that there are no consequences to ignoring a command—by giving up or by repeating the command—he'll start testing you in other ways.

Doggy Do's/ Doggy Don'ts

Don't yell "No" at your dog all the time. It quickly becomes one of those words that goes in one Beagle ear and out the other without ever registering. And it's usually yelled too late—after the misdeed has occurred. Instead use "No!" to head off misbehavior.

Say a command once and require that he comply. If he doesn't, use your disapproval noise—"Aaaght"—and show him what you want. This may mean shaping him into a sit, as you learned in puppy kindergarten or obedience class, or actually going over and getting him if he doesn't come when you call. Be matter-of-fact, not angry, when you do this. You want your Beagle to enjoy working with you.

In the beginning, reward your dog consistently every time he does something right. Once he knows a command, you can start withholding rewards until he gives a better performance: a straighter "Sit" or a faster "Down."

Timing Is Crucial

For a correction to mean anything, it must occur exactly at the time of the misdeed. Yelling at your dog after he's done something wrong is useless. He's not capable of understanding that you're scolding him for something he did hours or even minutes ago.

"But he looks guilty! He knows he did something wrong!" Dogs do not have a concept of guilt. They can, however, anticipate, and they know that when you come home, they get yelled at. They don't know why, but it's something they can learn to expect. If you come

Doggy Do's/ Doggy Don'ts

Encourage your Beagle to roll over for tummy rubs. A dog that will bare his belly to you is one who recognizes you as leader. For a good relationship, get in a couple of good tummy rubs a day.

home and find an accident or something destroyed, simply ignore the dog and clean it up. Your correction will have to wait until you can catch him in the act.

If you do catch your dog in the process of, say, chewing on something he shouldn't or squatting on the carpet, act fast! Say "Aaaght!" or use a shake can or squirt bottle to distract him. If he stops, give him a toy to chew on or hurry him outside to do his business. Then reward him with praise or a treat if one is handy. He's learned a very important thing, which is to turn his attention away from his actions to see what you want.

A Beagle is much more than just a cute, tri-color bundle of love. With patient, positive training, he can be a versatile companion and loving friend.

The Least You Need to Know

- Set down clear behavior guidelines for your Beagle from day one.

- Moderate your tone of voice until you find the right pitch to get his attention.

- Always reward your dog when you catch him doing something right. Treats and praise are favorite Beagle rewards.

- Show your dog what you want rather than punishing him for doing wrong.

- Use the crate for timeouts—not punishment—when your Beagle is overexcited or destructive. Never hit your dog.

The Juvenile Beaglinquent

In This Chapter

- 🏠 Baffled by barking
- 🏠 Coping with chewing
- 🏠 Dealing with digging
- 🏠 Eliminating escaping
- 🏠 Sorting out separation anxiety
- 🏠 Avoiding aggression
- 🏠 Biting basics

Beagles are generally nice dogs, but as I've noted before, when they get bored or lonely, beware! For a relatively small dog, the Beagle can be incredibly destructive and troublesome. Boredom isn't the only problem.

The onset of adolescence—a time of testing boundaries in any species—often brings an increase in behavior problems as young Beagles set out to establish their place in the family pack. Adolescence can begin as early as four months of age and can last until the dog is one to three years old, depending on the individual. During this time, they may start to mark territory by lifting their legs, display sexual behaviors such as humping, and challenge their people's authority by breaking rules or ignoring commands.

Behavior problems that can become magnified in response to lack of attention, lack of exercise, or adolescence include barking, chewing, digging, and running away. Beagles can also develop separation anxiety or become aggressive in some way. These are all tough behavior problems to deal with, but they can be corrected if you're willing to put forth the effort. And, of course, it's best not to let them develop in the first place!

Before we begin, though, let's remember that barking, chewing, digging, and roaming are perfectly normal dog behaviors, especially in the case of a Beagle. A certain amount of these behaviors is only to be expected. You know, fish gotta swim, birds gotta fly, Beagles gotta bark. It's when these behaviors become excessive that problems develop.

Mouthing Off

Beagles bark for any number of reasons. They bark when someone approaches their territory or when they see other dogs or when they hear sirens. They bark at squirrels and rabbits. They bark in excitement, when they know they're going for a walk or a car ride or getting their dinner. Sometimes they bark because they're stressed from being left alone too often. And sometimes they bark just because they're bored.

The act of barking isn't bad in and of itself. Many people get Beagles because they want a dog that will alert them to visitors or prowlers. It's when barking becomes excessive that the noise turns into a real headache, not only for owners but also their neighbors.

Before Things Get Out of Hand

Take steps to teach your Beagle when it's okay to bark and when he should stop. If you want him to bark when people approach the house, enlist your kids, spouse, or a neighbor to help out with the training. Ask the helper to come to the front door and knock or ring the doorbell. If your dog doesn't bark at the noise, encourage him by asking "Who's there? Is someone at the door?" Use an excited tone of voice. Praise him when he barks at the sound.

Once your Beagle knows to bark to alert you, teach him when to stop. After he gives a couple of barks, hold up your hand and say "Quiet." If he stops barking, praise him—"Good quiet"—and pop a treat into his mouth. Often showing him the treat may be distraction enough to stop the barking. Say "Quiet," and give him the treat after he's silent for several seconds. As your dog starts to learn what the word quiet means, lengthen the amount of time between the command and the reward.

Some trainers recommend wrapping a hand around the dog's muzzle and saying "Quiet" or "No bark." You risk a bite, however, if your Beagle doesn't see your hand coming and chomps down at the wrong time. Instead interrupt the barking by giving the "Down" command. Remember, dogs lying down hardly ever bark. As always, praise your Beagle when he's quiet and give him a treat.

Why Is He Barking So Much?

If barking has become a problem, you're going to have to do a little detective work. You need to figure out why the dog is barking. If he's bored, you need to change his environment rather than punish him. The best way to solve most barking problems is to get the dog inside the house where he can be with his people and away from the distractions that cause barking.

If your Beagle simply won't stop barking when people come to the door—or in other situations when you're present—and techniques such as teaching the

Doggy Do's/ Doggy Don'ts

Any time you use a shake can or water squirter, don't let the dog see that you're the source of the correction. It should come as if out of nowhere, giving him the idea that his actions are what prompted the noise or squirt.

"Quiet" command or putting him in a down are ineffective, try turning up the intensity. Squirt him with water from a spray bottle, toss a throw pillow at him, or throw a shake can in his direction (don't hit him with it!). Your Beagle needs to learn that nonstop barking brings disagreeable consequences.

Another reason dogs bark is because they want something. They want to eat, they want to go out, they want to play. Don't let your Beagle train you to respond to his barked commands. Wait until he has been quiet for a good 30 seconds before you feed him, let him out of his crate, open the door so he can go outside, or toss his ball. If you give in even once, your dog will learn that he can manipulate you by barking, and it will take a long time to retrain him.

Beagle Bonus

Teaching a dog to be quiet requires a lot of practice. Set up situations that give you the opportunity to show your Beagle what you want from him. It can take a while to teach a dog to be quiet on command, so don't give up.

Chew, Chew, Chew

Young Beagles, like all dogs, have a physiological need to chew. Chewing exercises develop their jaws, and it's a favorite form of play. Some dogs outgrow this chewing behavior, but others retain their enjoyment of it throughout life. We sit in front of the boob tube when we're bored. Dogs chew.

Beagle Bonus

Like babies, dogs go through a teething stage. Their teeth fall out so they can be replaced by the permanent teeth. Don't be shocked if you find one of your puppy's teeth on the floor; just pick it up and save it for his puppy book. Or maybe the tooth fairy will bring him a dog biscuit.

Your Beagle puppy is going to chew everything he can get his teeth on. Besides being entertaining, chewing is simply his way of exploring his territory. When your puppy decides to chew on an electrical cord, it's because he doesn't know that the cord isn't a toy like his hard rubber ball or bone. You can't afford to let him discover that on his own, so correct the behavior instantly, making it so unpleasant that he won't even want to try chewing cords again.

Doggy Do's/Doggy Don'ts

Praise your Beagle every time you see him chewing on a toy. Give each toy a name—"Good ball" or "Good bone" and rotate toys on a regular basis so he doesn't get bored. Handle toys frequently so they have your scent, and make hollow or hard rubber toys more appealing by stuffing them with treats or peanut butter.

Give an immediate verbal warning—"Aaaack" or "No!"—that what he's doing is wrong. Quickly follow the verbal warning with a physical correction. Squirt him with a spray bottle or toss a small, soft throw pillow in his direction. When he drops the cord and turns to you, give him a chew toy and praise him for chewing on it.

Doggy Do's/Doggy Don'ts

Prevent chewing by confining your Beagle when you can't be there to supervise. Crating your dog protects your belongings and protects him from a scolding that he won't understand. Be sure you give him a safe chew toy stuffed with goodies so he'll have something to occupy himself with while you're gone.

Preventing inappropriate chewing isn't just good for your furniture and clothing; it can save your dog's life. Dogs that chew electrical cords run the risk of death by electrocution. Dogs that steal garbage, especially fatty foods, are at risk for pancreatitis, a potentially fatal inflammation of the pancreas, or choking to death. Dogs that eat socks or rocks can suffer life-threatening intestinal blockages.

The Hole Truth

The good news is that Beagles aren't terriers, the world champions of digging. The bad news is that any Beagle who's bored enough can take up the habit of digging, once he tires of barking and chewing.

If your Beagle decides to take up excavation as a career, try to find ways to satisfy his need for activity that won't ruin your yard. These can include taking him for more or longer walks, getting him involved in a canine sport, confining him to a run where he can dig to his heart's content, or providing him with a specific digging area in an out-of-the-way place in the yard.

To prepare a Beagle digging area, choose a spot, surround it with railroad ties or some other type of border, and fill it with sand. Spike the area with favorite toys and treats such as hard biscuits for your dog to bury and dig up. Take him to his new play area and encourage him to dig there. When he does, say "Good dig!" and give him a treat. Any time you see him digging in a forbidden area, call him to you, reward him for coming, and then take him to his own spot.

Beagle Bonus

Keeping your Beagle busy or active will wear him out so he doesn't have the energy or inclination to dig. Teaching him to dig in a specific area is also a good solution.

The Runaway

As the Boss might say, Beagles are born to run. They'll run out the front door before you can stop them, they'll jump out of cars, and they'll go through or over fences if they possibly can. Beagles are exploring fools, so work hard to prevent wandering through training and secure fencing.

As you learned in Chapter 7, it's important to make sure there's no way your Beagle can go over or under your fence. Check to see that gates latch securely and that loose boards or holes don't offer a way out. If you have a digger, line the bottom of the fence with rocks or concrete.

Beagle Lingo

The most common release word is "Okay," but you can choose any word that works for you. Some trainers advise against using "Okay" because you may inadvertently release the dog when using the word in casual conversation.

Just as important is to teach the "Wait" command. "Wait" means stay in this area until I release you. Think of it as an informal "Stay."

Practice "Wait" at every doorway and gate you go through. With your Beagle on-leash, stand in front of the door and say "Wait." Reinforce the verbal command with a hand signal, placing your hand palm up in front of the dog's nose. If your dog tries to leave, put him back in position and repeat the command. If he holds the wait for a few seconds, praise him—"Good wait!"—and release him. If you can see that he's about to break the command, praise him and release him before he does.

Gradually increase the amount of time you require him to stay before you release him. Practice this command several times a day until you're sure your dog knows it, and use it regularly so he doesn't forget.

Home Alone

Beagles are smart, social animals who need and enjoy activity and companionship. When they're left alone frequently for long periods, the result can be psychological stress in the form of separation anxiety. The anxious Beagle panics when he's left alone and often engages in destructive chewing and digging, not to mention nonstop barking. In his frenzy, he may dig through carpets, chew through doors, or bark until he's hoarse.

Separation anxiety sometimes develops when the family routine changes. Changes that can spark it include a move to a new home, a new work schedule, or a new baby in the house.

If your Beagle shows signs of separation anxiety, take him to the veterinarian first to rule out a possible medical cause. If his physical health isn't a problem, ask the veterinarian to refer you to a behaviorist. Severe cases may require the use of medication in conjunction with behavior modification.

Easing Your Dog's Fears

Beagles are observant, and they know instantly when we're about to leave. Telltale signs such as getting dressed a certain way, putting items in a purse, or turning lights on or off all indicate that we're on the way out.

You might think it's a good idea to play with your dog just before you leave, but this is actually a good way to develop a full-blown case of separation anxiety. Think about it: You leave, and the good times go with you. No wonder your Beagle gets frustrated. Take him for a walk or have playtime a good half hour or more before you leave. The actual departure should be calm and matter-of-fact.

Instead of giving him the run of the house, consider leaving your dog in his safe room or in a crate if you'll be gone less than four hours. Dogs younger than two years shouldn't be considered responsible enough to be left on their own, and even older dogs can become anxious when they're left in charge of the entire "den." Give them a small space where they can be comfortable. Remember, a dog who's confined can't get into trouble and won't get yelled at when you come home.

Doggy Do's/ Doggy Don'ts

Don't scold your Beagle when you come home and find that he's destroyed something. That only makes him more anxious every time you leave.

Preventing Separation Anxiety

Introduce your Beagle gradually to the idea of being left alone. Try leaving him alone in a room for no more than five minutes, then come back. As he becomes comfortable with your absence, lengthen the amount of time you stay gone.

Provide favorite toys to keep your Beagle occupied, such as interactive toys that you can load with treats or stuffed toys that you've scented with your hands or dirty laundry.

Try leaving the radio or television on; calm talk shows or classical music are good choices.

Don't make a big fuss over the dog when you leave or return, or the lack of attention after you leave will be even more noticeable.

Wait until you've been home a few minutes before you feed your Beagle or take him for a walk, or he will associate your return with these special activities.

An Aggressive Beagle?

It's rare for Beagles to be aggressive. It's just not in their nature. Pack life deals harshly with animals that overstep the bounds of the group.

Nonetheless, some Beagles can develop guarding behaviors, especially when food or favorite toys are involved. Signs of this type of aggression include growling or freezing in position when the food or object is approached.

To prevent aggression from developing, begin early in a Beagle pup's life. Teach him to enjoy trading one thing for another. Offer a treat or a different toy in exchange for the one he has.

Doggy Do's/ Doggy Don'ts
Teach your children not to grab toys or bones from dogs and not to stick their hands into the dog's food bowl.

After he complies, give the first toy back. He'll learn that letting you take things from him brings rewards.

At meal times, drop goodies into his food bowl while he's eating. Or take his dish away, put something good in it, and give it back. Associating treats with people being near or taking his food bowl is a great way to avoid food-guarding behavior.

Similar techniques work with dogs that guard objects such as toys. Practice taking the toy away and replacing it with a treat or a different toy. Associate a command such as "Give" or "Drop It" with the action of taking the item away. Then return the original object. Repeat the exercise several times in a row, several times a day.

Types of Aggression

Aggression takes many forms. It can be linked to dominance, fear, play behavior, territoriality, predatory behavior, maternal instincts, and pain. Sometimes medical conditions are behind aggressive behavior.

Veterinary behaviorists commonly see dominance aggression in dogs. Body language that indicates dominant behavior includes standing tall, staring, protecting food or toys, and snarling.

Fear aggression is a response to unfamiliar people, animals, or situations, or people, animals, or situations that the dog associates with a previous unpleasant experience. Usually when a dog is faced with something he's afraid of, he runs, but if he's cornered or restrained his only option—in his mind—is to attack. Fear aggression can usually be dealt with through behavior modification, sometimes with the help of drug therapy.

Young dogs are most likely to show play aggression, usually toward people or other pets. They get overly excited, grabbing, nipping, or biting at clothes or hands. Teach your children not to play games that involve running or shrieking with a puppy or young dog. Chases often lead to nips.

This is normal behavior, but it can get out of control. Stop the mouthing behavior by screeching "Ouch!" in a loud, high-pitched tone of voice and walking away. Do the same thing if play gets too rough: walk away. Your Beagle will soon learn to tone it down if he doesn't want playtime to end.

Bet You Didn't Know

Counterconditioning involves changing a dog's negative reaction to a certain stimulus to a positive one. For instance, a Beagle that's afraid of, say, rabbits, might be given treats while a caged rabbit sits some distance away. The cage is gradually moved closer as the Beagle continues being rewarded with his favorite snacks. Eventually, he'll accept the rabbit's presence without any fear.

Beagles can be territorial. The most common territorial behavior in Beagles is barking. Beagles that spend a lot of time outdoors are more likely to bark in a territorial way because they're exposed to squirrels, birds, the cat next door, people walking down the street, delivery drivers, and other potential invaders of the home territory.

Keeping the dog indoors when you're away from home is the best way to cut down on territorial barking. If your Beagle must stay outdoors, try to reduce the amount of noise and visual stimulation he receives. Add more landscaping, put up a visually opaque privacy fence, or weave vinyl strips through your chainlink fence. If he's indoors and still barks territorially, keep the blinds drawn to limit outside stimulation. Leave the radio or television on to provide background noise.

Doggy Do's/ Doggy Don'ts
Never ask or expect your Beagle to obey a command that he doesn't understand or that he can evade.

To prevent territorial aggression toward visitors to the home, teach your Beagle to sit when people come to the door. Give him a treat when he obeys. Beagles are smart and will soon associate the arrival of guests with the chance for a yummy snack.

Beagles are born to hunt rabbits, so predatory aggression toward small, furry animals is certainly a possibility with this breed. Predatory behaviors include stalking, chasing, and attacking. Beagles can learn to distinguish between household pets such as cats or rabbits and potential prey, but training should begin when they're young. Ways to deal with predatory aggression include the use of a head collar, confining the dog to an escape-proof run when he's outdoors, and behavior modification.

A bitch with puppies can be fiercely protective when people approach them. Known as maternal aggression, this behavior disappears once the pups are weaned. It never develops, of course, if a female is spayed and doesn't produce a litter. If maternal aggression is a problem, use food rewards to lure Mom Beagle away from her litter so the pups can be handled without interference. If necessary, a behaviorist can help you use *desensitization* and counterconditioning techniques to teach the dog to allow her pups to be approached and handled.

Beagle Lingo

Desensitization is a behavior modification technique that involves frequent repeated stimulation so that certain sights and sounds lose their significance to an animal and no longer cause a reaction. The stimulus—a recording of thunder, for instance—is introduced gradually, at very low levels that don't bother the dog. When he becomes accustomed to that level of sound, it's increased a little more and a little more until the dog can hear it at a normal level without getting upset.

Pain from an injury or certain medical conditions such as dental disease or arthritis can trigger aggression. Other health problems that might cause aggression include hypothyroidism, epilepsy, or decreased eyesight or hearing. If your Beagle shows aggressive behavior for no apparent reason, he needs a complete physical to rule out any health problems that might be causing the problem.

Any form of aggression is serious and should be dealt with immediately. If aggression isn't caused by a health problem, seek the advice of a veterinary behaviorist or applied animal therapist who can help you recognize and treat your Beagle's aggressive behavior.

Doggy Do's/ Doggy Don'ts
Teach your Beagle that he can't get attention any time he wants it. If your dog is nagging you and you're busy, put him in his crate with a treat and a toy. To establish your leadership, require him to perform a command before you respond to his request for playtime.

Watch Those Teeth!

Teaching your Beagle not to use his teeth on people is the most important lesson he'll learn. In some communities, a single bite spells a dog's death warrant, so don't neglect this training.

Puppy teeth are as sharp as little needles, and puppies haven't learned yet how to control their bite strength. They've had some lessons from Mom and their littermates about not biting down too hard, but now it's your job to teach them never to use their teeth on people. To do that, you're going to have to suffer a little pain by letting the puppy experiment with using his mouth on you and learning from your reaction.

Any time he mouths you and bites down hard, screech "Ouch!" and leave the room. Your puppy learns that if he bites down too hard, you refuse to play with him. Let him practice using his teeth carefully by offering pieces of kibble held in your fingers. Again, if you feel pressure from teeth, screech and take the kibble away. Use this same method during games of tug or fetch. Kids, don't try this at home. This is a training technique for adults only.

The other aspect of bite prevention is lots and lots of socialization. Make sure your Beagle meets all kinds of people in all kinds of places. He should become familiar with people of both genders, as well as people of various ages, races, and sizes. Expose him to people in wheelchairs and on crutches, people riding skateboards and bicycles, people pushing grocery carts, and people wearing uniforms. Socialization is the one thing you can't overdo.

The real solution to all of these behavior problems is active training with positive reinforcement for appropriate actions. Close interaction with people is the best way to prevent problems. The dogs most likely to get in trouble for these behaviors are those isolated from the family.

Your Beagle is always learning, not just when you're training him. Recognize his intelligence and begin teaching appropriate behavior as soon as you bring him home.

The Least You Need to Know

- Even though barking, chewing, digging, and roaming are normal dog behaviors, your Beagle needs to learn to control them if he's to live happily in your household.

- Chewing is a necessary part of puppy development, so give your Beagle a variety of toys so he won't take his teeth to your furniture and clothing.

- Always be consistent. If you are inconsistent in what you expect of your Beagle, he will be equally inconsistent in his reaction to your commands.

- Help prevent separation anxiety by gradually introducing your Beagle to time alone at home and by providing him a comfortable, interesting environment while you're gone.

- Beagles should not be aggressive. At any sign of aggressive behavior, seek the advice of a qualified veterinary behaviorist or applied animal therapist.

Part 4
A Healthy Beagle Is a Happy Beagle

Among the many responsibilities of Beagle ownership are veterinary care, feeding, and home health care, including grooming, parasite control, and dental care. It's a good idea to know some emergency first aid, too. Beagles are curious explorers after all, and they're likely to suffer the occasional injury or run-in with a snake. The more you know about caring for your Beagle, the happier and healthier he'll be.

In this section, you'll learn how to find and choose a veterinarian, develop a home health care routine, and select a food from among the numerous diets available for dogs. Taking good care of your Beagle isn't difficult at all, if you know what you're doing.

Your Friendly Neighborhood Veterinarian

In This Chapter

- Finding a veterinarian
- Important vaccinations
- Breeding your Beagle: Yes or No?
- Recognizing health problems
- Down the hatch!
- Emergency situations

When you acquire a dog for the first time or move to a new community, one of the most important items on your to-do list should be finding a veterinarian. By choosing a pet health practitioner in advance, you can avoid the need to find one in a hurry if your Beagle becomes ill unexpectedly. This is especially important if you prefer a specific approach to canine health, such as holistic or homeopathic care.

Things to Consider

It's really important to find a veterinarian and hospital that suit your needs. They should provide the level of care you want and the attitude you like not only in a veterinarian but also in a lay staff.

Some people like a veterinarian who's personable and chatty, while others prefer a more academic, formal approach. That's all a matter of taste, and you should be willing to look until you find what you're looking for.

Other aspects of a practice are important as well. Do you want a high-tech clinic or a family practice? Can you get referrals for specialty care if it's needed? What's the procedure if your Beagle has an emergency in the middle of the night? Are the hours and location convenient for you?

You and your veterinarian should agree philosophically on issues that are important to you—or at least be willing to keep an open mind with each other. Such things might include the administration and frequency of vaccinations or how the vet feels about raw or homemade diets.

Consider, too, whether the veterinarian is affiliated with a professional organization, such as the American Animal Hospital Association or a holistic or homeopathic veterinary medical association. Such organizations usually have a set of standards that veterinarians must meet to maintain their membership.

Where to Look

There are a number of ways you can set about finding a veterinarian. You can go to whatever clinic is closest, you can close your eyes and point to a name in the phone book, or you can ask other people for referrals. Let's take a look at some of the best methods for finding a veterinarian.

Word of Mouth

This is probably how most people find the vet they go to. If you're moving to another part of town or to a different city, your current veterinarian may be able to refer you to a colleague she trusts.

If your new Beagle is your first dog, you probably don't have a veterinarian. Some good ways to find one include asking the breeder or dog-loving friends, neighbors, relatives, or co-workers for recommendations. Get the dirt on why they like their vet as well as the good and bad points about the staff and clinic facilities. A referral from someone you trust is a good start.

Doggy Do's/ Doggy Don'ts

For a first veterinary visit, take your Beagle in for a physical only. This should simply be a "getting to know you" visit and shouldn't include anything painful, such as vaccinations.

Organizational Leads

Another way to find a veterinarian is to contact the American Animal Hospital Association (see Appendix B for contact information). This organization inspects hospitals and staff to ensure that certain standards are met.

To find a veterinarian with a natural bent, visit www.altvetmed. com, which lists the directories of a number of associations for complementary and alternative veterinary medicine. These include the Academy of Veterinary Homeopathy, the American Academy of Veterinary Acupuncture, the American Holistic Veterinary Medical Association, the American Veterinary Chiropractic Association, and the International Veterinary Acupuncture Society. (See Appendix B for more contact information.)

The Interview

When you have the names of a few veterinarians, set up an appointment to meet the veterinarians and tour their hospitals. It's a good idea to interview several veterinarians to make sure you have the same health care philosophy.

Here are some things to look for during the tour and interview:

🏠 Does the office have overnight facilities for boarding, treatment, or observation?

🏠 Are the facilities clean, with fresh water and food provided to the animals staying there?

🏠 Are the veterinarian's fees within your budget?

Some other factors to consider follow in the next sections.

Petside Manner

Besides agreeing on treatment philosophies, you should like the way the veterinarian communicates with you. Look for someone who speaks in terms you can understand, who's willing to entertain questions without seeming hurried or annoyed, and who will return your phone calls within a reasonable time frame.

You aren't the only one who should feel comfortable with the veterinarian. Your Beagle should like him as well. Does the vet speak to your dog and get him relaxed or does he abruptly move right into an exam?

Expect the same good relationship with the veterinarian's staff. When you call, you should get a pleasant greeting. If you ask a question that can't be answered right away, you should get a phone call back by the next business day.

 When to Call the Vet
Take a stool sample in for evaluation if you ever notice blood or wriggly white specks that look like rice. Blood can be a sign of whipworms or other intestinal problems, and those rice specks are tapeworm segments.

Fees

Your veterinarian isn't in business just for his health. He attended school just as long as your doctor did, and he deserves to make a good living in his profession. While veterinary fees may seem high to you, they're much less expensive than doctor visits. Among other things, they reflect the veterinarian's cost for hospital maintenance, employee salaries and benefits, equipment, continuing education, and professional memberships. And remember, you probably have insurance to cover many of your costs.

When you interview the veterinarian, ask about the charges for common treatments and procedures, such as spay/neuter surgery, vaccinations, office visits, and medication for parasites. You want to be sure you can afford everything your Beagle will need, and you don't want to be surprised when you're presented with the bill. Find out if you can pay by credit card or if time payments can be arranged in the event of a serious and costly emergency.

The hospital tour and a meeting with the veterinarian and the staff will help you make a good decision. Remember, not every hospital—even if it's a good one—is going to suit everyone.

Bet You Didn't Know

You can get health insurance for your dog. It won't cover routine exams or vaccinations, but if your Beagle gets injured or has a serious illness, pet health insurance can help you cover the costs.

Vaccinations: The Latest Advice

Vaccination is one of the most controversial issues facing dog owners today. In question are the frequency of vaccinations, the safety of vaccines, and whether certain vaccines are necessary. Some people choose not to vaccinate at all.

What Are Vaccinations?

The body's immune system protects against disease. Puppies are born with temporary immunity conferred by their mother through her milk, but this protection lasts for only a few weeks.

Immunization, or vaccination, is a way to trigger what is known as acquired immunity. Acquired immunity provides long-term protection against specific diseases, such as parvovirus or distemper. Immunization involves giving small doses of an antigen—such as weakened live viruses or dead viruses—to activate the immune system's memory. Specialized white blood cells develop that are able to recognize the antigen and fight it off whenever it enters the body.

Various types of vaccines are available. Weakened live virus vaccines are long lasting, but they can cause problems in dogs with weak immune systems. Killed-virus vaccines are just that: vaccines in which an inactivated virus or bacteria is used to stimulate the immune system. These are safe for dogs with weakened immune systems.

Which Shots Are Most Important?

The most current advice is that core vaccines—distemper, adenovirus, parvovirus, and rabies—are essential for all dogs. Most boarding kennels require dogs to have bordetella vaccinations administered within six months of boarding. The administration of other vaccines, such as those for leptospirosis, coronavirus, giardia, parainfluenza, and Lyme disease, should be limited to dogs that are realistically at risk of exposure to the specific infectious agent.

In the case of Lyme disease, for instance, tick control is often more effective than vaccination. If your Beagle goes hunting or participates in field trials, however, the Lyme disease vaccination is probably a good idea.

What If My Beagle Has a Reaction?

While vaccination is generally safe, it's not without risk. Possible adverse effects include allergic reactions and, in rare cases, seizures. Reactions usually occur anywhere from 20 minutes to 24 hours after vaccination, so keep an eye on your Beagle any time he gets a vaccine shot.

Signs of vaccine reactions include facial swelling and hives; lumps, hair loss, or hair discoloration at the vaccination site; fever; and lethargy. If your Beagle has one of these reactions, the most important thing to know is that he may have more severe reactions with future vaccinations. You and your veterinarian will want to make note of any reactions so you can take steps to prevent them the next time. A more serious reaction that can affect the entire body is anaphylactic shock, which can be severe and sometimes fatal if not treated quickly. Signs of severe anaphylactic shock include diarrhea, agitation, vomiting, difficulty breathing, and weakness.

Bet You Didn't Know _____

The leptospirosis vaccine commonly causes reactions in dogs. Many veterinarians don't even give it anymore unless the dog is at high risk for the disease, which is unlikely. Some areas of the country, especially the East Coast, have a higher incidence of leptospirosis, but this form of leptospirosis is not the same as the one affected by the vaccine.

Other reactions aren't common, but as a well-informed Beagle owner, you should be aware of the possibilities. In some cases, vaccines can cause the very infections they're designed to prevent. That's why it's important that your Beagle be healthy and well nourished before being given any vaccines. Diseases that have been associated with the administration of vaccines include autoimmune hemolytic anemia, autoimmune thrombocytopenia, autoimmune thyroiditis, and encephalitis. Modified-live vaccines can cause pregnant dogs to lose their litters.

If you're concerned about vaccinating your Beagle, remember the seriousness of the diseases vaccines prevent. Instead of abandoning vaccination altogether and exposing your Beagle to the risk of disease, it's better to avoid unnecessary vaccines and too frequent administration of essential vaccines. Some of the problems associated with vaccines are thought to be related to combination shots that include antigens against more than one disease. Ask your veterinarian about vaccinating for each disease separately.

How Often Should My Beagle Be Vaccinated?

You have several options when it comes to deciding which vaccines to get for your Beagle and how often to get them. You can vaccinate annually with core vaccines and use non-core vaccines if your Beagle is at risk for a certain condition, such as Lyme disease. You can get core vaccines every two to three years, which is what many veterinary colleges are now recommending. Your veterinarian can give you specific advice based on the disease rate and conditions in your area. A rabies vaccination is required annually or every three years, depending on the vaccine used and the laws of your state.

A third option is to have *titers* tested annually. Titers have not always been cost-effective, and their results may vary from lab to lab. The good news is that a reliable and affordable clinical test has been developed that should be in veterinary offices soon. It will allow your veterinarian to measure distemper, parvovirus, and adenovirus titers within 15 minutes.

Beagle Lingo

A **titer** measures the concentration of an antibody in blood serum. Antibodies are proteins produced by the immune system in response to the presence of antigens, substances the immune system recognizes as a threat, and they help defend the body against disease. Antibody titers can give important information regarding your Beagle's current immunity to disease.

More good news is that researchers will soon complete a study on duration of immunity. The results will provide data on the length of immunity provided by vaccines for canine distemper, parvovirus, and hepatitis. The new information will help veterinarians give more precise advice on how often your Beagle should be vaccinated. Generally, vaccinations for viruses such as rabies and parvo tend to last longer than vaccinations for bacterial diseases such as leptospirosis.

Allergies

Four types of allergies generally affect dogs:

🏠 Inhalant allergies. These are triggered by dust mites, grasses, molds, and pollen.

🏠 Flea-allergy dermatitis (FAD for short). This is caused by fleas and other biting insects.

🏠 Contact allergies. These are caused by chemicals or irritants that touch the dog; they affect areas of the body where the skin isn't well protected by hair.

🏠 Food allergies. Some dogs are allergic to certain foods. Luckily for Beagles, they don't usually suffer from food allergies, but inhalant, contact, and flea allergies are common in the breed.

The most common sign of allergies is itchy skin, accompanied by frequent scratching. The itch-scratch cycle leads to inflamed skin and red bumps that look like pimples. The miserable dog chews at himself, causing raw or bald spots. Dry, scaly skin is another sign of allergies. The dog may lick his paws constantly, rub his face on the carpet, or develop watery eyes and a runny nose. Chronic ear infections can also suggest allergies.

The most effective treatment depends on the type of allergy. If you find fleas on your itchy dog, treat your home and dog to get rid of the fleas and then put your Beagle on a regular flea-treatment program to keep the problem from recurring. See Chapter 13 for more information on flea control methods.

If fleas aren't the problem, you and your veterinarian will need to dig a little deeper to identify the source of the allergy. Among the many causes of contact allergies are soaps and shampoos, flea collars, plastic and rubber dishes or toys, and carpet dyes.

Ask yourself whether you've tried a new shampoo on your dog, laundered his bedding in a new detergent, put a flea collar on him, or installed new carpeting in your home. Any one of these situations could trigger contact allergies.

Go back to the old shampoo or detergent, remove the flea collar, or lay a blanket over the new carpet so your Beagle doesn't touch it. If one of these steps solves the problem, you'll know what caused the allergy and can take steps to avoid it. In the meantime, your veterinarian may prescribe a topical antibiotic ointment for the skin infection and short-term corticosteroids to relieve itching and inflammation.

Beagle Bonus

While corticosteroids are great for stopping itching fast, long-term use is not recommended. Side effects include increased appetite (hard to imagine that a Beagle could want to eat even more!) and increased thirst, followed by (what else?) increased urination. High doses or frequent use of corticosteroids can also suppress the immune system—not a good thing. It's okay to use them for two or three days to control itching, but don't bug your veterinarian to give them for longer periods.

Inhalant allergies can be difficult to diagnose. Skin scrapings, skin tests (which involve injecting small amounts of common allergens to see if they provoke a reaction), and bacterial and fungal cultures are among the steps your veterinarian may take to identify the problem.

The best solution, of course, is to change the dog's environment so that he's no longer exposed to the allergen, but that's not always possible. Antihistamines and other medications prescribed by your veterinarian can help control itching and scratching. Fish oil fatty acid supplements sometimes have good results. Special shampoos can help improve the condition of the skin. If medical treatment doesn't work, allergy shots may help.

Beagle Birth Control

If you paid a lot of money for your Beagle, you may be tempted to breed her. After all, sale of the puppies could help you earn back her original cost. But as you learned in Chapter 4, there's a lot of expense involved in producing a nice litter. Before you try your hand at it, remember that breeding dogs is more of a money pit than a money fountain.

And things can go wrong. Among the complications you can face in whelping a litter are a stuck puppy that necessitates a caesarean section, and stillborn or deformed puppies. Giving birth isn't an easy, natural process that your Beagle can handle on her own. She'll need your help in what is a messy, nerve-racking situation. If complications occur, she can die, or all her puppies can die. Or you could be stuck hand-feeding 10 puppies because she doesn't produce any milk. Those people who all vowed that they'd love to have one of Belle's puppies vanish into the woodwork when it comes time to find homes for them. The next thing you know, your backyard is full of six-month-old howling Beagles. Think twice before deciding to breed your Beagle, and then think again.

Bet You Didn't Know

The average size of a Beagle litter is 7 pups, but it can range from 2 to 14 pups.

The Benefits of Spay/Neuter Surgery

For bitches, spaying before their first heat reduces their risk of mammary—breast—cancer by about 99 percent. If you let her go through one heat cycle and then spay her, the risk is still reduced, but only by about 65 percent. You won't have to keep your female confined when she's in heat, and you won't have to deal with any unwanted litters. Because the uterus is removed, she won't develop uterine cancer or a uterine infection.

There are benefits for males as well. They're less likely to urine mark their territory, and the smell of their urine is less strong. Neutered males are calmer and less prone to roaming, and they won't be slapped with any paternity suits. Spayed or neutered dogs can't be shown in conformation, but they can still participate in performance events such as agility and obedience trials.

When to Spay or Neuter

Usually this surgery is done at six months of age, as the dog enters adolescence. If a Beagle boy has a retained testicle (cryptorchid), your veterinarian may advise waiting until he's nine months old to see if the other testicle drops, making surgery easier. While its benefits are most obvious when performed during a dog's adolescence, spay or neuter surgery can be performed at any age.

How Do I Know If My Beagle Is Sick?

Lack of appetite is the most obvious sign. Any Beagle that turns up his nose at food likely isn't feeling well (unless, of course, you have one of the rare finicky Beagles). If your Beagle refuses to eat for more than a day, it's a good idea to take him to the vet for a checkup.

Doggy Do's/ Doggy Don'ts

Never give your Beagle any medication without first checking with your veterinarian. Common pain relievers such as acetaminophen and ibuprofen are toxic to dogs and even a small amount can be fatal.

Another sign of illness is a lower than normal activity level. It might not be that noticeable in an adult Beagle, but a lethargic puppy isn't normal. Other signs are pale, whitish gums, dull eyes, and a dull coat.

More obvious indications that something's wrong are vomiting and diarrhea. A single instance of either isn't reason to run to the vet, but if your Beagle is experiencing projectile vomiting or if diarrhea continues for more than a day, go to the vet. Eye injuries also require quick veterinary attention.

Your Beagle's Vital Signs

Vital signs are just that: signs of life. Specifically, they are body temperature, pulse rate, and respiratory rate. Your Beagle's vital signs are important indicators of his health. It's a good idea to check vital signs when your Beagle is healthy so you'll have a standard to measure against if he seems sick.

Temperature

A dog's normal temperature is 101.5 degrees Fahrenheit, but a normal temperature can range from 100.2 degrees to 102.8 degrees.

To take your Beagle's temperature, use a plastic digital thermometer labeled for rectal use. Look for one that beeps when a constant temperature is reached. Lube up the thermometer with K-Y Jelly or petroleum jelly, and get someone to hold the dog still while you insert the thermometer gently about an inch into the rectum. When the thermometer indicates completion, remove it, note the temperature, and clean the thermometer with rubbing alcohol.

An inactive Beagle is more likely to have a temperature in the low normal range, while an excited or active Beagle is more likely to have a temperature in the high normal range. If your Beagle's temperature is lower than 100 degrees or higher than 103.5 degrees, he needs emergency veterinary care.

Lower than normal body temperature can indicate hypothermia from exposure to the cold, or conditions such as heart disease, shock, or kidney failure. A fever can be caused by heatstroke, bacterial or viral infections, inflammatory diseases such as pancreatitis, autoimmune disease, certain cancers, or uncontrolled seizures.

Pulse Rate

The normal canine pulse rate ranges from 75 to 120 beats per minute (bpm), depending on the dog's size, age, and condition. To take your Beagle's pulse rate, press your finger against the blood vessel in the

Beagle Bonus

Signs of good health are pink gums that refill rapidly with color when pressed, clean-smelling ears and skin, a healthy coat, and clear, bright eyes.

V formed where the undersides of the hind legs attach to the body. Count the beats for 10 seconds and multiply that number by 6 to get the total bpm.

If your dog's pulse rate is unusually low or high, check it again a little later. If it remains abnormal, contact your veterinarian.

Respiratory Rate

Healthy dogs have a respiratory rate of 15 to 20 breaths per minute. Extended shallow or rapid breathing is cause for concern. Check with your veterinarian.

Giving Medication

If your Beagle does get sick, you'll probably have to give him some form of medication. Pills, liquid medicines, ear drops, eye drops, and ointments all make up the veterinarian's arsenal against disease. Know how to give them effectively so your Beagle will get well quickly. The better you are at it, the easier it will be. Don't forget to give your Beagle a treat or praise afterward. Mary Poppins had the right idea about that figurative spoonful of sugar helping the medicine go down.

Doggy Do's/Doggy Don'ts

Be sure to ask your veterinarian whether your Beagle's meds need to be given with food or on an empty stomach. Take note of whether the medication is to be given orally (by mouth) or topically (on the skin). Give the entire course of medication, even if your Beagle seems to be feeling better before it's all gone.

Pills

The easiest way to give a Beagle a pill is to encase it in something yummy, like peanut butter or cream cheese. Some Beagles will just eat whatever's put into their food bowl without stopping to see what it is. Just check to make sure he actually swallows the pill. Some dogs have been known to eat the yummy stuff surrounding the pill and then spit the pill out when you're not looking.

If your Beagle has lost his appetite, though, or must take his medication on an empty stomach, try the following techniques. (If you're lefthanded, just reverse the directions.)

Put the pill in your right hand and use your left first and middle fingers to gently open his jaws. Place the pill far back on the tongue, close the mouth, and stroke the throat to help the pill go down.

Another way is to hold the dog's head in your left hand, tipping the head back until he's looking straight up. In your right hand, hold the pill between your thumb and forefinger, and use the middle finger to hold the mouth open. Drop the pill at the back of the tongue, close the mouth, and blow softly into your dog's nose. This makes him lick and triggers the swallowing reflex.

Bet You Didn't Know

Some pills taste bad when they're broken, so try to give them whole instead of breaking them in half.

Liquids

Load up a plastic needle-free syringe or medicine dropper with the recommended dose. Tilting your Beagle's head upward, open his mouth and aim the dropper at the cheek pouch. When it's properly situated, hold his mouth closed around the dropper and squeeze slowly until it's empty. He'll swallow automatically when it reaches the back of his mouth. Administer a large dose slowly, giving your dog time to swallow, or he might gag or choke.

Ear Drops

Droopy-eared Beagles often need to have their ears cleaned or medicated. To keep them from shaking their heads and scattering the drops all over you, put the drops in and then gently hold the earflap closed. Massage the cartilage at the base of the ear to work in the medication. Be gentle in case your Beagle's ears are tender and he'll probably enjoy the massage.

Eye Drops

To avoid poking your Beagle in the eye, hold his head firmly in your left hand and tilt it upward. With your right hand, squeeze the drops into the inner corner of the affected eye, directly on the eyeball. Try not to touch the eye with the applicator tip. Close and open the eyelids to distribute the drops evenly.

Ointments

Some eye or ear conditions require the use of ointment rather than drops. You can apply it the same way you would eye or ear drops.

Storing Medication

Don't let bottles or tubes sit out in the sun. Heat can spoil their effectiveness. Ask your veterinarian if liquids need to be refrigerated. Finally, remember that certain factors affect a medication's effectiveness. Your Beagle's age, overall health, and weight can all play a role in how well or how quickly a treatment works.

Basic Emergency Care

Common injuries seen in Beagles, especially field dogs, are ruptured intervertebral discs, eye injuries, broken toenails, ruptured ligaments, and cuts and bruises. You could compare the list to those afflictions common to professional athletes.

Injuries or conditions that require immediate veterinary care are poisonings, trauma such as being hit by a car, bleeding that doesn't stop with pressure easily, seizures, collapse, and eye injuries.

With any luck at all, you'll never have to face a traumatic injury to your Beagle, but hey, it never hurts to know what to do—just in case. Following are some potential injuries and how to handle them.

Bleeding

If bright red blood is spurting from a wound, apply pressure fast! An artery is involved, and you need to stop the bleeding quickly. Press down firmly with a towel, t-shirt, or whatever's handy.

Don't try to make a tourniquet; you can do more harm than good. Get the dog to the veterinarian as quickly as possible to minimize blood loss.

Bet You Didn't Know

There are blood banks for dogs. The usual donors are retired racing Greyhounds, because they have very high red blood cell counts (among other reasons), but any dog can donate blood.

Broken Limbs

A Beagle can break a leg in the field if he puts a foot wrong in a hole. Beagles in the 'burbs run the risk of being hit by cars if they escape from the yard and are following a trail without paying attention to what's going on around them.

Your Beagle's leg may be broken if he can't stand on it, if it's sticking out at an abnormal angle, or if it's swelling rapidly. Try to immobilize the limb, using a stick or something similar as a splint, but don't mess with it too much. If the break is high on the leg, leave it alone. You don't want to make things worse. Keep the dog quiet and warm, and get him to the veterinarian.

Burns

Bathe the area with cool water. Ice can damage the skin, and butter or ointment lock heat in rather than soothing the burn. If the burn is over a large area of the body, layer gauze over it, keep the dog warm to prevent shock, and get to the veterinarian as soon as possible.

Treat chemical burns from cleaners or battery acid in the same way. Flush the burned area with cool water, and be sure to protect your hands with rubber gloves. Then take your Beagle to the veterinarian for further treatment.

Bet You Didn't Know

You can give CPR to dogs. Ask your veterinarian to show you how. Never give CPR unless you're sure the heart has stopped, or you could injure your dog.

Electrical burns on the corners of the mouth or the tongue and palate are most common in curious puppies and adolescent dogs. A severe electrical shock can result in convulsions, loss of consciousness, or slowed breathing. The heart may even stop beating. Switch off the electrical source or unplug the cord before touching your pet, and get your dog to a veterinarian right away.

Choking

The nosey Beagle will try to eat anything on the off chance that it might be food. If you see your Beagle coughing, gagging, or pawing at his mouth, check to make sure nothing's caught in his throat. Press your thumb and forefingers into the upper cheeks to open his mouth. Don't forget to check the roof of the mouth when you're looking. Sometimes small sticks can get lodged there crossways. If you see something, gently try to remove it with your fingers or a pair of needle-nose pliers.

If that doesn't work, bring on the Heimlich maneuver. From behind your dog, encircle his abdomen with your arms, placing them just beneath the rib cage. Squeeze and release the chest until your Beagle coughs up the obstruction. If neither technique works, don't waste time. Get the dog to the vet as soon as possible.

Eye Injuries

Beagles can injure those big ole brown eyes by running through brush or coming in contact with an irritant. If the eye looks red or irritated, flush it with saline solution. If you see that the eye has been punctured or lacerated, don't try to treat it. Get the dog to the vet immediately. Some eye injuries, such as a poke with a cactus needle, may require the services of a veterinarian who specializes in ophthalmology.

Frostbite

This painful injury can occur in Beagles that spend long hours in bitter cold conditions. Ear tips, footpads, and tail are most at risk. Pale skin that reddens and becomes hot and painful to the touch is the first sign of frostbite. Later skin layers may swell and then peel.

Thaw frostbitten areas slowly by applying warm, moist towels. Change the towels frequently, and avoid massaging the skin or applying hot compresses. You can stop warming the skin once it regains its normal color. Take the dog to the veterinarian for further treatment.

Doggy Do's/ Doggy Don'ts

To prevent shock after a serious injury, keep your dog warm and quiet. Wrap him in a blanket and speak soothingly to him.

Heatstroke

If your Beagle becomes overheated, his body may be unable to cool itself quickly enough. The result can be a dangerously high body temperature—far higher than the normal 101.5 degrees Fahrenheit. Heatstroke is especially common when dogs are left in cars on hot days. Even with the windows cracked, the temperature can become unbearable in the space of a few minutes.

Bet You Didn't Know

Dogs have a few sweat glands, but by themselves they aren't enough to keep a dog cool. Dogs control their body temperature by panting, which causes heat to dissipate through evaporation from the mouth.

If your Beagle starts vomiting or collapses from heatstroke or heat exhaustion brought on by high temperatures or too much activity on a hot day, cool him off by bathing him with cool—not cold—water. Once his condition is stabilized, take him to the veterinarian. Don't delay; heatstroke can be fatal if left untreated.

Insect Stings

Stings or bites from creatures such as bees, wasps, ants, spiders, and scorpions are just as painful in dogs as they are in people, and they have the same potential for side effects, from mild (swelling at the bite site, itching or redness) to serious (vomiting, diarrhea, respiratory failure, and collapse).

Bites on the head are most serious because they can cause the face and neck to swell, sometimes enough to cut off breathing. Obviously this is an emergency situation. If your Beagle's head is swelling up to the size of a cantaloupe, get the dog to the vet immediately. For a sting that's painful but not life threatening, apply a cool compress or a soothing paste of baking soda and water.

Poison

The inquisitive Beagle finds it hard to resist tasting anything new, and unfortunately he doesn't recognize the significance of the skull and crossbones that indicate poison. Household cleansers, certain plants, rat or snail bait, and yard treatments are all potential poisons. Even flea treatments that are meant to be applied to the dog can be toxic if applied too heavily, too frequently, or in combination with an incompatible product.

Signs of poisoning include drooling, vomiting, convulsions, diarrhea, or collapse. The eyes, mouth, or skin may appear irritated. If you suspect that your Beagle has eaten something poisonous, get him to the veterinarian immediately. Bring the package label of the suspected poison or a sample of anything the dog has vomited.

If a veterinarian isn't available, call the National Animal Poison Control Center for advice. The NAPCC's phone number is listed in Appendix B.

Doggy Do's/Doggy Don'ts

Don't induce vomiting unless you know what the dog has eaten and the vet gives you the okay. Depending on the substance, inducing vomiting can sometimes make the situation worse. Charcoal tablets given orally can help bind some of the poisons to the charcoal, preventing it from circulating through the bloodstream.

If the poison has been absorbed through the skin, put on rubber gloves and wash the affected area with warm water. Then take the dog to the vet.

The Least You Need to Know

🏠 Choose a veterinarian as carefully as you would your own doctor.

🏠 Keep your vet's phone number easily accessible and know the hours, location, and phone number of the nearest emergency veterinary hospital.

🏠 Spay or neuter your Beagle to prevent unwanted litters and to reduce or prevent the likelihood of certain cancers.

🏠 Give the complete course of medication your vet prescribes, even if your dog seems to be well before you use up all the medication.

🏠 In the event of a serious injury, apply first aid as needed to stabilize your Beagle and then get him to the veterinarian as soon as possible.

🏠 Know your Beagle's normal behavior and vital signs, so you can recognize potential illness or injury early on.

Chapter 13

Routine Health Care

In This Chapter

- 🏠 Flee, fleas
- 🏠 Tick talk
- 🏠 Worms away
- 🏠 Toothy topics
- 🏠 Beagle beautiful: brushing, bathing, and nail care
- 🏠 Keeping those floppy ears healthy

The day-to-day care of a Beagle is pretty simple. His short coat is easy to groom, and unless he rolls in something stinky he doesn't need to be bathed very often. Nonetheless, he needs some routine maintenance to keep him in best Beagle order. This includes parasite control, regular dental care, ear cleaning, nail trimming, and brushing.

Pesky Parasites

It used to be that dogs were host to a party of parasites. Fleas and ticks fed on them, and intestinal worms settled down inside them. People used to keep dogs just so the fleas would stay off of them!

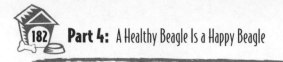

Bet You Didn't Know

Flea saliva is the substance that makes dogs itch when they're bitten.

We are fortunate these days that pharmaceutical advances have made parasite control much simpler and more effective. By instituting a parasite control program right from the start, you can help keep your Beagle (and yourself) comfortable and itch-free.

The Beagle Flea Circus

The bite of a single flea can send your Beagle into a fit of scratching and biting. Imagine how uncomfortable it must be for him to suffer with large numbers of fleas! Fleas transmit tapeworms, too, another reason to stamp them out.

To keep fleas at bay, check your Beagle for them regularly and treat him with a product that will put fleas on the run. This is especially important if you live in a warm, humid climate, the flea's favorite environment.

Finding Fleas

Run a fine-toothed flea comb through your Beagle's short coat. Flea-combing alone won't get rid of the pests, but it will allow you to determine if your Beagle is infested. If you find one or two fleas, you can bet that many more have settled in your home.

When to Call the Vet

Signs of flea allergy dermatitis are itchy, crusty sores on the body and thickening of the skin. If your Beagle is constantly biting and scratching, take him to the vet before secondary bacterial skin infections develop.

You can also establish the presence of fleas by brushing your Beagle while he's standing over a white towel or piece of paper. See if any small black flecks fall out of his coat. Moisten them with water. If they turn red, you've got fleas. Those black flecks are flea dirt, blood excreted by the flea after feeding on your dog.

Flea-Control Products

It used to be that the treatments for fleas were almost as bad as the fleas themselves. Getting rid of fleas required spraying, dipping, or powdering the dog with powerful poisons. The latest products are easy to apply and are much more toxic to the flea than to the dog. They attack the flea's nervous system or reproductive ability.

Your veterinarian can help you decide which product is best for your Beagle, depending on the local climate and your dog's lifestyle. Beagles that spend a lot of time in the field may need a different regimen than those who spend most of their time at home or traveling to dog shows.

There's an amazing variety of flea-control products available, either from your veterinarian or over-the-counter at the pet supply store. Developments in flea control include insect growth regulators (known as IGRs), which prevent larvae from reaching adulthood, and pills and topical applications that enter the dog's system and kill the flea when it touches or bites the dog. These new products, sold under the names FrontLine, Advantage, Revolution, and Program, are given only on a monthly or bimonthly basis, which makes them more convenient.

And there are the old standbys: the sprays, shampoos, powders, and dips. The first three usually kill only the fleas that are on the dog at the time of application. Flea-fighting foams and creme rinses may have a brief residual effect. Dips last longest, but they're also the most toxic.

The least toxic sprays, shampoos, powders, and dips contain pyrethrins or pyrethroids. Pyrethrins are derived from chrysanthemum plants; pyrethroids are synthetic versions of pyrethrins. The advantage to a pyrethrin product is that it works quickly but doesn't remain in the environment for very long.

Doggy Do's/ Doggy Don'ts

Before using any flea-control product, read the directions carefully and don't deviate from them.

Dips, flea collars, and yard sprays often contain more powerful and long-lasting chemicals. They're found under the names Carbaryl, Diazinon, Dursban, Fenthion, Malathion, and Sevin. Use them sparingly if at all on and around your Beagle; more is definitely not better.

Getting Rid of Fleas

If you find fleas on your Beagle or another pet, you'll need to treat all the animals, as well as your home and yard. A full-on assault is the only way to permanently get rid of fleas. Send your pets out for flea baths; launder all bedding, including your own, in hot water; and vacuum thoroughly to remove fleas and their eggs. One pass with a vacuum can remove 50 percent of the flea eggs in carpets. Sprinkle some flea powder on the carpet before vacuuming. The flea powder will kill any fleas that hatch from eggs you've vacuumed. You may also want to have your carpet professionally cleaned and treated with a nontoxic powder containing borax to suck the life out of the fleas.

Then use an IGR premise spray in your home and a yard spray outdoors. Be sure to spray along baseboards, at doors leading in and out of the house, around your fence, and under and around decks. Rake up any leaves or other debris that could provide an attractive home for fleas and their eggs. Don't forget to spray the doghouse and the inside of your car.

Once you've eliminated fleas in the environment, use a product such as FrontLine, Advantage, Revolution, or Program to keep the nasty little bloodsuckers from coming back.

Doggy Do's/ Doggy Don'ts

Never use a premise or yard spray on your Beagle. Only use products that are specifically formulated for use on dogs. Read the label carefully to make sure they are safe for puppies or old dogs. By the same token, don't use your dog's flea-control products on your cat, ferret, or rabbit.

Natural Flea-Control Remedies

What if you prefer not to use any type of chemical on or in your Beagle? There are a number of natural products you can try. No studies have shown any of them to be effective, but they are generally safe.

The most popular such remedy is garlic. Your Beagle doesn't have to wear a clove around his neck, but you can chop it fresh into his food or give him garlic pills. Brewer's yeast is another common natural remedy that's believed to ward off fleas. It too comes in pill form.

To rid your yard of fleas, consider using one of the new nematode products. Nematodes are worms that live on flea larvae. They're nontoxic and don't harm people or other animals. Simply spread the product in the areas of your yard that stay warm and moist. One brand name, Interrupt, is available through veterinarians, or ask about such products at your local nursery.

Tick Attack

These unpleasant spider-like creatures latch on to dogs and people (and other animals) and feed on their blood. They're found in most areas of the United States and are commonly encountered in tall grasses, fields, and forests. Ticks transmit Lyme disease, Rocky Mountain spotted fever, and other diseases, so you'll want to keep them off your Beagle, not to mention yourself.

Bet You Didn't Know

The body of an adult female deer tick is about the size of a sesame seed. Ticks are usually brown or black in color.

Finding Ticks

Tick season runs from spring through early fall. Any time your Beagle has been outdoors, especially if you've been hiking or hunting, examine him from head to tail for ticks when you get home.

Ticks usually attach around the head, neck, ears, or feet, so be extra thorough when you check those areas. Wear gloves to protect yourself, and carefully part the fur so you can see down to the skin. Unless they're swollen with blood, ticks are easy to miss, especially on dogs with dark coats.

Removing Ticks

Using tweezers, grasp the tick's head. Pull slowly and firmly, straight away from the dog's body, so that you get the entire tick. You don't want to leave its head buried in your Beagle. When it's out, flush the tick down the toilet or drop it in alcohol to kill it. Remember not to touch a tick with your bare hands. The spirochete that causes Lyme disease can enter through your skin.

Bet You Didn't Know

The ticks most commonly found on dogs are the brown dog tick and the American dog tick, but the deer tick and the western black-legged tick—both of which transmit Lyme disease—also feed on dogs.

Ignore people who suggest burning the tick off or suffocating it with nail polish, petroleum jelly, kerosene, or gasoline. These "techniques" are as harmful to your Beagle as they are to the tick.

Tick-Control Products

If you don't live in an area that's heavily tick-infested, a topical flea-control product such as Frontline Plus or Advantage is probably enough to protect your dog. Otherwise, use a product such as Kiltix, the Preventic collar, Defend Ex-Spot, or BioSpot, along with Advantage, Frontline, or Revolution and daily tick inspection. Always check with your veterinarian before using a combination of products on your Beagle.

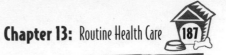

Intestinal Worms

Even though you can't see them, internal parasites are just as unpleasant and troublesome as external parasites. They include roundworms, tapeworms, hookworms, and whipworms. Worms can affect your Beagle's condition, causing dull fur, a potbellied appearance, and internal bleeding, among other things. Most pups are born with some kind of worm infection, acquired from their mother while they're in the womb, so a deworming schedule is important right from the get-go. This is not only for your Beagle's good health, but also for your own. Many worms can be transmitted to humans.

Detecting Worms

Most intestinal parasite infections are diagnosed through a fecal exam. Sometimes tapeworm segments can be seen wriggling in a dog's feces, but usually worm eggs can't be detected with the naked eye and must be seen under a microscope. It can sometimes require several fecal exams before the presence of worms is confirmed.

Bet You Didn't Know

When parasites aren't the cause of an itchy rear, have your Beagle checked for impacted anal glands, a food allergy, or some other skin problem.

If you see your Beagle scooting his rear on the ground, he may be itchy because of a parasite infection. Take in a fecal sample for testing.

Treating and Preventing Worms

Different worms usually require different treatments. Don't just assume that an over-the-counter product will take care of the problem. Get a definite diagnosis and appropriate treatment so you get rid of the problem the first time around. A regular course of heartworm medication also prevents most intestinal worms.

Regular handwashing will help you and your family avoid accidentally ingesting microscopic roundworm eggs. It's also a good idea to wear gloves when you're working in the garden. Hookworm larvae can enter the body through the skin. Avoid going barefoot in areas where hookworms are endemic, such as the southern United States. Your veterinarian or the local public health authority can advise you.

Heartworm Disease

Heartworm disease is transmitted by female mosquitoes through their bite (don't worry; dogs and cats get it, but not people). Your Beagle is at risk, even if he spends more time indoors than outdoors.

How Heartworms Develop

The mosquito's bite deposits infective heartworm larvae, which penetrate the skin until they reach the bloodstream. Over the next few months, the larvae develop, and eventually their ride through the bloodstream takes them to the dog's heart, where they can grow as long as 14 inches. Not surprisingly, a mass of these worms can significantly damage your Beagle's heart, lungs, and other organs, eventually causing his death if they're not gotten rid of.

An Ounce of Prevention ...

The treatment for heartworm disease is not only expensive, it's almost as dangerous as the condition itself. To kill the heartworms, your veterinarian must administer a highly toxic drug intravenously twice a day for two days. Side effects can include appetite loss, vomiting, diarrhea, kidney failure, and even death. Some dogs with severe infestation or congestive heart failure are poor candidates for drug treatment and must have worms removed surgically, a procedure that requires special skill. Prevention is without a doubt the way to go.

A simple blood test is all it takes to check for heartworm disease. If your Beagle tests clear, your veterinarian can prescribe a preventive medication. Depending on the product, preventives are given daily or monthly. Most preventives also protect your dog from other intestinal parasites such as roundworms, hookworms, and whipworms, and at least one also protects against fleas.

Bet You Didn't Know

Heartworm disease used to be found primarily in the southern United States, but it has now spread throughout the country. Don't assume that heartworm isn't a problem in your area.

Pearly Whites

The following are the most common signs of dental disease:

- Odor. If your dog's breath smells like the inside of a garbage can, something's wrong. Normal dog breath smells nice.

- Lack of appetite. Dogs with dental problems have trouble eating. They may pick up food and then drop it or stop eating altogether. Check your dog's water dish for bits of food as well.

- Pawing at the mouth. This can be a sign that the area is painful or that something is stuck inside. In either case, have your dog checked out by a veterinarian.

Brushing your Beagle's teeth daily, starting in puppyhood at four to six months of age, is the best thing you can do to ensure good dental health, but even brushing three times a week or weekly can help. The more often you look at your dog's mouth, the more likely you are to spot problems early.

Just like people, dogs need regular dental cleanings, even if their teeth are brushed regularly. There's nothing like a good dental scaling to get rid of plaque and tartar buildup. Routine periodontal treatment performed by a veterinarian typically includes ultrasonic scaling, manual scaling below the gumline, and polishing.

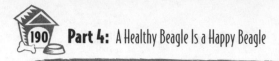

The key to good dental health is to start young and be consistent and positive. Your Beagle's toothy grin is your best reward.

Brush and Bathe

There's a story going round that dogs have a certain smell. It's true that some breeds, such as Bloodhounds, have a particular musty odor, but the majority of dogs, including Beagles, don't have a doggy scent.

> **Beagle Bonus**
> While it's pretty easy to keep a pet Beagle looking sharp, grooming a Beagle for the show ring is a whole other story. Current trends include trimming, stripping (the removal of dead hair using the finger and thumb or a specialized tool), and sometimes even clippering the coat to neaten the dog's appearance and create a stylish outline.

If your Beagle smells bad, don't just assume it's doggy odor. There are several reasons for a Beagle to smell bad, some innocuous, some more serious. For instance, unspayed females have a vaginal discharge that may have an odor. This is normal. Beagles also like to roll in or on stinky dead things. It's their way of trying out the season's newest perfumes. This calls for a bath, but it's nothing to worry about. Beagles that spend all their time outdoors may not smell as sweet as they could. An ear infection can also cause your Beagle to smell bad. Check the ears first if you're wondering about the source of an odor.

But if your Beagle suddenly develops an odor and you can't find a cause for it, take him to the veterinarian. He may have an infection or other health problem such as hypothyroidism.

The average Beagle needs a bath only a couple of times a year to keep him sweet-smelling. Bathe your Beagle only when he's noticeably dirty; otherwise, regular brushing once or twice a week will keep his skin and coat in good condition. While you're brushing, check for lumps, bumps, or sores that could indicate an injury, infection, or tumor.

ShamPoochie

Any gentle shampoo formulated for dogs will clean your Beagle's coat. Serious fanciers like to use dry, no-rinse blue shampoos because they brighten the dog's coat. These are also great for quick cleanups, whether or not your Beagle is a show dog. Besides, who says he can't at least look like one?

Is it okay to use your own shampoo to bathe your Beagle? Generally this isn't a good idea. Shampoos formulated for people can strip the oil out of a dog's coat, leaving it too dry.

Hair, Hair Everywhere!

Yes, your Beagle will shed or, as dog people say, blow coat. Females blow coat twice a year, after each heat cycle, and males go through a major shed annually, usually in the spring.

To help keep shedding under control, give your Beagle a warm bath when the coat starts to loosen. Brush him as you blow him dry to remove the excess coat.

Hear, Hear!

Give special attention to your Beagle's ears. Because they hang down, they can trap moisture and warmth, making them an inviting location for ear mites and bacteria.

Check your Beagle's ears weekly, and clean them with mineral oil or a solution recommended by your veterinarian. Use a cotton ball rather than probing the ears with a cotton swab. You don't want to puncture an eardrum.

Common ear conditions include infections of the ear canal, ear mites, and foreign bodies in the ear. A nasty or sour smell from the ear is often the first sign of a problem.

(© Kristine Kraeuter)

Because their long, floppy ears don't get a lot of air circulation inside, Beagles are prone to ear infections. Check and clean the ears regularly to prevent problems.

Several types of infections can affect your Beagle's ears. They include bacterial otitis and fungal and yeast infections. Staphylococcus bacteria are the usual culprits in bacterial otitis. A moist, brown discharge is your clue that these bacteria have invaded. Other bacteria that can cause ear infections are pseudomonas or proteus (identifiable by their yellow or green discharge) and sometimes several bacteria are at play at the same time. Once he's identified the species of bacteria, your veterinarian can prescribe an appropriate antibiotic.

Fungal and yeast infections often accompany bacterial infections and can spread to the middle ear if left uncontrolled. Treatment involves cleaning and drying out the ear canals, followed by medication.

Tiny ear mites settle into the ear canal and feed by biting the dog's skin. They're highly contagious from dog to dog and between

dogs and cats. Signs of ear mites are red, scabby ear flaps and a brown, crumbly, waxy discharge that's described as looking like coffee grounds. Accompanying ear infections can cause the ears to smell bad.

To diagnose ear mites, your veterinarian will look at the discharge under the microscope, to see if she can spot moving white specks about the size of a pinhead. To rid your Beagle of ear mites, the ear canal is thoroughly cleaned. Then you'll need to apply a medication prescribed by the veterinarian to kill the mites. All the dogs and cats in your household will need to be treated, whether they show signs or not.

In the average veterinary practice, ear problems make up 20 percent of the veterinarian's cases. Take good care of your floppy-eared Beagle so he doesn't become a statistic.

Nailing the Pedicure

Beagles wear down their toenails through their normal everyday activity, but feet still need regular attention to keep them in good shape. Check nails weekly to see if they need trimming.

Use a guillotine-style trimmer with a sharp edge to make the job easier. Clip just at the curve of the nail to avoid the quick. If your Beagle has light-colored nails, you can see the dark line of the quick and take care to avoid it. Keep some styptic powder such as QuickStop on hand in case you miscalculate. In a pinch, cornstarch can help stop bleeding.

When to Call the Vet

If you accidentally cut your Beagle's quick, the yelping and bleeding should stop in five to seven minutes. If bleeding doesn't show any sign of slowing, even with the use of styptic powder, give your vet a call.

The Eyes Have It

Your Beagle's eyes shouldn't need any special care to keep them bright and shining. Just wipe away the "sleepies" in the corners of the eyes with a moistened cotton ball. When you're cleaning them, you can glance to make sure the eyes don't seem red or irritated. If you see your Beagle pawing at his eye, check to see that there's nothing irritating it. Take him to the veterinarian if signs of irritation continue or if he has an unusual discharge.

The Least You Need to Know

- Fleas, ticks, and internal parasites can carry disease or make your Beagle sick. Control them not only on your dog but also in the surrounding environment, indoors and outdoors.

- Use parasite-control products that are made for use on dogs, and check with your veterinarian to make sure you're not mixing products that could be toxic when combined.

- Regular dental care prevents periodontal disease and associated bodily infections. Brush your Beagle's teeth!

- Beagles do not have an unpleasant body odor. Take your Beagle to the veterinarian if he suddenly starts to smell bad and you know he hasn't rolled in anything nasty.

- Brush your Beagle once or twice a week to keep his skin and fur healthy and clean.

Chapter 14

Chow Time!

In This Chapter

- 🐾 Choosing a balanced diet
- 🐾 Making sense of labels
- 🐾 Foods for each life stage
- 🐾 Preventing obesity

If your Beagle could read, this would be his favorite chapter. Food is very important to Beagles, and they'll do just about anything to get it. "More, more, more" is their motto, even if they've just been fed. Oh, once in a while you'll run into a picky Beagle, but these are few and far between.

To keep your Beagle in peak health, though, you'll want to regulate the type and amount of food he gets. Obesity is a serious problem in this breed and can lead to associated health problems such as diabetes or joint disorders. Understanding how much your Beagle needs to eat to maintain good health, the need for a complete and balanced diet, and just what those labels really say will all help you provide your Beagle pal with a nutritious diet.

What Does "Complete and Balanced" Mean?

The nutrients your Beagle requires for good health are an appropriate mix of protein, fat, carbohydrates, vitamins, and minerals. Dogs are meat eaters, but in the wild they also eat vegetable matter, grasses, fruits, and roots. Because dogs can survive and thrive on such a varied diet, they are classified as omnivores rather than carnivores.

Since it's not really practical for the modern Beagle to go out hunting for any kind of food on a regular basis, researchers have developed commercial diets that are complete and balanced for a dog's needs. When a diet is complete, that means it contains all the nutrients that dogs are known to need. When dogs don't get enough of a particular essential nutrient, they become susceptible to problems related to that nutrient's functions. For instance, vitamin A supports normal vision, proper skeletal development, healthy skin, and normal immune function.

Bet You Didn't Know

An omnivore is an animal that can subsist on both plants and animals while a carnivore is an animal that subsists on flesh.

A diet that's balanced contains nutrients in appropriate proportions to one another, and the nutrients are balanced to the diet's energy level. For instance, the energy level provided by a puppy food is much higher than that provided by a senior diet. The body is designed to deal with nutrient excesses and deficiencies on a short-term basis, but over the long term, an unbalanced diet leads to health problems.

How do you know if a food is complete and balanced? It says so right on the label. But there's more to it than that. Pay attention to how the manufacturer figured out that the food was complete and balanced.

Nutrient profiles for dogs in all life stages—growth, adult maintenance, pregnancy and lactation—are set by a group called the American Association of Feed Control Officials (AAFCO). Manufacturers can develop a food simply by throwing in a little of this and a little of that until the recipe matches the AAFCO nutri-

Bet You Didn't Know

Many of the dogs used in feeding trials are, natch, Beagles! Beagles are popular for this purpose because of their small size and good appetite.

ent profiles. That's the easy way. Manufacturers who really want to know if their foods meet dogs' needs (not to mention tastes good to dogs) conduct feeding trials based on AAFCO standards. If the dogs thrive on the diet and eat it eagerly (Mikey likes it!), then it's ready to go.

Any time you have a choice, choose a food whose label states that feeding tests are behind the claim for complete and balanced nutrition. The nutritional adequacy statement should read something like "This food is complete and balanced for adult dogs [or puppies] based on AAFCO feeding trials." If a food doesn't state that it was tested in feeding trials, you have no way of knowing whether the food tastes good to dogs or if the nutrients are digestible and available for the dog to use.

Picking the Right Food

From the early manufactured dog foods, which have been commercially widespread for only the past 50 years or so, canine diets have blossomed into a multitude of categories, with special foods for puppies, old dogs, large dogs, small dogs, fat dogs, working dogs, dogs with allergies, and dogs with diseases. While it's nice to have a selection, the almost bewildering variety can make it difficult to choose. Knowing how the dog's body uses and responds to nutrients can make the decision a little easier.

Reading the Label

Understanding how pet foods are labeled can also help you choose an appropriate food. Federal and state regulations call for very specific descriptions of ingredients and quantities in pet foods.

What's in a Name?

The product name is the first clue. If a food is called Uncle Joe's Beef for Beagles, the food must contain 95 percent beef, not counting the water used for processing. Taking the water into account, the food must still contain at least 70 percent beef. Because ingredients must be listed in order by weight, beef would be the first ingredient listed on the label, followed by water, vitamins, and minerals. If the name includes a combination of ingredients, such as Uncle Joe's Beef and Chicken for Beagles, beef and chicken must make up 95 percent of the total weight (excluding water), and the food must contain more beef than chicken.

Let's say that the food is called Uncle Joe's Beef Dinner for Beagles. Whether the food is canned or dry, the named ingredient must make up at least 25 percent of the product, exclusive of water. In other words, any time a food contains at least 25 percent of a named ingredient but less than 95 percent, it must include a qualifying description such as dinner, platter, entrée, nuggets, or formula. When you look at the label for this food, the beef will probably be third or fourth on the ingredient list. What if Uncle Joe's makes a Beef and Chicken Dinner? Together, the two named ingredients must total 25 percent of the product, with at least 3 percent chicken. There will always be more of the ingredient that's listed first.

Sometimes manufacturers like to highlight a minor ingredient such as bacon or cheese. They can do this if the food contains at least 3 percent of the highlighted ingredient. If you see Uncle Joe's Chicken Dinner for Beagles "with bacon," you know that it contains at least 3 percent bacon. If it reads "with bacon and cheese," it must contain at least 3 percent of each ingredient.

What does it mean if a food is named Uncle Joe's Chicken Flavor Beagle Food? A food with the word "flavor" in the name isn't required to have a specific percentage of the given flavor, but it must be detectable. Expect to see

Beagle Lingo

Digests are materials treated with heat, enzymes, and acids to form concentrated natural flavors.

chicken meal, chicken by-products, or chicken *digests* listed on the label to provide flavor. With the exception of artificial smoke or bacon flavors, which are often added to treats, pet foods rarely contain artificial flavors.

The Ingredient List

Pay attention to the way ingredients are listed on the side of the bag or can. As mentioned earlier, they must be listed in order by weight. Read the label carefully to make sure an ingredient hasn't been scattered throughout the listing to make it look as if there's less of it than there really is. For instance, a label that lists ground corn, yellow corn meal, corn gluten, and corn gluten meal has a lot more corn than might appear at first glance. In fact, if you were to add up the complete amount of corn, it might well turn out to be the food's main ingredient. Corn is an acceptable form of protein, but it's not as good as meat or eggs. Choose a food that has more meat-based protein than grain-based protein.

More Useful Info

Other information you can find on the label is the manufacturer's name and address, the guaranteed analysis, and feeding directions. The manufacturer's contact information is important in case you have a question about or problem with the food. Most manufacturers provide a toll-free number you can call with questions.

The guaranteed analysis states minimum percentages of crude protein and crude fat and maximum percentages of crude fiber and moisture. It may include guarantees for other nutrients such as

Bet You Didn't Know _____ The maximum moisture content for pet foods is 78 percent. Exceptions to this rule are products labeled "stew," "in sauce," or "in gravy." Remember that you're paying for all that extra water.

calcium, phosphorus, sodium, and linoleic acid. If you want to know about a particular nutrient, contact the company. Because of differences in moisture contents, the levels of crude protein and most other nutrients are lower for canned foods (75 to 78 percent moisture) than for dry foods (10 to 12 percent water). To compare nutrient levels between particular canned and dry foods, multiply the guarantees for the canned product by four.

The feeding directions tell you how much of the food to give. Use them only as a rough guideline. Your Beagle needs only 1 to 2 cups of food each day. Let his condition tell you whether he needs more or less. Remember, working Beagles, puppies, and pregnant or lactating bitches need more food than couch potatoes.

Who's It For?

Look for the nutritional adequacy statement to find out whether a food is appropriate for a puppy or an adult dog. If the food is labeled "for growth," it meets the needs of a growing pup. A food labeled "maintenance" is formulated for an adult dog with a normal activity level. You can feed an "all life stages" food to an adult dog, but a maintenance food wouldn't provide a puppy with the energy and nutrients he needs.

Foods have also been developed for overweight dogs, older dogs, and dogs with allergies.

Lifestyle Equals Energy Needs

Factors to consider include your Beagle's energy level and size. Active, high-energy dogs need a diet that's high in caloric density, meaning that it's high in fat and highly digestible. This is a good choice for a hunting or field trial dog, a show dog, or a dog that gets lots of long walks or competes in agility or some other active sport. Couch potato Beagles that get most of their exercise walking to and from the food bowl need a much lower calorie diet or they'll get fat.

(© Janet Nieland)

Growing puppies need to eat about twice as much volume of food per pound of their body weight as adult Beagles. As your pup reaches adulthood, gradually decrease the amount of food he receives.

Bet You Didn't Know

The dog's body uses protein to create more protein, as well as to provide energy. If the amount of fat and carbohydrate in a diet isn't balanced to the amount of protein, then the protein ends up being used for energy instead of to make new protein.

A dog's energy requirements are also related to its size. Smaller dogs, such as Beagles, need more calories per unit of body weight than large dogs. In general, they do better with a higher energy food. The exception is the dog that's prone to obesity from lack of exercise or because he's genetically programmed to pack on the pounds.

Dry, Canned, or Semimoist?

You can find pros and cons for just about anything, and dog food is no exception. The three varieties most commonly available are dry (kibble), canned (wet), and semimoist (meatlike food in a pouch).

Most Beagles will chow down on anything, but given a choice they're likely to prefer canned food. Canned food tastes good and smells good, both of which are a Beagle's most important criteria. Canned food is expensive, though, so your wallet will take a hit if you feed it as your Beagle's primary diet. It's also high in water, which makes it difficult to justify paying a lot for it. Canned food sticks to teeth and aids in the formation of plaque. The other drawbacks to canned food are that it's messy and must be refrigerated after being opened so it doesn't go bad.

Dry food's main advantages are price and convenience. Dry food costs less than canned food, and it's easy to store and dish out. Many veterinarians recommend dry food because its hard texture helps prevent plaque and tartar from building up on teeth.

Beagle Bonus

It's okay to mix dry and canned foods if you want to give your Beagle a bit of a taste sensation without the high price. Choose foods from the same manufacturer for best results.

Semimoist food tastes good like canned food and is convenient like dry food. Those are its only advantages, however. It's high in sugar and additives, making it a poor nutritional choice. Think of it as the fast food of dog dinners and limit it accordingly. It's best used in small quantities as a treat.

Feeding Your Puppy

Dogs have different nutritional requirements at different times in their lives. As puppies, they need energy for growth. Your Beagle will multiply his birth weight several times before he's fully grown. He needs a high-quality, nutrient-dense food that's specially designed to meet his needs.

Until they're about four weeks old, puppies receive all their nourishment from mother's milk. Then the breeder begins to introduce a mushy cereal and eventually weans them onto puppy food. When you take your new Beagle home, you'll want to continue feeding him the same food or gradually switch him over to the puppy food of your choice. Look for a food that contains about 24 percent protein and 18 percent fat. The first ingredient listed should be meat, such as chicken or lamb. Many foods come in small-bite sizes, and these are a good choice for your Beagle pup.

Choose a food that's formulated for puppies, and feed it until your Beagle is nine months to a year old. Puppy foods contain the nutrients needed to provide the slow growth a puppy's body needs to develop properly. Faster and fatter is not better! Puppies that put on weight too quickly are more prone to skeletal, joint, and ligament problems. Do not give calcium or other supplements. Too many supplements, especially calcium, can cause serious skeletal and joint development problems.

Feed him three or four times a day until he's about four months old. Puppies have small stomachs, so they're not able to make-do with two meals a day the way an adult dog can. Ask the breeder or your veterinarian how much he should receive at each meal. Mixing dry and canned food will create a tasty blend he'll enjoy. As he grows older, you can gradually reduce the number of meals he gets until he's eating only in the morning and evening. When he's a year old, you can begin feeding a diet formulated for adult dogs. As you would with any dietary change, mix the new food with the old diet gradually, over a period of a week to 10 days.

Feed your puppy (and your adult Beagle) on a schedule. Put down a measured amount of food at specific times each day and take it up after 20 to 30 minutes. Free-feeding (leaving food out all the time) often leads to obesity.

Doggy Do's/ Doggy Don'ts
Provide your Beagle with fresh water every day. Water is one of the most important nutrients your dog needs.

Help! My Beagle Is Fat

Because they're such chowhounds, obesity is a major problem in Beagles. Not only do they get their regular meals, they're masters at wheedling treats from anyone who crosses their path. And when they can't get food by begging, they're not above stealing it. Being overweight isn't healthy, though, so if your Beagle starts packing on the pounds, take steps to reverse the situation.

(© Janet Nieland)

A fat Beagle is not pretty, cute, or healthy. Obesity is a serious problem in the breed, so watch your Beagle's weight carefully. This dog ballooned to 65 pounds—twice the breed's appropriate weight—before six months of diet and exercise brought her down to 32 pounds.

To tell if he's too fat, give your Beagle the hug test. When you place your arms around him, you should be able to feel his ribs beneath the skin and muscle. If you can see his ribs, he's right: You do need to give him more food! If his ribs aren't anywhere to be found, because they're buried beneath a thick layer of fat, it's time for a diet. Another way to check his condition is to look down at him. From above, you should see an obvious waist. If he's a solid cylinder from front to back, a little waist whittling is in order.

Doggy Do's/Doggy Don'ts

Weigh your Beagle regularly to track his weight. You can take him to the vet to be weighed (there should be no office charge for this service) or you can weigh him at home. Stand on the scale to get your weight and then pick up your Beagle and weigh yourself again. The difference is how much your Beagle weighs.

Doggy Diet

Your Beagle can lose weight one of two ways. You can give him a food formulated for weight loss. These diets are usually labeled "lite" or "reduced calorie." The benefit to these diets is that your Beagle still gets the same amount of food, so he won't feel deprived. The drawback, some veterinarians say, is that while lite foods have restricted fat levels to reduce calories, they have increased levels of carbohydrates, which stimulate insulin secretion. The result is that the body stores unused calories as fat.

The alternative is to feed a reduced quantity of your dog's regular food so that he takes in fewer total calories than he's using for his daily energy needs. To do this, reduce the amount you're giving him by ⅓ cup. So if you're feeding him 2 cups of food every day, reduce it to one and ⅔ cups. Don't forget to reduce all the treats and table scraps you've been sneaking him on the side! After two weeks, weigh him. If he's lost weight, even just a little bit, continue giving the same amount. If his weight is the same as it was at the beginning of the diet, reduce the amount you're feeding by another ⅓ cup. Weigh again in two weeks to track his progress. If he still hasn't lost weight, start giving him only 1 cup of food daily, ½ cup in the morning and ½ cup in the evening. Remember, Beagles are relatively small dogs and what looks like a minuscule amount to you is plenty for them (no matter how much they protest to the contrary).

And any self-respecting Beagle will protest having the amount of his food reduced. If your Beagle puts on the starving act, you can supplement his food with canned green beans (low-sodium, please) or canned pumpkin (not the sweetened kind you'd use for pie). Green beans and pumpkin are low in calories and high in fiber, and they'll help your Beagle feel full.

Bet You Didn't Know _____

Many of the ingredients that sound like chemicals on dog food labels are actually vitamins, minerals, or other nutrients. Sometimes they're artificial colors, stabilizers, or preservatives such as BHA and BHT. Any such additive must be approved for its intended use (as a preservative, for instance) or Generally Recognized as Safe (GRAS).

If you want your Beagle's diet to be successful, don't give up, and make sure other family members aren't sabotaging the diet by sneaking him food when you're not looking.

Exercise

Another prescription for weight loss is more exercise. If your Beagle is grossly overweight, start slowly, walking him daily for only a few minutes. As he begins to lose weight, you can increase the length and pace of the walks. If you live in a hot, humid climate, schedule walks for cool mornings and evenings so you don't stress your Beagle unnecessarily.

Veterinary Supervision

Before beginning any diet or exercise program, take your Beagle to the veterinarian for a checkup. You want to make sure he doesn't have a health problem that's causing the obesity or that would be adversely affected by a change in diet or exercise level.

Watch for Weight Loss

On a diet, your Beagle should lose weight slowly. Rapid weight loss isn't healthy. If your Beagle, fat or not, suddenly begins to lose weight, even though he's eating the same amount of food and getting the same level of exercise, take him to the veterinarian. He could have a serious health problem.

The Perfect Food

Is there a balanced diet that's right for every dog? The answer is no. Dogs are individuals, and while most of them might do quite well on a given diet, there will always be a few with special needs, such as weight loss or a health condition, or who simply do better on a different formulation. Stress, environment, and other factors can also affect a dog's dietary needs.

If you're unsure whether a food is right for your Beagle, just take a look at him and let his condition be your guide. If his coat looks great, his energy level is high, his eyes are clear, and his stool is small and firm, you can be reasonably sure his overall health is good.

When to Call the Vet

If your Beagle has chronic ear infections, loose stools, a poor-quality coat, and itchy skin, take him to the veterinarian. He may have a nutritional deficiency or food allergy.

The Least You Need to Know

- Buy the highest quality food you can afford. In the long run, it will be less expensive, because your Beagle will have fewer health problems.

- Learn how to read dog food labels so you know exactly what's in your Beagle's diet.

- Choose a food that has been proven in AAFCO feeding trials.

- Feed your Beagle no more than 1 to 2 cups of food each day. The recommendations on dog food labels are usually overstated.

- Puppies need three or four meals daily until they're about four months old. Then they can taper off to two meals a day.

- To help prevent obesity, avoid free-feeding your Beagle. An obese Beagle needs to lose weight slowly and steadily, not rapidly.

Part 5

Fun with Beagles!

Now that you know how to train and care for your Beagle, it's time for the fun stuff. With his smart and exuberant nature, there's no end to the good times you can have with a Beagle. The only limits are your imagination and energy level.

The following chapters will introduce you to dog sports, therapy work, and the intricacies of beagling.

Chapter 15

A Beagling We Shall Go

In This Chapter

- 🏠 Pack hunts
- 🏠 Field trials
- 🏠 Size comparisons
- 🏠 Work styles
- 🏠 The Triple Challenge

Almost any activity done with a Beagle has been called Beagling at one time or another, but to be perfectly accurate, the term is limited to activities in the field, such as hunting or field trials. In its truest form, the word Beagling refers to traditional pack hunts, which are very different from hunting with a single Beagle or the field trials held to evaluate the qualities of individual hounds. In this chapter, we'll explore the different types of field events available to Beaglers.

Tally Ho!

Watching a Beagle pack work is a rare pleasure. An early morning walk outdoors, participating in a centuries-old tradition, with dogs bred for generations to do this one thing: It's not something that many of us will ever experience, but foot hunting with a pack of Beagles is an opportunity well worth seeking out.

The joy of watching a pack work is seeing the hounds cooperate to achieve their goal. They are to move in such unison that a blanket could be thrown over the entire pack, says one commentator on the sport. A pack consists of as few as two couples (four hounds) or as many as 20 couples (40 hounds). While they all work closely together, each Beagle brings a unique ability to the field. Couples are closely matched in size and speed to ensure smooth running.

> **Beagle Bonus**
>
> To learn more about how packs are put together, look for a little book called *Hounds for a Pack* by Comte E. de Vezins, translated by J. Allen. The book is out of print, but it's not difficult to find at a reasonable price on a book search site such as www.bookfinder.com.

The Quarry

The pack's quarry may be the snowshoe or European hare, or the cottontail rabbit. Each requires a dog with a different working style.

Snowshoe and European hares tend to remain above ground, and they usually live in deep forests or on open plow lands. Their style of running is to move straight away through their home territory or to make large circles. Hare have been known to cover several miles during a single run. With each leap, hares cover quite a bit of ground, so the scent they leave behind is spaced farther apart than that left by a rabbit. Beagles on hares are more likely to follow an air scent than a ground scent. Beagles used for hare hunting need lots of speed and endurance, plus the ability to efficiently cover rough, open ground. If they fail to work quickly, the hare is likely to leave them far behind.

> **Beagle Bonus**
>
> Pack masters want a hound that will last all day long and not come in lame the next day, so sound structure and good movement are important.

Cottontail rabbits, native to America, tend to circle, twist, turn, and double back rather than run straight out, and they'll go to ground (hide in a hole) to escape their pursuers. The Beagle in hot pursuit must be able to gear down and keep close contact with the ground trail to stay on top of the rabbit's scent. He needs patience and perseverance to puzzle out a confusing scent and decide which way to go. Rabbits prefer environments with thick, protective cover, interspersed with fields or grassy areas where they can feed. Beagles that hunt rabbits must be small enough to wiggle through heavy brush or large enough to force their way through.

If you're worried about the bunny's safety, don't be, enthusiasts say. In this country, the quarry is rarely harmed. When the rabbit gets tired of the chase, he simply goes to ground.

Size Matters

While Beagles of either variety (13-inch or 15-inch) can do well on different types of game, their size and work style needs to be matched to the terrain as well as the quarry's habits. Smaller Beagles can squeeze through tight places when hunting rabbits in thick cover. The 13-inch Beagles tend to be a little slower than their larger brethren, but they can go through a fence more easily. Slightly larger Beagles are usually favored for hunting over rough ground.

In a pack situation, a similarity in size helps the dogs run together and function more smoothly. The two varieties can be mixed in a pack as long as there's not too much disparity in size. A large pack of 15-inch Beagles really moves.

In the end, what matters most is what you like in a dog.

The Hunt Scene

A pack hunt is a highly ritualistic and formal event, complete with horns and livery. Directing the proceedings is the huntsman, attired in a bottle green coat with a velvet collar in the colors of the packs, white pants, and a white shirt with a stock or tie. The huntsman decides where the hunt will start and *casts* the hounds. During the hunt, he signals the hounds with his voice or horn. His (or her) assistants, the *whippers-in*, wear the same livery, making them easy to identify. The whippers-in help keep the pack together, alert the huntsman to any problems, and signal when the quarry is spotted.

> ### Beagle Lingo
>
> To **cast** hounds is to start them off on the search for a rabbit or hare to track. It isn't always practical to wait for the dogs to find their own quarry, so beaters (the people who "beat" the brush to start the rabbit running) may be used to flush rabbits for the dogs in small pack and SPO trials. Beaters are always used in brace trials. **Whipper-in** is a huntsman's assistant; this individual ensures that dogs stay together.

(© Kristine Kraeuter)

The hunting season for organized Beagle packs usually begins in October of each year with a formal opening day hunt, including the traditional blessing of the hounds by a priest. Sometimes a puppy show and hunt tea are part of the opening day festivities. Meets usually take place on weekends or holidays. The season ends in early spring.

Spectators, known as the gallery, stay well behind the hounds and hunt staff. They may shout "Tally ho" if they spy the rabbit or hare before the hunt staff does. Otherwise the gallery stays still and quiet while the Beagles work out the scent. Once the Beagles are off and running, the gallery follows, some at a jog or run, others at a more sedate pace.

Bet You Didn't Know _____

Beagles are referred to as foot hounds because, unlike fox hunting, they are followed on foot. An exception is the judging of the Three Hour Stakes Class of the NBC Triple Challenge. During this event, judges are mounted on horseback so they can get a better view of the pack and more accurately evaluate the individual hounds in competition. The handlers and gallery, however, follow the hounds on foot. Beagles may also be followed on horseback by people whose age or infirmity makes it difficult for them to keep up on foot.

Occasionally the pack falls silent, trying to figure out which way the quarry went. Talking can distract them, so the gallery is urged to remain quiet. As the Beagles pick up the scent again, they sing out and are on their way. When the rabbit finally goes to ground, the huntsman signals the end of the hunt by sounding a few long, wavering notes on the horn.

Field Trials

Pack hunts require hounds to work closely together and are in essence social events. Field trials, on the other hand, are competitive performance events in which dogs compete against each other for placements and points toward field championships. More than 60,000 Beagles compete each year in AKC-licensed field trials. The United Kennel Club, the American Rabbit Hunters Association, and the United Gundog Beagle Federation also hold field trials.

Bet You Didn't Know

Once a title is earned, it becomes part of the dog's name. A Beagle field champion would have a registered name that looks like this: FC Baxter Run Rabbit Run.

The AKC has licensed Beagle field trials for more than 105 years, and the following descriptions apply to AKC field trials. Field trials test different aspects of the Beagle's function as a hunting dog, but boldness and desire to hunt are foremost. At least two judges score the dogs. Beagles can compete in three types of trials:

- Large pack on hare
- Small pack or small pack option (SPO)
- Brace

Because Beagles come in two sizes, classes are divided by height as well as sex. Following are the four classes:

- Open dogs not exceeding 13 inches in height
- Open bitches not exceeding 13 inches in height
- Open dogs over 13 inches but not exceeding 15 inches
- Open bitches over 13 inches but not exceeding 15 inches

If fewer than six hounds of a particular sex are entered in any class, both sexes can run in a single class. Spayed or neutered dogs are not eligible to compete in field trials, because they aren't able to pass on their working ability. The intent of field trials (and conformation shows) is to choose the best breeding stock to produce the next generation of dogs.

No matter which class or trial they're in, Beagles are judged on their ability to find game and pursue it energetically and decisively. Quality of performance is more important than how often the Beagle finds game.

Besides eagerness and determination, judges look for certain desirable qualities, listed as follows:

- Searching ability

- Willingness to explore rough cover

- Independence

- Good range

Other qualities of a good scenthound are stamina, adaptability to changes in trail and scenting conditions, and the ability to work well with other hounds. Hounds are also tested for gun-shyness, with a blank cartridge used to simulate gunfire.

Beagle Bonus

The United Beagle Gundog Federation offers a Certified Hunting Beagle (CHB) program, which emphasizes not only hunting ability but also proper Beagle conformation. The UBGF has two components to its field trials, performance and conformation, raising the awareness among field trialers of the importance of not only a good hunting hound but also a well-made hound.

Beagle trials have no time limit and continue through several rounds until the judges make their placements. First- through fourth-place dogs earn championship points, with the number of points determined by the placement. A field championship title requires 3 first-place wins and 120 points.

In any type of pack trial, handlers want a Beagle that can last a long time, all day if necessary. This calls for a dog with good conformation. The past 10 to 15 years have seen many changes for the better in the conformation of field trial dogs.

At pack trials, competitors draw the order in which they'll go a week or so ahead of time. Each pack has a certain amount of time for their hunt. The amount of time depends in part on the size of the entry. The trial usually starts at 7 A.M., and the handlers are directed to the starting spot, where they present the pack to the judges. The Beagles must find their own hare or rabbit and run it with as little help as possible from the staff. When a pack's time is up, the Beagles must stop, even if they're hot on a trail. The next pack comes to that spot, the hounds are presented to the judges, and they go on from there.

Large Pack Trials

In large pack trials, only hares are tracked. Some large pack trials are specialized, with the dogs pursuing snowshoe hares in New England or swamp rabbits in the Southern United States. Rabbits or hares can be pursued in small pack and small pack option (SPO) trials.

Large pack on hare classes can last all day and test a dog's endurance as well as scenting ability. Pack dogs are expected to move freely and cover ground effortlessly. The large pack classes usually consist of 30 to 60 or more dogs. The dogs are cast to find their quarry and are judged on their ability to do so.

Small Pack Trials

Small pack and SPO trials move quickly, making them exciting to watch. Small pack field trials cast dogs in packs of three to seven hounds, while in SPO trials the dogs are usually divided into packs of five to nine dogs. If only eight or nine dogs are entered, they may all be run together as a pack.

Bet You Didn't Know

SPO trials are the fastest growing segment of the field trial community. They're described as coming closest to simulating actual hunting conditions.

Like large pack trials, small pack and SPO trials require the hounds to be cast. Because the pack moves quickly, judges often follow on horseback so they can better follow the action.

During the trial, poorly performing dogs are pulled and a new round, or series, begins. In SPO classes, no penalties are levied on Beagles that trail game other than what's announced—rabbit instead of hare, for instance. Dogs are penalized or eliminated for any actions that impede the smooth running of the pack. The last dogs remaining run in what's called the winners' pack, from which final placements are made.

Brace Trials

Brace Beagling is the oldest of the types of field trials. Brace trials emphasize a Beagle's hunting style and accuracy. Unlike pack dogs, which require speed, successful brace trial Beagles are slow and methodical. At one point, brace trial Beagles were considered useless for real hunting, because they couldn't last all day in the field and go again the next day.

In brace trials, which almost always take place in fenced areas to prevent the dogs from getting lost, dogs are cast in braces (pairs) or trios in the first series. Braces are chosen randomly and judged in order.

The field marshall calls "first brace" or "next brace" and beaters flush a rabbit. Whoever sees the rabbit shouts "Tally ho" and if necessary indicates where the rabbit came from and which direction it went. Handlers are then told where to take their dogs and may encourage the dogs to find the rabbit's trail, or line. Once the handler releases the dogs, however, no more instructions are permitted and the handler must stay behind the judges.

Bet You Didn't Know

In addition to rabbit and hare, Beagles have also been used to hunt game birds, foxes, deer, and even wild pigs.

Beagle Bonus

Common faults in brace Beagles are excessive length, too much bone, crooked legs, and bad feet.

Each brace may work for only a few minutes. When the judges are satisfied with what they've seen, they instruct the handlers to "pick up the dog." Sometimes they call for another rabbit for the same brace; otherwise, they ask for the next brace. When each brace has run, the first series is complete, and the judges make their picks for the second series. This continues until the judges decide all their placements.

The Triple Challenge

The National Beagle Club's Triple Challenge competition was developed in response to concerns that different types of Beagles were moving too far afield, so to speak, from each other. Show Beagles had little or no field ability, and even field dogs had increasingly divergent appearances and hunting styles.

To bring the various types together and encourage development of the all-rounder Beagle, the NBC came up with the Triple Challenge, open to show champions, field champions, or members of NBC-recognized hunting packs. Each Beagle entered must compete in a brace trial, a three-hour stake, and in the conformation ring. The dog with the highest combined score wins.

The Triple Challenge, which began in 1996, takes place over a single weekend and is now a popular, prestigious event among Beaglers of all stripes, from organized pack, field trial, hunting, and show backgrounds. Through its variety, the event promotes the versatile Beagle. In the brace trial, individual hounds are evaluated. The stakes class tests a Beagle's ability to contribute to the work of a pack afield. And conformation, movement, condition, soundness, and temperament are judged in the show ring.

The Triple Challenge brace trial follows the format of an AKC Beagle field trial. Dogs in the first series usually run as trios. In second or subsequent series, they run as braces. The goal is to score each hound and rank it from first place on down.

In the three-hour stakes class, judges evaluate a Beagle's field ability as well as cooperation and contribution to the work of the pack. All the hounds entered are cast, hunted, and judged as a single pack. For best viewing, judges observe from horseback. All hounds are placed from first to last.

(© *John Kraeuter*)

Pack dogs must be in top physical condition with sound running gear and functional conformation to successfully meet the physical demands of their sport.

Last, but not least, is the conformation show. Judges examine each hound entered and score and rank all of them. In each competition, high-scoring hounds from each variety are chosen. The Beagle with the highest combined score wins. All hounds with combined total scores of 200 or more receive a certificate of versatility.

To enter the Triple Challenge, a Beagle must meet one of five criteria:

- Have earned points toward an AKC field or conformation championship
- Be a member of an NBC-registered Beagle pack
- Have the ARHA title of Rabbit Champion, Grand Rabbit Champion, or Hound of the Year

🏠 Have the UKC title of Hunting Champion or Grand Hunting Champion

🏠 Have the title of CKC (Canadian) Field Trial Champion

All hounds entered must be registered with the AKC or entered into the NBC stud books.

The Least You Need to Know

🏠 The word Beagling can be applied to any activity done with Beagles, but traditionally it's used to refer to pack hunts.

🏠 The traditional quarry for Beagles is rabbits or hares, but Beagles have also been used to hunt other game, including birds, foxes, and deer.

🏠 Rabbits and hares live in different environments and have different running styles, so hunting them requires Beagles with specific skills.

🏠 Field trials are competitive performance events that are not open to spayed or neutered Beagles.

🏠 There are three types of field trials: large pack on hare, small pack or small pack option, and brace trials.

🏠 The Triple Challenge rewards versatile Beagles that have hunting ability and good conformation.

Chapter 16

Games Beagles Play

In This Chapter

- 🏠 Dog sports, from agility to tracking
- 🏠 Playing at the park
- 🏠 Jogging and other exercise
- 🏠 Therapy hound
- 🏠 The wild life
- 🏠 Winter fun

His powerful nose makes the Beagle a natural at tracking or hide-and-seek games, and thanks to motivational training techniques that emphasize positive reinforcement, more and more Beagles are excelling in obedience and agility. Learn about all the sports and activities that you and your Beagle can enjoy.

Tuning in to CSN (Canine Sports Network)

Playing with a dog used to mean tossing a ball for him to chase and retrieve or playing tug-of-war. Now there are actual dog sports, and some of them are even televised. Turn on Animal Planet, and you're likely to see an agility competition, a dog show, a flyball

demonstration, or a flying-disc championship. Switch to the Out-door Living Network or ESPN, and you'll see field dogs in action. There's a sport for every dog, and Beagles can excel at many of them—if they have a foundation of extensive socialization and basic training. At least three Beagles have earned AKC titles in multiple sports: conformation, obedience, agility, and tracking. Let's take a look at the possibilities for your dog.

Agility

Think of agility as a canine obstacle course. The idea for the sport was based on equine show-jumping competitions: you know, the ones where the horses gallop through a course and leap tall walls and water hazards in a single bound. Well, agility doesn't have any water hazards, but it does have lots of jumps, an A-frame dogs must scale, teeter totters and dog walks (like a balance beam) to cross, weave poles to thread, and tunnels to navigate.

Agility requires a dog and handler to navigate this obstacle course in a given amount of time. The dogs work off-leash, with the handler (you!) directing them through the course. Speed, accuracy, and communication between dog and person are essential. Dogs compete in divisions according to their height, so Beagles compete against other Beagle-size dogs. The dog with the fastest time and fewest faults wins its class or height division.

Bet You Didn't Know

Agility began in England in 1977 as a way of filling time between conformation classes at the world-famous Crufts dog show. It was so much fun and such a crowd-pleaser that the activity evolved into the popular sport it is today.

Medium-size dogs with good working ability and lots of enthusiasm do best in agility. Beagles have the potential to do well, but they're often distracted by their noses. Training a Beagle for agility can be fun, but it requires a bit more effort and patience on your part than it would if you were working with, say, a Border Collie or Shetland Sheepdog.

Nonetheless, Beagles can and have performed well, even earning titles.

Knowing what motivates your Beagle is the secret to effective training. In most cases it's food, but a favorite toy can work as well. Whatever it is, use what works best. If your Beagle prefers cheese to liver, save the cheese for agility training sessions and don't give it at any other time. This makes the treat extra-special, and your Beagle will be willing to work harder to get it. The same goes for that favorite toy. Bring it out only during training time.

Before beginning agility training, your Beagle needs to know the commands sit, down, stay, and come. Even if he doesn't know them perfectly, he'll get better at them as training progresses, especially if he's having a good time.

Avoid using negative corrections such as training collars (choke or prong collars) or leash jerks. The idea is for the two of you to have fun. Remember Beagles always respond best to positive reinforcement. If you must correct your dog for an error, do it by withholding his treat, toy, or praise.

Beagle Bonus

As you learned in previous chapters, Beagles work best when their stomachs are empty, so they'll work harder for their rewards. Even if your Beagle prefers toys or praise to food, schedule meals for after your agility class or training session. You want him to be alert, not lethargic.

While it's not that difficult to keep your Beagle's attention when he's in your own backyard, it's another story when he's surrounded by other dogs and people, the scent of treats everywhere, and a new environment with lots of new smells. You'll have to work hard to make yourself and the equipment the most interesting thing out there! To help ensure a minimum of distractions by sniffing, relax and stay happy. If you're having fun, your Beagle will be more interested in having fun with you than in going off and doing her own thing.

If your Beagle seems to take longer than other dogs to learn certain obstacles or techniques, remember that each dog is an individual. Your Beagle is just as smart as other dogs, but he has a distinct learning style and won't do things just because you want him to. He has to see what's in it for him. Maintain a positive attitude, and your Beagle will excel at this fun sport.

Beagle Bonus

Squiggles, a Beagle owned by Marietta Huber, has earned the AKC's highest agility title, MACH (Master Agility Champion). Squiggles took fifth place in the 16-inch category in the 2001 AKC National Agility Championships, placing ahead of two Shetland Sheepdogs and a Soft-Coated Wheaten Terrier, and won the Hound Group category.

Begin training your Beagle for agility when he's eight or nine months old. He can't compete in agility trials until he's at least one year old. The age limit helps prevent injuries to a pup's still developing skeletal system. Start with very low jump heights and gradually increase them to avoid physical problems.

Because of the equipment and level of training required to participate in agility, you'll need to find a club or trainer that specializes in this sport. See Appendix B for information on contacting agility organizations and for a recommendation of a book on agility training.

Conformation

Looks and flair will help your Beagle succeed in the show ring. This is where breeders go to show off the fruits of their breeding programs. You don't have to be a breeder to show your Beagle, but you do need a dog who strongly resembles the ideal called for in the breed standard, because the dogs are judged against the standard, not each other. Because Beagles are such a popular breed, competition is keen in the Beagle show ring.

Besides looks, the qualities of a show dog are balance, attitude, and—what else?—showmanship. Balance means that your Beagle should look as if he could go all day in the field. The conformation that would allow him to do that includes a well laid back shoulder, a strong, powerful rear, and a good long ribcage so the heart and lungs can work well to provide stamina. A good show dog is confident. He moves smoothly and alertly and projects himself to gain the judge's attention. The best show dogs have a certain amount of pizzazz that draws people's eyes to them.

To earn a championship, a dog must garner 15 points under 3 different judges. The number of points a dog earns at a show depends on the number of other dogs he defeats. A 3-, 4- or 5-point win is called a major. Dogs must earn at least 2, 3-point majors under 2 different judges to earn a championship.

Like most scenthounds, the Beagle doesn't always see the benefit of parading around a show ring on his best behavior. You'll need to provide special incentives to hold his attention. Squeaky toys and liver bait are favorite attention-getters used by scenthound handlers. Use food or a toy to get and keep your Beagle's attention. He should know you have it, but he shouldn't be so distracted by it that he doesn't focus on what he's doing.

To prepare a Beagle for the show ring, it's a good idea to attend a handling class offered by a local dog club. Your Beagle will learn to stand properly for examination, gait nicely without pulling on the lead, and pay attention to the handler. You will learn how to *stack*, gait, and groom your dog, among other things. If you plan to handle the dog yourself, a handling class is a great place to pick up tips.

When you're moving your Beagle in the ring, remember that judges like to see the Beagle on a loose leash with his neck extended.

Doggy Do's/ Doggy Don'ts

Don't give your Beagle food while the judge is examining him. Instead hold a tiny treat in the palm of your hand away from the dog's face. This will help him to look attentive.

Lots of people hold the leash too tightly, jerking the dog's head up, because they don't want the Beagle's nose down on the floor, but this can affect the dog's movement. It can hide movement faults, but savvy judges will insist on seeing the dog move naturally.

To find a handling class, contact the AKC (listed in Appendix B) for a referral to a local all-breed or Beagle club. Many dog clubs offer handling classes for newcomers.

Beagle Bonus

To present a Beagle so his outline can be seen is called **stacking.** Some dogs are really good at stacking themselves, but others need a little help from their friends, namely you or the handler if you're using one. A free-stacking Beagle is a rarity. Expect to stack your Beagle yourself and hold him in a pose.

(© Janiece Harrison)

You can start training your puppy at an early age to stack himself for the show ring.

Take your Beagle around the ring at a walking pace. Remember, he's meant to accompany hunters on foot. A moderate pace is best. Don't lollygag, but don't race around the ring either. More important than how fast your Beagle moves is the number of steps he requires to cover a given amount of ground.

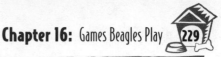

Flyball

Flyball is a team relay race over hurdles. Each team has 4 dogs, and each dog in turn races over 4 hurdles spaced 10 feet apart. At the end of the jumps is a box with a lever. The dog must press the lever, triggering a tennis ball that shoots out of the box. The dog catches the ball and goes back over the jumps, where the next dog is anxiously awaiting his turn. The team with the best time and fewest faults wins. Hurdle height is based on the shortest dog on the team, so smaller dogs such as Beagles are welcome teammates. Titles your Beagle can earn in this sport range from Flyball Dog (FD) to Flyball Grand Champion (FGD Ch.). (Various flyball titles are listed in Appendix B.)

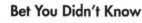

Bet You Didn't Know

A Beagle named Maddie has performed flyball demonstrations at pregame and halftime shows for the Harlem Globetrotters, San Francisco 49ers, and Oakland Raiders. She was the first Beagle to earn Flyball Master (FM) and Flyball Master Excellent (FMX) awards and at this writing was the top ranked Beagle in the North American Flyball Association.

Beagles don't have a reputation for excelling at flyball, but if your Beagle has a retrieving gene, he might love this sport. With their speed and jumping ability, Beagles can do well, as long as they aren't distracted by an interesting scent. To keep them focused, apply the same techniques discussed previously in the section on agility. When Maddie first started training for flyball, her owner had to make sure people at the sidelines weren't eating, because Maddie would run over and try to steal their food!

As with agility, wait to start jumping your Beagle until he's eight or nine months old, and start slowly with low jumps. Your Beagle should know and respond to basic obedience commands—especially "Come!" before he begins flyball training.

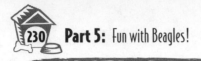

To learn more about flyball, contact the North American Flyball Association (NAFA), listed in Appendix B.

Obedience Trials

While Beagles aren't commonly seen in the obedience ring, they have been known to earn titles in this sport. Obedience requires precision, which isn't the Beagle's strong point, but if you're patient and persistent, there's no reason why you and your Beagle can't earn an obedience title or two. Some talented Beagles and their people have achieved high scores indeed, including High in Trial (HIT) designations, as well as advanced titles. Obedience titles range from CD (Companion Dog) at the Novice level to OTCH (Obedience Trial Champion) at the very pinnacle of competition.

To succeed in the obedience ring, your Beagle must perform a defined set of exercises, scoring more than 50 percent of the possible points for each exercise (ranging from 20 to 40), with a total score of at least 170 out of a possible 200. Each time a dog scores 170 or higher, he earns a "leg" toward an obedience title. Three legs and he has a title! Then he can move on to competition at the next level. The three levels of obedience are novice, open, and utility.

 Doggy Do's/Doggy Don'ts _____

> Be willing to move backward if your Beagle seems to have hit a training wall. Moving forward too quickly with a lesson can stop a dog in his tracks. Step back and review previous lessons with a dog to make sure he fully understands and is comfortable with what you're asking.

Novice-level exercises are simply the skills every well-mannered dog should know:

- 🐾 Heeling on- and off-leash at different speeds
- 🐾 Coming when called

🏠 Performing the sit or down and staying when told

🏠 Standing for a physical exam by the judge

The Open level is a little more difficult. Your Beagle must perform many of the same commands, but off-leash and for longer periods, plus jumping and retrieving exercises. Utility-level exercises include scent-discrimination work, where the Beagle excels. Top-level competitors can attempt Utility Dog Excellent (UDX) and OTCH titles. Talk to your trainer or contact a local dog club to find out more about obedience competition.

Tracking

Now this is a sport where Beagles rule. In tracking tests, which are noncompetitive, they demonstrate their natural ability to follow a trail—specifically, a human scent trail. To earn a Tracking Dog (TD) title, your Beagle need successfully complete only one track.

(© *Kristine Kraeuter*)

Tracking is one sport where the Beagle is sure to excel.

A beginner-level track is 440 to 500 yards long and must be at least 30 minutes old and at most 2 hours old. To earn a Tracking Dog Excellent (TDX) title, a dog must follow an older and longer track. At this level, the track must go for 800 to 1,000 yards and be 3 to 5 hours old. This track has more turns than one for a TD title and may include physical obstacles such as fallen trees or scenting obstacles such as false scent items lying along the trail.

Versatile Beagles can learn to follow tracks over different surfaces, from asphalt to dirt or grass. To earn a Variable Surface Tracking (VST) title, your Beagle must follow a track that's three to five hours old, which may take him through streets and into buildings.

Tracking training can begin at any age, although your Beagle won't be able to earn a title until he's six months old. Play hide and seek games (ask your trainer how) at home to reinforce this skill. Someone at your local dog club or Beagle club can help you get started if you want to put a tracking title on your Beagle, and books on tracking training are listed in Appendix B. Equipment you'll need is minimal: a nonrestrictive harness, a 20- to 40-foot leash, items for the dog to find such as a leather glove or old wallet or sock, flags to mark starts and turns, treats to reward your dog, and a notebook and pencil for drawing a map of the track. If you're working out in a field, you'll need to wear appropriate clothing and bring water for yourself and your dog.

Canine Good Citizen

If the previous sports sound like more effort than you and your Beagle want to put forth, consider going for a Canine Good Citizen® title instead. Any dog with good manners can earn the AKC's CGC designation.

For a CGC, your Beagle must meet 10 simple requirements:

🐾 Accepting the approach of a friendly stranger

- Sitting politely for petting without showing shyness or resentment

- Having a healthy, well-groomed appearance and a willingness to be combed or brushed and examined by the judge

- Walking nicely on a loose lead

- Walking politely through a crowd

- Performing the sit and down on command and staying when told

- Coming when called

- Behaving politely around other dogs

- Reacting without panic or aggression to common distractions such as a dropped item or a person running by

- Staying nicely with a stranger while the owner moves out of sight

You can provide praise and encouragement during the test and petting between exercises. No treats or toys are permitted, though; your Beagle must perform solely for love of you.

That's it! Ten easy steps to a CGC title. Your Beagle doesn't even have to dress up. The only items he needs are his regular leash, a buckle or slip collar (no prong collars or head halters, please), his own brush or comb for the judge to use on him, and written proof of rabies vaccination and license. Ask your trainer or contact the AKC to find out where and when CGC tests are scheduled in your area.

Doggy Do's/ Doggy Don'ts

Be sure your Beagle potties before any competition or test, including the CGC. Most sports fail dogs or at least take points away if the dog eliminates in the ring or during testing.

Jogging

Because Beagles have been bred for centuries to chase rabbits over hill and dale all the livelong day, they can make great jogging companions. Don't make the mistake, however, of running your puppy before he reaches physical maturity. The pounding of feet on the ground can be very damaging to skeletal and joint development.

Beagle Bonus

Beagles were made for outdoor activities. If you and your family enjoy hiking, camping, and swimming, your Beagle will be right there with you, leading the way on the trail or into the lake.

Wait until your Beagle is at least one year old before you start him on a running program. Begin slowly, gradually increasing the length and pace of the run. It's always a good idea to ask your veterinarian's advice before beginning any extensive exercise program with your dog.

Hiking

Beagles are capable of hiking distances of 10 to 12 miles without flagging. As with running, wait until your Beagle is fully mature—at least a year old—before you take him on any long-distance hikes. Start with short hikes and gradually increase the length and difficulty of your outings.

Bet You Didn't Know

Dogs can get sunburned, especially if they have short or light-colored coats. Limit your Beagle's sun exposure on hot days and apply sunblock to his ears and nose 30 minutes before going outside.

Remember that your Beagle is a hunter at heart. Use a long or retractable leash so he can explore, but do keep him connected to you. If your dog hightails it after a rabbit, he can end up miles away in a short amount of time. And no, he won't be able to sniff his way back. Unless you're fully confident in his response to the "Come" command—something few Beagle

owners can say—keep him leashed for his safety and your peace of mind.

Use common sense on the trail. If it's a hot day, rest frequently and give your Beagle plenty of water. Remember that you and your dog are walking at different levels. You might be getting a cool breeze on your face, while he's only getting hot sun. Dogs will do their best to keep up; be attentive to your Beagle's condition so that he doesn't run the risk of heatstroke.

Swimming

Many Beagles are avid swimmers. They'll happily join you in pool, lake, or ocean. Swimming is great exercise for Beagles and is a good way for them to retain a svelte physique.

Many Beagles enjoy playing in the water. Make sure your dog knows how to get safely in and out of the pool.

Dogs aren't born knowing how to swim. If your Beagle is a water novice, introduce him to the wet stuff gradually. You didn't

learn to swim automatically when your big brother threw you in the pool and neither will your Beagle. Instead of tossing your Beagle in the water and letting him sink or swim, start in shallow water and coax him in with a treat or toy. The presence of another dog that already swims may also lure him in. Whatever the case, your dog should always be within reach so you can help him if necessary.

Your Beagle will probably start to dog paddle with his front legs on his own. To give him the idea of using his whole body, lift his hind legs and help him float. Make sure he knows how to use the steps to get out of the pool. Keep the pool covered or the gate to it closed when you can't be there to act as lifeguard.

Just as you would with a child, be aware of water conditions. Jellyfish, sea lice, and strong currents can all pose hazards to your Beagle. Check with a lifeguard or read posted notices before either of you go into the water.

At the beach or at home, provide your Beagle with access to plenty of cool, fresh water. Drinking salt water can make him sick, and river and lake water contains parasites that can cause giardia, an unpleasant condition that involves lots of vomiting and diarrhea. Give your dog bottled water or water from your tap at home.

Doggy Do's/ Doggy Don'ts

Running on sand is strenuous. If your Beagle is out of shape, curb his activity on sand so he doesn't pull a muscle or tendon.

Any time your Beagle has been in the pool or ocean, rinse him off with fresh water. Chlorine and salt aren't good for his skin or fur, so you'll want to make sure he's thoroughly rinsed.

Swimming is a great form of exercise, but don't let your dog overdo it. He will be using new muscles and may tire quickly.

A Soothing Paw

If sports just aren't your bag, baby, but you'd still like to participate in an activity with your Beagle, consider therapy work. The same traits that make the Beagle a great pet—friendly nature, medium size, and easy-care coat—make him a super therapy dog as well. Therapy dogs make visits to children's hospitals, nursing homes, and schools, where they spread their own brand of health-giving good cheer. As we all know, laughter is the best medicine, and Beagles have the gift of bringing smiles to faces. And numerous studies have shown that stroking a dog helps to lower blood pressure and relieve stress. If your Beagle can pass a CGC test, he has all the makings of a therapy dog.

It takes a true Beagle Scout to become a therapy dog. Your Beagle should be clean, neat, and parasite-free, with trimmed nails that won't scratch a patient's skin. He must be gentle, friendly, and able and willing to get along with other dogs and people. Jumping up on people and stealing food are no-nos. His vaccinations should be up to date, and he should respond to basic obedience commands. Some organizations offer therapy dog training classes. Among other things, such classes can help your Beagle become accustomed to wheelchairs, crutches, canes, and walkers.

Therapy Beagles get lots of petting as they make their rounds, and sometimes they're invited to give kisses. Often they inspire people to talk about pets they had as children or pets they have at home. Some Beagles entertain by performing tricks or obedience routines.

Therapy work is a wonderful way to spread the happiness your Beagle brings you. For more information about getting involved, contact Therapy Dogs Incorporated or Therapy Dogs International. Contact information is listed in Appendix B.

The Least You Need to Know

- 🏠 Beagles can excel in dog sports if they're given patient, persistent training using positive reinforcement.

- 🏠 Obedience trials require precise responses, but if your Beagle can make it to the Utility level, he can show off his scent-discrimination ability.

- 🏠 To get the most out of your show Beagle, use treats or toys to keep his attention in the ring.

- 🏠 Beagles love to go hiking and camping, but they need to stay on-leash so they don't take off after a rabbit or squirrel and disappear into the wilderness.

- 🏠 If your Beagle stays outside for extended times, make sure he's well protected from temperature extremes that can cause sunburn or frostbite.

- 🏠 The Beagle's gentle, friendly nature and moderate size make him a fabulous therapy dog.

Fun for Kids and Beagles

In This Chapter

- AKC dog showing for kids
- 4-H dog activities
- Agility
- Tricky Beagle

For the right child, a Beagle can be the perfect friend. Beagles love kids (not least because they're often smeared with food), and an active child and Beagle can spend hours learning tricks together, exploring the neighborhood, playing ball, and more.

Structured activities can keep them both busy as well. Junior showmanship, 4-H, and agility are just some of the ways that children can get involved in competitive events with their Beagles. Training for these activities is a wonderful way for the two to spend time together and build a lasting relationship.

AKC Junior Showmanship

Lots of professional handlers (people who show dogs for a living) and breeders got their start showing dogs as kids. The American

Kennel Club has a program called Junior Showmanship that allows children to compete with others in their age group. Besides Traditional Junior Showmanship, where children are judged on how well they present their dog, kids can also participate in obedience, agility, and other performance events. The handling skills, confidence, and good sportsmanship learned will last a lifetime.

Kids 10 to 18 years old can participate in Junior Showmanship. Beginners start out in Novice classes, which are limited to children who haven't yet won three first-place awards in a Novice class. More experienced children move on to Open classes. Novice-level handlers can pick up some great tips by watching the kids in the Open classes perform.

(© Kristine Kraeuter)

Junior Showmanship is a great way for kids to be active with their Beagles.

Junior Showmanship judges base their decisions on the child's ability to show the dog properly, just as he would be presented in the breed ring. The handler's dress and conduct and the dog's well-groomed appearance all play a role. The dog's conformation isn't judged in Junior classes, so a child with a pet-quality dog stands just as much chance of succeeding as one handling a finished champion. The dog must be an AKC-recognized purebred (a Beagle, in this case), owned by the child or the child's family.

Beagles in Junior Showmanship

Many Beagles are handled by kids whose families already have Beagle show dogs. The family's retired champions get a second chance in the spotlight in the Juniors' ring. Others choose Beagles because of their small size and sturdiness. Another plus is that Beagles get along well with other dogs.

Because Beagles do have that stubborn, independent streak, the best choice for a beginner is usually an already trained finished champion. Once a child has some experience in training and handling a Beagle, she can move on to a puppy.

Grooming a Beagle for the show ring is fairly painless. He'll need a bath and a nail trim, plus a little trimming and clipping to neaten his appearance. Depending on the expertise of the Junior groomer, the trimming and clipping take 20 to 45 minutes. Mom and Dad may need to help young children with grooming.

As far as trainability, each Beagle is different. Most Juniors experience some stubbornness with their Beagles—that's just typical of the breed. Others luck out because their hounds are already trained for the show ring, so they have less difficulty getting the dog to strut his stuff. Some Beagles are natural hams and love being in the ring, while others would rather be scenting on the sidelines.

Beagle Bonus

It's not unusual for a Beagle to suddenly "forget" something he's known how to do perfectly for months. The independent Beagle, especially one with a dominant nature, can be unpredictable in the show ring, so he needs a patient handler, whether child or adult.

One advantage of the Beagle as a show dog is that he's easy to transport, presenting few problems with car or air travel. And a Beagle is not likely to lose his appetite just because he's in a strange place.

Getting Started

To get an idea of what's involved in Junior Showmanship, go to a local dog show and watch the Juniors classes. Many dog clubs offer weekly handling classes for Juniors and adults, which are a great way to meet other kids and learn the ropes. Most Juniors are very willing to help newcomers to the sport.

Handling classes take about an hour a week. Most Juniors work with their dogs between class, spending 10 minutes several times a week on training. Of course, training a puppy or other dog new to the show ring takes more time.

To get a free copy of the AKC's Rules and Regulations for Junior Showmanship, a geographical list of dog clubs, or an AKC Junior Handler Number (which is a must for getting started), contact the AKC at 5580 Centerview Dr., Raleigh, NC 27606; (919) 816-3595; www.akc.org.

4-H Fun

The 4-H program is the youth education branch of the Cooperative Extension Service (part of the U.S. Department of Agriculture). Every state and county has a CES office. Look for the CES listing in the government section of the phone book's white pages.

Among the many activities sponsored by 4-H is a dog project. Children who sign up for the 4-H dog project can train their dogs for showmanship, obedience, the Canine Good Citizen test, therapy work, or agility. Any dog can participate, so Beagles and Beagle mixes are welcome.

In showmanship classes, 4-H members learn how to present their dogs and themselves, working as a team. The dog must appear well-groomed, alert, and under control. Handlers are judged on their confidence and

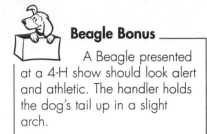

Beagle Bonus

A Beagle presented at a 4-H show should look alert and athletic. The handler holds the dog's tail up in a slight arch.

ability to groom and show the dog. As in AKC Junior Showmanship, only handling ability is judged, not the dog's conformation.

The 4-H program offers a number of classes for young dog owners. Which class is entered depends on the child's and dog's level of experience. For instance, a dog with more than 10 weeks of training must be entered in a Beginner B obedience class instead of a Beginner A class. Kids ages nine or older can train in Beginner A or B classes (not both) for only one year. Then it's time to move on to a Graduate Beginner or higher class.

Other 4-H programs teach aspects of responsible dog ownership. These include choosing a dog, understanding dog behavior, nutrition, canine anatomy, and keeping dogs healthy.

Agility for Kids

If you read about agility in the previous chapter, you know how much fun it is. Just think what a great sport it would be for a kid and Beagle. All of the national organizations that sponsor agility trials have Junior classes for kids and their dogs. Sponsoring organizations are the AKC, the United Kennel Club, the United States Dog Agility Association, and the North American Dog Agility Council.

AKC Agility

The AKC doesn't have a special Juniors class for agility, but Juniors who put an agility title on a dog receive a certificate recognizing their participation in a performance event. (The same is true of obedience and field trials.)

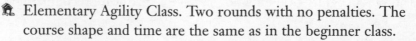

Doggy Do's/Doggy Don'ts _____

Wait until your Beagle is old enough to concentrate before you begin training him seriously for agility. He also needs to have completed his skeletal development, which usually occurs at 9 to 12 months of age. AKC doesn't permit dogs younger than one year to compete in agility trials. However, young puppies can start learning many agility techniques, such as going through tunnels and crossing dog walks and teeter-totters. Your adult Beagle should be healthy and in good shape—no fatties—before he starts training for agility.

Juniors simply enter their Beagle in the class in which he would normally compete. The dog is scored on his performance, and when he earns a title his young handler receives a certificate and pin. To receive the award, the handler needs to obtain the proper certification forms, fill them out, and have them signed by the judge.

UKC Agility

The United Kennel Club permits handlers of any age to compete in all agility trial classes. The only requirement is that the dog be under the handler's control.

USDAA Agility

The USDAA junior handlers program is for youngsters 18 years and younger. They can participate at four different levels of competition:

- 🐾 Beginner Agility Class. The course has 10 obstacles arranged in a simple horseshoe or S shape. Teams must complete 1 round of competition in 60 seconds with no penalties.

- 🐾 Elementary Agility Class. Two rounds with no penalties. The course shape and time are the same as in the beginner class.

Intermediate Agility Class. The course is more challenging. A team must complete 3 rounds with no penalties in a course time of 75 seconds.

 Senior Agility Class. This is the most difficult. The course has 13 to 15 obstacles, and the team must complete 3 penalty-free rounds in 75 seconds.

NADAC Agility

The Junior division is open to any dog whose handler is 17 years or younger. Juniors compete only in regular or jumpers classes, where they can earn Novice, Open, and Elite agility certificates.

Dogs entered in NADAC Junior classes have jump heights that are set four inches lower than the regular jump height. Course time—the time allowed to complete the course—is increased by 10 percent.

Bet You Didn't Know

Regular classes demonstrate the dog's ability to perform all agility obstacles. Jumpers classes demonstrate the dog and handler's ability to work as a fast-moving team and highlight the dog's natural jumping ability.

Tricks Are for Beagles

Tricks are great fun for kids to teach and Beagles to learn. Trick training is how lots of movie and TV dogs get their start. The stunts they perform often are simply a series of tricks that have been linked to create actions the dog needs to know for his role. Any dog can learn to do tricks—even an old one. Keep training fun and use lots of treats. Remember that successful training of even a single trick usually takes weeks, not days. Praise and reward your Beagle for any behavior that comes close to what you want him to do. Be patient and persistent, and your Beagle will soon be rolling over, jumping through hoops, speaking on command, and more.

(© Kristine Kraeuter)

Beagles tend to be hams. They enjoy learning tricks because it lets them show off.

You don't need a lot of fancy equipment to teach tricks. A good supply of treats is a must. Choose yummy, stinky foods like cheese or liver. Don't give a large treat; just a small bite is enough to reward your Beagle. You don't want him to get fat, after all.

Beagle Bonus _____

Many tricks are useful to teach if you plan to get involved with your Beagle in agility, obedience, or tracking. These include weave heeling, circle, and find it. For some tricks, you may need a prop. For instance, if you want to teach your Beagle to jump through a hoop, a Hula Hoop is a good choice.

A clicker is useful, too. Look for one at a toy store or pet supply store. Give a click when your Beagle does something you like. Then reward him with a treat. He'll quickly learn that a click means good things are coming and will work to earn more clicks. To find more sources on clicker training, see Appendix B.

Jump Over an Object

Place a low object on the ground, such as a small trashcan on its side. If possible, set it up between a door and a wall or two other barriers so your Beagle doesn't have the option of going around it. Hold a clicker in your left hand and a treat in your right hand (or the reverse if that's more comfortable). With your Beagle on one side of the object to be jumped, get down on your knees on the other side. Hold out the hand with the treat and move it back toward you, encouraging your Beagle to jump over the object to get to the treat. If he jumps over, click as he's jumping. Give the treat when the jump is completed. If he tries to go around, don't yell at him or say no. Just put him back in place and start over. As he starts to get the hang of this trick, give it a name. Say "Over!" as he's jumping and "Good over!" when he completes the jump. Teach him to go over the jump from both sides. When he gets good at this trick, you can make it more interesting by teaching him to jump over another dog (one that's good at the "Down-Stay" command) or your brother or sister.

Speak

This is a good trick to teach Beagles that like to bark. Once you can teach them to bark on command, you can then teach them to be quiet on command, something every Beagle should know.

To teach "Speak," click and treat every time your dog barks. Say "Good speak!" as he barks. With practice, he'll learn to associate the command "Speak" with a bark. Then you can add a hand signal, such as an "Okay" signal (closed thumb and forefinger, resembling an open mouth).

Doggy Do's/ Doggy Don'ts
Keep clickers and treats stashed around the house or in your pockets so you're always prepared to reward a good behavior.

If your Beagle doesn't bark often (a good thing, usually), you'll have to be ready to click and treat any time he does. Pay attention to the times he does bark. What triggers it? A knock at the front door? A squirrel? Some dogs mumble and grumble when they can't reach toys underneath the bed or other furniture. Be ready, and click and treat for those sounds.

Bet You Didn't Know

If your Beagle is barking and won't stop, give the "Down" command (if he knows it). Dogs usually don't bark when they're lying down. When he's down and quiet, say "Good quiet" and give him a treat.

Quiet

Once your Beagle knows how to speak on command, teach him to be quiet on command. The instant he stops barking, click and treat. (The treat in his mouth will help keep him quiet.) Say "Good quiet!" as he's enjoying his cheese or liver.

Weave Heeling

This trick involves some fancy footwork. It can take time to learn, so don't lose patience. Practice for just a couple of minutes each day. Your Beagle should know "Sit" before you try this trick.

Stand with your Beagle sitting at your left side. Hold a treat in each hand. Take a big step forward with your right foot and lure your Beagle under your leg, holding your right hand behind and under your leg. As he goes under, say "Weave." When he's on your right side, give him a treat and say "Good weave." Then take a big step forward with your left foot and repeat. Continue.

Circle

This trick will come in handy in agility—it teaches your Beagle good turning and directional skills and improves his flexibility. It also teaches him to focus closely on you.

Start with your Beagle sitting at your left side. With a treat in your hand, move your hand around your body as far as it will go, encouraging your dog to follow the motion. Have a treat in your other hand so you can complete the circle. As he goes around you, say "Circle me" and reward him when he completes the circle. As he gets good at this, start moving forward while you say "Circle me." Practice circling in both directions. When your Beagle has learned "Circle me" and "Weave," you can combine the actions into a fun routine. Kind of like a Beagle square dance.

Dance

As your Beagle stands in front of you, hold a treat above him and encourage him to prance on his hind legs in a circle. As he does this, put a name to the action, such as "Dance" or "Spin." Click and treat him when he completes a circle.

Doggy Do's/ Doggy Don'ts

If you have a Beagle with a bad back, avoid teaching tricks that involve standing on the hind legs.

Gradually teach him to "Dance" for longer periods. If you want to teach him to dance from a distance, use a cat fishing-pole toy to get him moving in circles. Lots of dogs love these toys, especially if there's a furry lure on the end. Teach this trick on a safe surface, such as carpet, not a slick one like a wood, tile, or linoleum floor.

Wave

This is an easy trick to teach, especially if your Beagle likes to use his paws a lot. To teach "Wave," start with your dog in a sit. Wait until he moves his paw, then click and reward him for the motion. (You may have to gently nudge some dogs to get them to lift a paw.) When he learns that lifting his paw gets a reward, start clicking and reward for higher paw lifts. As your Beagle gets good at this trick, give the action a name: "Wave!" When he associates the word with the action of lifting his paw, practice giving him the command from a distance.

Find It!

This is the perfect trick to teach a nosy Beagle. It's also something of an intelligence test. Will your Beagle figure out to look under or behind something to get his treat? This is good practice for tracking training. You'll need a towel or a clear plastic container as props.

Use cheese or liver—anything with a strong smell—for this trick. Start with your Beagle in a sit. Show him the treat and tell him to stay. Walk away a few steps and hide the treat beneath the towel or plastic container. Be sure your Beagle sees you hide it. Walk back, let him sniff your hand, and say "Find it!" He should zoom off in search of the treat. When he uncovers it and eats it, say "Good find it!"

Gradually increase the difficulty of this trick by placing the treat farther under the towel or beneath an opaque container (one the dog can't see through). When he's figured those out, make it really tough by hiding the treat without the dog watching where you put it. Eventually you can teach him to find and retrieve other items, such as keys or a stuffed toy.

Doggy Do's/ Doggy Don'ts

Keep trick-training sessions brief. Beagles get bored fast. Five to 10 minutes is a good length of time to spend, but you can repeat these short training sessions several times a day. Schedule them before meals or several hours after a meal.

Balance the Treat

This is difficult to teach a Beagle, but cute when it's successful. You'll need to be patient because your Beagle will probably snarf a lot of treats before he figures out that he has to wait until you give the okay.

Put your Beagle in a sit and tell him to stay. Place a small treat on top of his nose, saying "Stay" as you do so. He'll probably tilt his head back in an attempt to get the treat off his nose, so be prepared to catch it and put it back in place before he eats it. At first, wait only a few seconds before telling him "Okay" or "Take it." Then he's allowed to flip it off and eat it. Gradually lengthen the amount of time he must hold the biscuit on his nose before you allow him to eat it.

Play Dead

Your Beagle should know the "Down" command before you try to teach this trick. Start with your Beagle in a sit. Point your index finger at him and move your hand downward. This looks a lot like the hand signal for "Down." If your Beagle knows that command, he should move into the down position. Once he's down, encourage him to roll over onto his side, saying "Bang!" or "Play dead" as he does. Click and treat when he's in position. Practice until he can do this in one smooth motion when you give the command.

Touch It

When your Beagle learns this trick, you can use it to teach him to go to or touch other items. You'll need a stick or wand of some sort for this trick. A clean bird perch works well. The stick should be 18 to 36 inches long.

Hold the stick out. If your Beagle noses or paws it, click and treat. (Don't reward him for biting the stick.) When he starts to understand what you want, add the command "Touch it." Increase the difficulty by holding the stick out in different directions—up, down, left, right—so your dog has to move a certain way to complete the touch. Then teach him to touch other items by pointing the stick at them and rewarding him when he touches them.

Shake

This trick is a lot like "Wave." Start with your dog in a sit. Say "Shake" and gently take his paw in your hand. Hold the paw briefly and then say "Good shake" and release the paw. Repeat this until he starts giving his paw when you say "Shake." Some dogs learn "Shake" very quickly while others may take a week or two.

More Tricks

Beagles can learn all kinds of tricks. If your dog enjoys trick training, look at the library or bookstore for books on teaching dogs tricks. Some good choices are listed in Appendix B.

Some of the other tricks you might learn to teach are beg, roll over, through (a hoop trick), kisses, and wag your tail.

The Least You Need to Know

- There are special classes for kids who want to show their Beagles in conformation, agility, and obedience. Kids can also show dogs in 4-H events.

- Children 8 to 18 can participate in various junior events.

- Junior showmanship classes are judged on how well the child presents the dog, not on the dog's looks.

- Beagles can learn numerous tricks and enjoy performing.

- Patience is the key to teaching a dog tricks.

Part 6

Special Needs

Like any dog, your Beagle may one day have some special needs. These may be related to genetic disorders that can affect the breed or they may come about naturally, as the result of old age.

Covered in this section are a discussion of some of the more common hereditary diseases that can strike Beagles and an explanation of the canine genome and how research into the genome may one day provide cures or treatments for some of those diseases. Finally, you'll learn what to expect as your Beagle ages and ways you can help him be more comfortable in his golden years.

Chapter 18

Genetic Disorders

In This Chapter

🐾 Hereditary problems common to Beagles

🐾 The canine genome unraveled

Beagles as a whole are a healthy breed. Because they've been bred for field performance, they tend to be quite athletic dogs, and most breeders do their best to produce sound, healthy puppies. Despite their efforts, however, genetic health problems can pop up from time to time.

General Genetics

Common health problems in the Beagle breed are for the most part the same as for dogs in general, with a few notable exceptions. This section covers some of the more common problems found in the breed. It is not inclusive and should not be used as a guide to diagnosis. Always ask your veterinarian about any health problem your Beagle develops.

Inherited diseases or conditions commonly seen in the Beagle include bleeding disorders, cherry eye, chondrodystrophy (dwarfism), epilepsy, glaucoma, heart disease, hypothyroidism, and intervertebral disc disease (IVDD). Each of these problems is described in the following sections.

Bleeding Disorders

Dogs can suffer from a number of bleeding disorders, some serious, some mild, and Beagles are no exception. Such disorders seen in Beagles are factor VII deficiency and factor VIII deficiency.

Factor VII is a component of blood. When it's missing, blood is slow to coagulate, or clot. The condition is present at birth. Beagles with factor VII deficiency may be prone to mild bruising.

Hemophilia A, also known as factor VIII deficiency, occurs when the blood has an absence of factor VIII. Dogs with this condition have trouble forming clots, so if they start bleeding, it's often difficult to stop the flow. Hemophilia A can first occur at birth. It's the most common severe inherited clotting disorder in both people and dogs. Hemophilia A is carried by females but occurs only in males.

Be sure to tell your veterinarian if your Beagle has a tendency to bleed easily, if bleeding continues for a long period after a small nick or cut, or if bleeding is difficult to stop.

Cherry Eye

Cherry eye occurs when one of the tear-producing glands located at the inner corner of the eye (your vet may refer to it as the medial canthus) slips out of place, or prolapses. The area becomes red and swollen, hence the name. Cherry eye can occur in one or both eyes and usually shows up during puppyhood. While it's not pretty to look at, it's not serious and is easily repaired with surgery to tack the gland back in place or remove all or part of the gland.

Bet You Didn't Know

Congenital defects—those a dog is born with—such as hare lips and hernias may or may not be genetic in origin.

Be aware that removing the entire gland or, conversely, not doing anything for the eye, can result in a condition called dry eye (keratoconjunctivitis sicca, for those of you into medical lingo).

Dry eye occurs when the source of tear production is removed, either through surgery or through lack of blood supply, thanks to the blocked tear duct. When dogs can't produce enough tears, their eyes become irritated and produce a thick, stringy discharge. These dogs may need to have daily doses of artificial tears prescribed by your veterinarian.

Chondrodystrophy

Dwarfism, or skeletal dysplasia, takes a number of different forms. Terms you may hear in reference to it include osteochondrodysplasia, chondrodysplasia, achondrodysplasia, and Chinese Beagle syndrome. These so-called "funny [in appearance] puppies" are smaller than normal and may have certain physical deformities, including associated heart defects. For instance, "Chinese" Beagles have wide skulls with wide-set eyes that look slightly slanted. Dwarfism is also discussed in Chapter 5.

(© John Kraeuter)

The puppy on the right has a form of hereditary dwarfism called chondrodystrophy. He's pictured with a normal littermate.

Epilepsy

Idiopathic (meaning the cause is unknown) epilepsy is a common condition that causes repeated seizures in affected dogs. Certain lines (families) of Beagles, both field and show, have had problems with epilepsy, and the disease appears to be a recessive trait in the breed.

Epilepsy is usually controllable with medication, but the main problem it presents to breeders is that it often shows up later in life, after the affected dogs have already produced litters. That means that all of their puppies are carriers, even if they don't have the disease themselves. No tests are yet available to identify dogs that are carriers of the disease, so the only thing breeders can do is to eliminate affected dogs from their breeding programs.

Beagle Bonus

Researchers supported by the AKC Canine Health Foundation are working with certain breeds, including Beagles, to identify markers linked with the idiopathic epilepsy trait in those breeds.

Glaucoma

Caused by increased fluid pressure inside the eye, often from inadequate drainage of fluid from the eye, glaucoma is one of the main causes of blindness in dogs. Signs of glaucoma include reddened eyes, tearing, sensitivity to light, or enlargement of the eye. The eye may look glassy or the pupil unusually dilated. Early diagnosis is critical to effective treatment. Without treatment, the pressure damages the eye, causing pain and eventually blindness.

Beagle Bonus

Some Beagles will suddenly go into a spasm of snorting. It's often referred to as a reverse sneeze, because it occurs during inhalation. Many new owners are very concerned when they first observe this until they are assured it is as harmless as a sneeze. This reverse sneeze may occur because the dogs have an elongated soft palate.

Heart Disease

One of the heart problems seen in the Beagle is pulmonic stenosis. This condition, which usually affects small breeds and occurs in puppyhood, is a narrowing of the connection between the right ventricle and the pulmonary artery. When this happens, it becomes more difficult for the right ventricle to pump blood. The right side of the heart becomes enlarged, just as any muscle does when it's worked. The first sign of pulmonic stenosis is usually a systolic murmur (one that occurs when the left and right ventricles of the heart are beating, making a sound like lup-shh-dup). The diagnosis is confirmed with chest x-rays and an electrocardiogram. In severe cases, pulmonic stenosis can be treated with a balloon valvuloplasty, which has a success rate of about 70 percent.

Other heart problems that may be seen in the Beagle are dilated cardiomyopathy (DCM) and ventricular septal defect (VSD). Signs of DCM include lack of stamina, shortness of breath, blue gums or a blue tongue after exertion, coughing, lack of appetite, and weight loss. When the vet listens to the heart, it may sound muffled. If detected early, DCM can be controlled with medication for a time.

A ventricular septal defect is a hole in the wall of the heart, causing poor circulation. It occurs at birth. A VSD doesn't always cause problems. Sometimes the hole in the heart wall is small enough that the only sign is a harmless heart murmur. A larger VSD may cause the left side of the heart to work too hard. If the heart becomes overworked, the result can be congestive heart failure.

If your Beagle pup has a murmur, the veterinarian may suspect VSD and order chest x-rays, an electrocardiogram, or heart ultrasound to confirm the diagnosis. If necessary, medication and surgery are available, but most dogs with a small VSD go on to live a long and normal life.

Hypothyroidism

This disease of the endocrine system (which controls hormone production and release) causes destruction of the thyroid gland. It's a common hormonal disorder of all dogs, but there seem to be more and more cases of thyroid dysfunction in brace Beagles, partly because they have been heavily *linebred* and *inbred*.

> **Beagle Lingo**
>
> **Inbreeding** refers to close breedings, such as mother/son, father/daughter, sister/brother. Inbreeding itself is not bad. The intent is to intensify good qualities, but of course it can also worsen bad traits. That's why it's important for breeders who choose to inbreed to use only the very best breeding stock. **Line breeding** is the mating of less closely related dogs, such as half sister/half brother or grandmother/grandson. An **outcross** means that the dogs are not related within three generations. All three types of breeding can produce healthy puppies.

When the level of thyroid hormones falls below normal, many different body systems are affected. Signs of thyroid disease are rough, scaly skin, hair loss, and unexplained weight gain. Skin infections, flea and food allergies, stinky ears, and chronic ear infections are also indicators. Hypothyroidism is easily controlled with medication.

Most cases of canine hypothyroidism result from autoimmune thyroiditis, meaning the body is being attacked by its own immune system. If breeders are going to reduce the incidence of this disease in Beagles, they need to test for the presence of TgAA (Thyroglobulin Autoantibody) in their breeding stock. About half the cases of hypothyroidism in dogs have been reported to be associated with a positive TgAA test result.

IVDD

Intervertebral disc disease affects a number of Beagles. Intervertebral discs lie between and cushion each vertebra. With their firm, rubbery exterior and soft, jellylike interior, they've been described as resembling vitamin E capsules.

Problems begin if the discs start to dehydrate. They become brittle, losing their flexibility. They begin to stick out and can even rupture. When the discs stick out or rupture, they press on the spinal cord, causing back pain, unsteadiness or clumsiness in the rear, and in severe cases paralysis. Ruptures can occur in neck, thoracic (chest), or lumbar (lower back) vertebrae. IVDD is usually age related, but it can occur in Beagles as young as one year old. Obese Beagles are especially prone to IVDD.

Suspect IVDD if your Beagle yelps when you pick him up, doesn't want to jump on or off furniture, or is reluctant to go up and down stairs. Diagnosis usually requires an MRI (magnetic resonance imaging) or a special type of radiograph (x-ray) called a myelogram, which involves injecting a dye into the spinal cord.

Beagle Bonus

To help your Beagle with IVDD be more comfortable, raise his food dishes so they are level with his head, reducing the pressure on his spine. Avoid tug-of-war games, and use a halter instead of a neck collar. If your dog has had surgery, allow three to six months of recovery time before returning him to normal activity level.

Mild cases of IVDD can improve with strict crate rest and steroids for two to four weeks, but severe cases may require surgery. Surgery is iffy. Some dogs return to normal; others are the same or worse. Your veterinarian can give you a more definite prognosis based on your individual dog.

The Least You Need to Know

🏠 An awareness of genetic disorders and their signs is important for every Beagle owner.

🏠 Beagles are a generally healthy breed, but they are prone to certain hereditary diseases.

- 🏠 The most common hereditary problems in Beagles are bleeding disorders, cherry eye, dwarfism, epilepsy, glaucoma, heart disease, hypothyroidism, and intervertebral disc disease.

- 🏠 Cherry eye is easily treatable with surgery.

- 🏠 Untreated glaucoma can lead to blindness.

- 🏠 The mapping of the canine genome will lead to development of new tests and treatments for hereditary problems.

Chapter  19

This Old Beagle

In This Chapter

- 🏠 Signs and problems of aging
- 🏠 Dealing with disabilities
- 🏠 Helping your old Beagle be more comfortable
- 🏠 When it's time to say good-bye

One of the great things about Beagles is their relatively long life-span. They usually live 10 to 15 years and some go on for even longer. Beagles also tend to retain their puppy-like looks and attitude well into their golden years.

Like all of us, however, Beagles tend to slow down a little and take life easier the older they get. They may develop age-related health problems or be more interested in a nap than a long walk. Often they have special nutritional needs. Life with a senior Beagle is a special time. Here are some ways you can make things easier for your dog and for yourself.

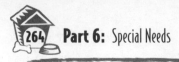

(© Janet Nieland)

With good care, Beagles can live well into their teens. These two are celebrating their sixteenth birthday.

What to Expect

Experts say that dogs spend 30 to 40 percent of their lives as seniors. Dogs usually start to show signs of age when they're seven years old. Beagles, being a smaller breed, may not appear to be aging much until they are about 10 years old.

The good news, veterinarians say, is that it's a great time to be an old dog. Available to them are special foods suited to their specific needs, new medications to treat common ailments of older dogs, and many products geared to help them live more comfortable lives. Let's take a look at the problems that can face older dogs and what can be done about them.

Arthritis

More than 8 million dogs in the United States have been diagnosed with arthritis, and of those, more than 80 percent are 7 years or older. Arthritis is a common and painful condition that can affect the hips, elbows, and other joints.

Dogs with arthritis may not show it much at first. A Beagle with creeping arthritis may slow down or become reluctant to walk as far, run, climb stairs, or jump on furniture. He may seem stiff when he gets up (like so many of us) or limp for a few steps after rising. Sometimes he yelps when he's touched in sensitive areas or even shows aggression. If your Beagle shows any of these signs, take him to the vet for an exam.

Doggy Do's/Doggy Don'ts _____

Never give your Beagle aspirin, Tylenol (acetaminophen), ibuprofen, or any other pain reliever without first checking with your veterinarian. Tylenol and other nonsteroidal anti-inflammatory drugs (NSAIDs) are toxic to dogs and just one or two can be fatal. Rimadyl is an NSAID made specifically for dogs and has been very helpful for many, but it can have side effects. Ask your veterinarian about them so you can make an informed decision.

If a Beagle is fat, weight loss can help reduce the pain from arthritis. Medications to relieve pain are also available, including supplements that contain glycosaminoglycans (GAGs) or glucosamine, chondroitin, and ester C to support joint flexibility and mobility.

Cancer

Beagles as a breed aren't necessarily prone to cancer, but older dogs in general are more likely to develop cancer. Common types of cancer seen in dogs are mammary cancer, skin tumors, testicular cancer, cancers of the mouth or nose, and lymphoma.

Many cancers today are treatable with surgery or chemotherapy, especially if they're diagnosed early. Check your Beagle's entire body often for suspicious lumps or bumps that could indicate tumors.

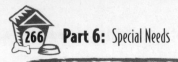

Is It Doggie Alzheimer's?

Yes, dogs can get senile. The condition of brain aging in dogs is called cognitive dysfunction syndrome (CDS). Most owners don't notice clinical signs of cognitive dysfunction until a dog is about 11 years old, but in the laboratory researchers see changes as early as 8, 9, or 10 years of age.

The effects of brain aging can be subtle, but signs of Beagle "senior moments" might include disorientation or confusion, interacting less often with family members or not recognizing them, changes in sleep or activity patterns, and housetraining accidents. For instance, a Beagle with CDS might wander aimlessly in the house, get "lost" in a corner, or pace or howl at night instead of sleeping soundly. Use the acronym DISH to remember signs of cognitive dysfunction:

🏠 Disorientation

🏠 Interaction changes

🏠 Sleep or activity changes

🏠 Housetraining is forgotten

Certain health problems such as thyroid, kidney, or adrenal gland disease can mimic the signs of CDS, so a thorough health workup is essential to properly diagnose CDS. If that's the problem, your veterinarian may be able to prescribe medication to lessen the problems associated with CDS. Choline supplements, available from holistic veterinarians or pet supply stores, may also help increase mental alertness.

Bet You Didn't Know

Besides CDS, possible reasons for behavioral changes include arthritis, loss of hearing or vision, or household changes such as a new pet or baby, a new home, a change in work schedule, or a divorce.

Diabetes

Diabetes, a common and serious problem in dogs, is a disorder of the pancreas gland, which produces a hormone called insulin. Insulin drives nutrients—specifically glucose, or blood sugar—into the cells.

Diabetes occurs when the pancreas stops producing insulin or doesn't produce enough insulin. Glucose levels build up in the bloodstream, causing high blood sugar. All that extra sugar spills into the urine, causing the affected dog to urinate more frequently. Because their bodies are losing so much water, diabetic dogs compensate by drinking a lot. And because their cells aren't getting the nutrients they need to function, diabetic dogs lose weight and become weak, even if they seem to be eating a lot.

Contributing factors to diabetes include genetic predisposition, gender, age, and obesity. Beagles are one of the breeds with a high incidence of the disease. Diabetes is seen more often in females than males and usually develops at six to nine years of age.

Although diabetes doesn't have a cure, it can be managed successfully. Treatment involves once- or twice-daily insulin injections, a high-fiber diet, and close regulation of the dog's mealtimes, as well as the amount of food he receives. Exercise can help the dog lose weight, which can improve a diabetic animal's condition.

Bet You Didn't Know

According to statistics from the American Veterinary Medical Association, there are about 18 million old dogs in the United States.

Hypothyroidism

This disease, which was discussed in more detail in the previous chapter, tends to be a problem of middle and old age. If your Beagle is diagnosed with hypothyroidism, your veterinarian will probably

prescribe a daily pill and recommend blood testing every six months to make sure the amount of medication being given is appropriate.

Kidney Disease

The kidneys remove waste products from the body and ensure that the body maintains an appropriate level of water, minerals, and Vitamin B. As dogs age, kidney function can begin to deteriorate.

Bet You Didn't Know

It's a myth that too much protein in the diet causes kidney disease. And low-protein diets won't prevent kidney disease from developing. There's no need to give your aging Beagle a low-protein diet unless your veterinarian recommends it.

Routine screening tests can help identify kidney disease in the early stages, before too much damage is done.

One sign of possible kidney disease that you might notice at home is increased water consumption. If your Beagle is diagnosed with kidney disease or kidney failure, a special low-protein diet can help.

Sensory Deprivation

One of the consequences of old age is that senses become less sharp. Sight, hearing, and even smell can all start to go. Fortunately dogs are pretty adaptable and can live well with these disabilities, as long as we make a few simple allowances for them.

Hearing Loss

Sometimes Beagles aren't exercising selective hearing. As they age, they can start to lose their hearing. Deafness can be partial, meaning the dog can hear only certain sounds, or it can be total.

Deafness has a number of causes, from congenital defects to inflammation or infection of the ear canal to nerve problems. In older dogs, it's usually degenerative changes in the dog's inner ear

that lead to hearing loss. You may notice that your Beagle no longer comes running from the back of the house when you're preparing his meal or that he doesn't come right away when you call him. Sometimes he's difficult to wake, even at the sound of a loud noise.

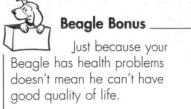

Beagle Bonus

Just because your Beagle has health problems doesn't mean he can't have good quality of life.

Get ahead of deafness when your Beagle is a puppy by teaching him hand signals along with verbal commands. If he ever loses his hearing, you'll still be able to communicate with him. To avoid startling your dog and risking an accidental bite, stomp your foot to wake him (he'll feel the vibrations) or make sure he sees you approaching him.

Loss of Vision

As Beagles age, their bright brown eyes can become hazy and gray, a condition called nuclear sclerosis. Fortunately, it doesn't seriously affect their vision.

Beagles do tend to be prone to cataracts, however. These opaque spots on the lens of the eye can cause partial or total vision loss. Some cataracts are hereditary, but others just come with age.

Cataracts can often be removed surgically, but if that's not possible, your Beagle will likely get along just fine with reduced vision or even no vision at all. Dogs don't need to read or watch television, so sight isn't as important to them as it is to us. They simply rely a little more heavily on their sense of smell.

Beagle Bonus

If your Beagle has lost his eyesight, make things easier on him by not moving furniture around. You can also spray perfume or other scent on furniture at Beagle nose height so he can use the smell to find his way around.

The Nose ... Doesn't Know?

Even Beagles can start to lose their sense of smell as they age. Often, this doesn't occur until they're very old, however. You may notice that your Beagle has trouble finding dropped bits of food or has a less ravenous appetite. To entice him to eat, try heating his food to enhance the aroma.

Golden-Age Exam

When your Beagle turns seven years old, ask your veterinarian about a baseline health workup. A golden-age checkup, as it's sometimes called, includes complete bloodwork, a urinalysis, and sometimes an EKG and chest and lung radiographs. A physical exam checks for stiffness, heart murmurs, bad breath, skin lesions, and other common signs of aging. This type of thorough going-over provides a baseline against which your Beagle's future health can be measured.

Because changes can occur rapidly in older dogs, many veterinarians now recommend that senior dogs be examined twice a year instead of annually. This can help catch problems such as kidney disease early, while they're most treatable. If your Beagle develops a health problem, don't just write it off to old age. With proper care, he can live well into his teens.

Doggy Do's/ Doggy Don'ts

Pay attention to small changes in your Beagle's appearance and behavior and report them to your veterinarian.

Upping the Comfort Level

There are a number of ways we can help old dogs stay comfortable and happy. For starters, your old Beagle will appreciate having his choice of warm spots to sleep. (It's harder to stay warm the older you get!) Place comfy beds around the house in sunny areas or near

the fireplace. Cover him with a blanket if it's a gray day and you don't have a fireplace. (He may kick it off or scrunch it up to his satisfaction, but at least you'll have made the effort.)

If your Beagle has a favorite sofa or chair, make it easier for him to climb up on it, especially if he has arthritis or IVDD. One couple lovingly made "Beagle aids" for their teen dog, including a ramp to the dog door, a step to the bed and the sofa, and a special low table on the back porch for sunning.

As your Beagle ages, grooming is more important than ever. Keep the ears clean and trim toenails weekly. Brushing stimulates the skin for good circulation, and it gives you an opportunity to regularly check for lumps and bumps, bad breath, tartar buildup on teeth, stinky ears, and the like. Don't let these problems go unchecked; an older dog is less able to deal with what may be seemingly minor health problems.

Finally keep up the loving and snuggling. That will make your Beagle happiest of all.

The Toughest Decision

One of the most difficult times in your life will be when your special Beagle is old or sick and no longer enjoying life. The kindest thing you can do is to release him from his suffering. A peaceful death is the best gift you can give to a dog who has provided many years of love and companionship.

How do you know when the time is right? Knowing the right time for euthanasia is an intensely personal decision because every Beagle-human relationship is different. If you can read the signals, however, your dog will let you know when he's ready to go.

The main thing to consider is quality of life. Appetite, attitude, activity level, elimination habits, comfort, and interaction with family members are all elements to think about. Talk to your family about their perceptions of the dog's quality of life. Questions to ask yourself include whether your Beagle has more good days than bad

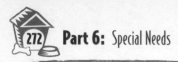

days, whether he can still do his favorite things, and whether he acts as if he's in pain.

Older dogs spend most of their time eating, sleeping, eliminating, and getting attention. When the time comes that they're not able to do those things, they're not enjoying life anymore. That's when you need to consider euthanasia.

Signs of deterioration can come on unexpectedly. A Beagle that has seemed to be going along well may simply appear to give up one day, refusing to eat or move. The suddenness of this type of change sometimes means that the decision to euthanize must be made before the entire family is really prepared. It's a good idea to talk about it in advance so that everyone understands and agrees on the standards for quality of life.

Deciding to euthanize a pet is rarely an easy or clear-cut decision. In making your decision, consider whether you and your Beagle can still enjoy each other's company. When the answer is no, you'll know it's time.

Another Beagle?

By now, you know what a great companion the right Beagle can be. His gentle nature and fun-loving personality almost always trump the trouble his nose can get him into. When your first Beagle goes, the greatest tribute you can pay him is to welcome another Beagle into your home and love him just like you did the first one. Your new Beagle can never replace the old one, but he'll earn his own special place in your heart.

The Least You Need to Know

🏠 The Beagle life span is 10 to 15 years and sometimes longer. Beagles are generally healthy, but are prone to certain problems of old age, including cataracts, hearing loss, hypothyroidism, kidney disease, and canine senility.

🏠 A baseline exam at age seven followed by annual blood tests thereafter can help your veterinarian identify problems early.

🏠 Use the acronym DISH to remember signs of cognitive dysfunction: Disorientation, Interaction changes, Sleep or activity changes, Housetraining is forgotten.

🏠 Provide ramps, comfy beds, good grooming, and lots of loving to help your Beagle sail through old age in style.

🏠 Euthanasia is a difficult and personal decision that can be made easier by considering quality of life issues.

Glossary

agility Demonstration of a dog's ability to negotiate a complex obstacle course in a given period of time.

AKC American Kennel Club.

babbling Excessive or unnecessary tonguing, usually done out of excitement.

backtracking Following the trail in the wrong direction.

baying The prolonged bark or howl of a hound on the trail.

beagling Any activity done with Beagles but most precisely applied to hunting on foot with a pack of Beagles.

beaters People employed to flush rabbits out of the brush for Beagles to chase.

bench show A dog show in which all dogs being shown must be displayed, or benched, when they're not in the show ring.

bitch A female dog.

bone In dog terms, bone is used to describe the amount of bone tissue in proportion to a dog's overall size; for instance, heavy-boned or light-boned.

brace This is a pair of Beagles.

brace trial A competition in which groups of two or sometimes three Beagles are judged on their ability to trail a rabbit.

casting Term used to indicate that the dogs must find a rabbit or hare on their own.

Cherry eye A condition that occurs when one of the tear-producing glands in the inner corner of the eye slips out of place.

Chinese Beagle Syndrome A type of skeletal disease that causes the dog to have slanted eyes and short outer toes.

chondrodysplasia Also referred to as dwarfism. This is a condition that results in a smaller than normal dog with certain physical deformities.

conformation A dog's form and structure as defined by the breed standard. Also used to refer to dog shows: a conformation show.

congenital condition A condition that exists from birth.

Cryptorchid A dog with retained testicles.

dam The mother of a litter of puppies.

desensitization A behavior modification technique that involves frequent repeated stimulation so that certain sights and sounds lose their significance to an animal and no longer cause a reaction.

field line A family of dogs bred to hunt rather than for conformation or pet qualities.

field trial A competition in which hounds are judged on their ability and style in finding game or following a trail.

full registration Papers that allow a dog's offspring to be registered with the AKC.

gait The way a dog moves.

genetic condition A condition that is inherited, or passed on from parent to offspring.

ghost trailing Pretending to follow a trail that's nonexistent.

giving tongue Barking, baying, or howling on the trail. Should be done only when the Beagle has a good scent to follow.

goes to ground Hides in a hole, or den.

hereditary condition A condition passed on from parents to offspring.

hip dysplasia A developmental disease of the hip joint, in which the hip doesn't fit properly in the socket.

Hocks The bones in the hind leg that form the dog's heel.

IGR Insect growth regulators, chemicals that prevent larvae from reaching adulthood.

Indefinite Listing Privilege (ILP) number   Assigned by the AKC to a dog that is obviously a particular breed but has no papers. An ILP number does not confer registration status but does permit the dog to compete in performance events.

Junior showmanship   Special conformation classes for children ages 10 to 18. The child is judged on his or her ability to correctly present a dog, rather than on how closely the dog meets the breed standard.

limited registration   Papers that confirm a dog's purebred ancestry but prohibit registration of his offspring. Some breeders give limited registration to pet-quality puppies to ensure that buyers don't breed dogs that are less than the best. Limited registration can be changed to full registration at the breeder's discretion.

line breeding   The mating of dogs that are not close relatives, such as half brother and half sister.

litter   The puppy or puppies produced by a bitch.

livery   Distinctive clothing worn to identify a pack's huntsman and whippers-in. Show livery recommended by the Beagle standard is a black velvet cap, white stock, green coat, white breeches or knickerbockers, green or black stockings, white spats, and black or dark brown shoes. Vest and gloves are optional. Ladies should wear the same outfit except for a white skirt instead of white breeches.

loin   A dog's hind end, behind the ribs but in front of the pelvic area.

Monorchid   A dog with only a single testicle.

mottled   A coat with dark roundish blotches on a light background.

muzzle   Made up of the nasal bones, nostrils, and jaws.

NADAC   North American Dog Agility Council.

NBC   National Beagle Club.

on the bench   Benched dogs are on display when they're not competing in the ring.

pack trial   A competition in which small or large groups of Beagles are sent out to hunt a hare or rabbit. Packs are judged on appearance as well as how cooperatively they work together.

pedigree   A dog's family tree.

pied   A coat with large patches of two or more colors.

puller   A dog that works by pulling a sled, cart, or other vehicle.

quarry   A dog's prey, such as a rabbit or hare.

running mute   Failing to give tongue.

scenthound   A dog that hunts by sense of smell.

show line   A family of dogs bred for conformation rather than hunting ability.

sire   The father of a litter of puppies.

skirt the trail   To take a shortcut to avoid heavy brush or other obstacles.

SPO   Small pack option, a type of Beagle field trial.

stacking   To display a dog's outline in the show ring.

standard   A description of the ideal member of a given breed.

stop   The indentation between the eyes where the nasal bones and cranium meet.

stud dog   A male dog used for breeding.

styptic powder   Used to stop bleeding.

Three-hour stake   A time-limited pack hunt.

ticked coat   One with small isolated areas of black hairs on a white background.

titer   A measurement of the concentration of antibodies in blood.

tongue   To bay or howl on the trail.

topline   A dog's back.

Triple Challenge   A competition held by the NBC to determine the best all-around Beagle: one with good conformation, good individual working ability, and good cooperation with pack members.

turned   When a rabbit takes a different direction.

type   The qualities that distinguish a particular breed.

UKC   United Kennel Club.

USDAA   United States Dog Agility Association.

whipper-in   Huntsman's assistant; ensures that dogs stay together.

withers   A dog's shoulders.

working titles   Titles awarded to dogs that prove their working ability in field or obedience trials.

Beagle Resources

Books and Periodicals

Bonham, Margaret H. *Introduction to Dog Agility*. Hauppauge: Barron's, 2000.

———— *The Simple Guide To Getting Active With Your Dog*. Neptune City: TFH Publications, 2002.

Burch, Mary R. *Volunteering With Your Pet: How To Get Involved in Animal-Assisted Therapy With Any Kind of Pet*. Hungry Minds, 1996.

Coile, D. Caroline. *Show Me! A Dog Showing Primer*. Barron's, 1997.

Copeland, Sue M. and John M. Hamil, D.V.M. *Hands-On Dog Care*. Doral Publishing, 2000.

Donaldson, Jean. *The Culture Clash*. Berkeley, CA: James & Kenneth Publishers, 1996.

Dunbar, Ian. *How To Teach a New Dog Old Tricks*. Berkeley, CA: James & Kenneth Publishers, 1998.

Giffin, M.D., James M. and Lisa D. Carlson, D.V.M. *Dog Owner's Home Veterinary Handbook, 3rd edition*. New York: Howell Book House, 2000.

Johnson, Glen R. *Tracking Dog: Theory & Methods, 4th edition*. Barkleigh Productions, 1999.

Kraeuter, Kristine. *Training Your Beagle*. Hauppauge: Barron's, 2001.

LaBelle, Charlene. *A Guide To Backpacking With Your Dog*. Alpine, 1992.

Mullally, Linda B. *Hiking With Dogs*. Falcon, 1999.

Musladin, Judith and Rosalind Hall, Marie Stuart, (contributors). *The New Beagle: A Dog for All Seasons, 2nd edition*. New York: Hungry Minds, 1998.

Olejniczak, Anne, and Denise Olezniczak; Luana Luther, (editor). *Best Junior Handler! A Guide to Showing Successfully in Junior Showmanship*. Doral Publishing, 1997.

Palika, Liz. *All Dogs Need Some Training*. New York: Howell, 1997.

Payne, Joan. *Flying High: The Complete Book of Flyball*. KDB Publishing Company, 1996.

Pryor, Karen. *Getting Started: Clicker Training for Dogs*. Waltham: Sunshine Books, 2001.

Siegal, Mordecai, Editor. *UC Davis Book of Dogs: The Complete Medical Reference Guide for Dogs and Puppies*. New York: Harper Collins, 1995.

Taunton, Stephanie, and Cheryl S. Smith. *The Trick Is In the Training: 25 Fun Tricks To Teach Your Dog*. Hauppauge: Barron's, 1998.

A good magazine you should check out: *Popular Dogs Beagles*. Available at pet supply stores or by calling toll free 1-888-738-2665, ext. 2102. $8.95.

Websites for Beagle Lovers

National Beagle Club (AKC parent club)
http://clubs.akc.org/NBC/index.htm

National Beagle Rescue Listings
http://clubs.akc.org/NBC/beagle_rescue.htm

Some Other Beagle Rescue Groups

Beagle Adoption and Rescue Center of Southern California
Janet Nieland
714-826-0928 or chbeagle@aol.com

Beagle Rescue, Education, and Welfare (BREW) of Northern Virginia
www.brewbeagles.org/index.php

TriBeagles, North Carolina
www.tribeagles.org

SOS Beagle Rescue, Kentucky and Tennessee
www.beagles-on-the-web.com/sos

Seattle Beagle Rescue
www.beaglerescue.org

Just for Fun

Aladar Beagles
www.aladarbeagles.com

Beagles on the Web
www.beagles-on-the-web.com

Beagles Unlimited
www.beaglesunlimited.com

Better Beagling
www.betrbeagling.com

Brushyrun Beagles
http://beagle.net/members/brushyrun

Merriewood
www.merriewood.com/arooooo

Titles and Abbreviations

A title becomes part of a Beagle's official name. Any championship title goes in front of the name; any working title goes after the name. For instance, the name of a Beagle with conformation and field championships, and obedience and agility titles would look like this: DC Ride Sally Ride CD, NA. All those letters mean that Miss Sally is a Dual Champion (DC) with a Companion Dog (CD) title and a Novice Agility (NA) title.

Listed alphabetically below are some of the many titles your Beagle can earn and how they're abbreviated.

> AM CH – American Champion (used when a dog has championship from more than one country: AM/CAN CH Baxter Run Rabbit Run)
>
> AX – Agility Excellent
>
> AXJ – Excellent Jumpers with Weaves
>
> BIS – Best In Show
>
> BISS – Best in Specialty Show
>
> BOB – Best of Breed
>
> CAN CH – Canadian Champion
>
> CD – Companion Dog
>
> CDX – Companion Dog Excellent
>
> CGC – Canine Good Citizen
>
> CH – Champion
>
> CT – Champion Tracker

DC – Dual Champion

FC – Field Champion

FD – Flyball Dog

FDX – Flyball Dog Excellent

FDCH – Flyball Dog Champion

FM – Flyball Master

FMX – Flyball Master Excellent

FMCH – Flyball Master Champion

FGDCH – Flyball Grand Champion

FTC – Canadian Field Trial Champion

IFC – International Field Champion (American and Canadian)

INT CH – International Champion

LPH – Large Pack on Hare*

MACH – Master Agility Champion

MX – Master Agility Excellent

MXJ – Master Excellent Jumpers with Weaves

NA – Novice Agility

NAJ – Novice Jumpers with Weaves

OA – Open Agility

OAJ – Open Jumpers with Weaves

OTCH – Obedience Trial Champion

SPO – Small Pack Option*

TC – Triple Champion

TD – Tracking Dog

TDX – Tracking Dog Excellent

TT – Temperament Tested

UD – Utility Dog

UDX – Utility Dog Excellent

VST – Variable Surface Tracking

*The letters SPO or LPH before an FC title indicate that the dog earned all of its points either under the Small Pack Option format or the Large Pack on Hare trials.

Organizations

ASPCA Animal Poison Control Center/National Animal Poison Control Center
1717 S. Philo, Suite 36
Urbana, IL 61802
1-888-426-4435
$45 per case, with as many follow-up calls as needed.
www.aspca.org/site/PageServer?pagename=apcc

American Kennel Club
5580 Centerview Drive
Raleigh, NC 27606-3390
919-233-9767
www.akc.org

Association of Pet Dog Trainers
17000 Commerce Parkway, Suite C
Mt. Laurel, NJ 08054
1-800-PET-DOGS
information@apdt.com
www.apdt.com

Love on a Leash (therapy dog organization)
PO Box 6308
Oceanside, CA 92058
www.loveonaleash.org

National Association of Dog Obedience Instructors
Corresponding Secretary
PMB #369
729 Grapevine Highway
Hurst, TX 76054-2085
www.nadoi.org.

National Beagle Club
Secretary, Susan Mills Stone
PO Box 13
Middleburg, VA 22117
http://clubs.akc.org/NBC

National Dog Registry (tattoo registry)
1-800-637-3647
www.natldogregistry.com

North American Dog Agility Council
11550 S. Highway 3
Cataldo, ID 83810
208-689-3803
www.nadac.com

North American Flyball Association (NAFA)
1400 W. Devon Avenue #512
Chicago, IL 60660
www.flyball.org
(Contact for information about clubs in your area. Send $10 for rules.)

Therapy Dogs Incorporated
PO Box 5868
Cheyenne, WY 82003
877-843-7364
www.therapydogs.com

Therapy Dogs International
88 Bartley Road
Flanders, NJ 07836
973-252-9800
www.tdi-dog.org

United Kennel Club
100 E. Kilgore Road
Kalamazoo, MI 49002-5584
616-343-9020
www.ukcdogs.com

United States Dog Agility Association
PO Box 850955
Richardson, TX 75085-0955
972-487-2200
www.usdaa.com

Veterinary Pet Insurance
PO Box 2344
Brea, CA 92822-2344
714-996-2311 or 1-800-USA-PETS
www.petinsurance.com

Index

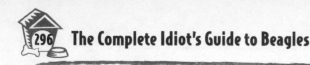